THE BOOK OF AIRSPORTS

THE BOOK OF AIRSPORTS

Ann Welch

drawings by Piers Bois

ARCO PUBLISHING COMPANY, INC.
New York

All rights reserved. No part of this publication may be reproduced in any form, or by any means, without permission from the Publishers.

ACKNOWLEDGMENT
The author and publishers wish to thank and acknowledge the kind help of the following with advice or photographs: AERO (fig 7.10); Air Portraits (fig 3.3a); Peter Bish (figs 5.3a, b, 5.4, 5.6, 5.7, 5.8a, 5.9 and colour plate 4b); British Gliding Association; Ciba-Geigy Plastics and Additives Company (fig 2.9); Kenneth Clark, Manpowered Aircraft Group; Ashley Doubtfire, British Hang Gliding Association; Philip Gladstone (figs 4.6b, 4.7); Theddy Heimgartner (fig 2.3); Kurt Lampert (fig 1.14); Stanley Lauder, Popular Flying Association; Rose-Marie Licher (colour plate 4a); Robert Lowe; Paul MacCready; Fred Marsh, Formula 1 Air Racing Association; S T Midson (fig 7.9); Lorna Minton (figs 2.10, 2.12, 2.14, 3.9e, and illustration on page 6); Don Monroe (figs 4.8, 4.9); Ron Moulton; Julian Nott, British Balloon and Airship Club; Bill Paul, British Parachute Association; Norman Pealing (fig 3.9a); Peter Pratelli; Roy and Ann Procter (figs 3.9b,c); Royal Aeronautical Society (figs 4.3, 4.4a,b,c, 4.5, 4.10); Tom Sage, Cameron Balloons; Kenneth Simmonds, Thunder Balloons; Soaring Society of America (fig 1.1b); Sound Stills (fig 5.2b); *Sunday Mirror* (fig 1.3); Andrew Wakelin, British Association of Parascending Clubs (figs 6.3a,b,c, 6.4a,b).

Published by Arco Publishing Company, Inc.
219 Park Avenue South, New York, N.Y. 10003

Copyright © 1978 by Ann Welch

Drawings copyright © 1978 by Piers Bois

All rights reserved

Printed in Great Britain

Library of Congress Cataloging in Publication Data

Welch, Ann Courtenay Edmonds, 1917–
   The book of airsports.

  Includes index.
  1. Aeronautical sports. I. Title.
GV755.W44   797.5   78–2600
ISBN 0–688–04628–7

Contents

	Introduction	page 7
1	Hang Gliding *and a few principles of flight*	9
2	Gliding *and doing it inexpensively*	26
3	Aeroplanes *and some map reading*	48
4	Man-powered Aircraft *and its new challenge*	66
5	Hot Air Ballooning *and a little more history*	77
6	Parachuting *and parascending*	92
7	Wind and Weather *and observing with models*	112
	Appendix I Rules of the Air	128
	Appendix II Example of Medical Standard (British Gliding Association)	130
	Appendix III Addresses	131
	Index	133

Introduction

Large jets and package tours have carried millions of people into the air but at the same time have kept them remote and insulated from the air itself. But flying is not all Heathrow, Gatwick and Kennedy. Some of the sky is there for everyone to use and to discover its delights for themselves, if they want to enough. The opportunities are greater than they may seem at first glance, in spite of the growing spread of controlled airspace, inflation and all the other limitations and restrictions of life. But flying for fun is not handed out on a plate; it has to be worked for with considerable determination and persistence. It eats up time and energy, it demands study of navigation and meteorology and, by no means least, it needs self-reliance and competence. Flying is not like watching the television: just switch off when bored. If you are in the air you have got to get yourself down because no one is there to help you.

If you do accept the challenge, the rewards are great, and the choice is wide. There is the physical rough and tumble of hang gliding, the high technology of soaring, the satisfaction of building and flying your own aeroplane or the peaceful drifting flight of a balloon. If none of these is quite what you want, you can experiment quietly with gossamer man-powered aircraft at a height of 10 feet, or you can dive from an aeroplane at 10,000 feet and can make patterns in the sky before opening your parachute. It depends what you want to do. Perhaps the largest problem if you want to fly is in getting started. It is not always easy to obtain information, flying sounds – and sometimes is – extremely expensive; and you cannot be sure if you are going to enjoy it. If you have a friend who flies or glides, tag along to see what it is like; if not, take a week's holiday and go on a course. The outlay will probably be no more than you would spend lying on a sunny beach, but at the same time you will not be committing yourself. At the end of the week you will know, one way or the other.

One of the surprising things about flying is that, although the choice is wide, many people seem to narrow it down by being interested in only their own favourite brand of aviation. This is a pity, because there is an almost infinite interrelationship not only between the pleasures and skills involved, but in the equipment and needs, such as instruments, airfields or forecasts. No branch of sport flying is superior to any other; the only difference is that you will enjoy one more than another. The greater the co-operation, the better are the chances of retaining fair shares in airspace; this means more flying for everyone.

Another marvellous thing about the wide choice in flying sports is that there is something for all ages. After 5 years or so of exciting parachuting, the jumper may like to change gear and to obtain a private pilot's aeroplane licence. Some years later again, he may find he has more time to spare and may decide to build himself an aeroplane.

This book gives only a brief introduction to what is possible. It does not include activities such as business or all-weather aeroplane flying or helicoptering; it does no more than touch on the enormous field of aeromodelling; however, some addresses are given from which information can be obtained. If you want to fly, it is no good waiting for it to come to you. However diffident you may feel, go and visit clubs and airfields, write letters for information, and, if you do not get a reply, write again. Most people who have been pilots or parachutists for some time are very ready to help newcomers, but they cannot do so if you do not make yourself known.

Figure 1.1. The attraction of hang gliding is its independence. You carry your own aircraft up the hill and fly without the need of any motor or helper. But you should not fly alone.

1 Hang Gliding

Throughout history there have been people who have wanted to fly, not in aerial carriages but like the birds. To use only their own energy to get airborne and to feel the air, warm or cool, on their bodies. There is a special excitement in such an individual personal flying because the sense of achievement is great. Pioneers, such as Lilienthal and Pilcher, loved their flying, but it was not for everyone since, as well as being pilots, they had to be both designers and constructors. Working on the far fringes of aeronautical knowledge their flying was dangerous, and finally both were killed by experimental aircraft. With the birth of the aeroplane the dream of flying like the birds was almost lost. A few individuals continued to build simple hang gliders out of bamboo and cotton sheets, but they were looked on as eccentrics: aviation, after all, was unconsciously in pursuit of the jumbo jet. By the time it had achieved the technology and the aeroplane to carry 350 passengers, flying had become extremely expensive, and the reality of simple personal flying seemed almost to have disappeared. But the dream still lived. In the 1960s, in the USA the simple hang glider was reborn, its father being Francis Rogallo who developed the flexible wing delta. The new hang gliders were also built of bamboo, covered with polythene, and they did not fly very well. But suddenly across the world the dream had become a reality. Hundreds, and then thousands, of people started building and flying hang gliders. As in the early days of aviation, pioneers were killed, but with such explosive energy development was rapid. Within the last 10 years a completely new dimension has been added to sport flying. There is a large range of excellent and beautiful hang gliders on the market, and clubs and schools have appeared to train the new flier. Hang gliding is also the cheapest way of getting into the air. It is quiet and immensely satisfying. It is also challenging, because it is so absolutely personal. The pilot is not backed up by air traffic controllers, meteorologists or pages of regulations. He is on his own and has to make his own decisions, and his neck is his own responsibility. But some people are not very good at looking after themselves. They attempt to fly from hills or in weather that is beyond their experience to cope with, or they indulge in 'show-off' flying – fast dives and steep wing-overs – that the simple hang glider was never designed to take. Hang gliding is fun, but like all aviation it is also a stern disciplinarian.

For the flier who is prepared to accept responsibility for himself, just as the birds have to, what could be more delightful than taking your own aircraft to the top of some beautiful hill on a spring afternoon, running a few steps and floating out over the valley. The air is clean and fresh, the trees and hedgerows coming into leaf and the sky above full of puffy white cumulus clouds. You swing your body to turn easily along the ridge, and immediately you feel the lift of the wind as it blows up over the hill to support you. You fly a mile along the ridge about 50 feet up, looking down at picnickers staring up, and formating momentarily with a seagull. All the time you are unconsciously adjusting your body to balance the little gusts and surges of the air and to keep in the narrow band of lift. You reach the trees at the end of the ridge, take a look at the nest-building rooks and turn back. An extra surge of lift hits you as a thermal upcurrent flows up the warm and sunny face of the hill, and you take it with your muscles, turning and perhaps slowing up a little to get the most out of this bonus fountain of lift. Ahead, and small on the hillside, are other colourful hang gliders, and as you watch one comes up to join you. You fly together for a while, chasing each other along the ridge or trying to get higher by the cunning use of the elusive surges of lift. Then you come in to land together, touching down lightly on the soft fresh-smelling grass of the hilltop and fold your wings.

The aircraft

Although hang gliders are the simplest aircraft that exist, they are precision built and have to be properly rigged and adjusted. Otherwise they will perform less well and also be less safe. They come in an increasing variety of shapes and sizes, ranging from the basic rogallo for club and school use to almost aeroplane planform hang gliders. In between are swallowtails, swept-wings without tails and even the occasional biplane.

Control ranges from pilot weight shift on the rogallos and most of the flexible wings to weight shift with tip-draggers to help turning on the swept-wings.

Some hang gliders with tails use weight shift and a movable rudder, and one or two have conventional aerodynamic controls like aeroplanes. Needless to say an inexperienced pilot should not consider changing from one type to another, as they all have different handling characteristics in the air. There are a wide range of simple rogallos available on the market, and even these have different methods of rigging and will feel different to fly, but basically the construction is the same. Aluminium tube – of the proper specification and quality – is used for the primary structure (Figures 1, 2). This is bolted together and held rigidly by bracing wires. The sail is held on to the tubes by sail pockets and is designed so that it will billow up to some extent on the two halves of the wing to provide stability. Fine adjustments are made to the rigging to provide a small amount of reflex in the keel to provide positive stability in pitch and to keep the long leading edge tubes straight in flight. This adjustment is made by means of wing wires or deflexers. It is very important that the hang glider is rigged according to the manufacturer's instructions and that no experimental adjustments are made without a proper understanding of aerodynamics. A few people build their own hang gliders, but this is not such a profitable exercise as may first appear. It is not even enough to copy faithfully the hang glider of a friend if the necessary aeronautical knowledge is not possessed. Unwittingly the design or construction may be slightly modified in some way that may not be perceived, and the hang glider may be weaker than intended. It is more likely that the performance will be less good than other similar aircraft on the hill, which will be disappointing. It is more sensible to buy a second-hand hang glider from a known and reputable source and to use that for gaining flying experience. But first of all it is necessary to learn to fly.

Starting to learn to fly

If you have never flown anything before, the first need is to put aside just for a while that dream of stepping lightly off a hilltop and formating high in the sky with the birds, because learning to fly a hang glider properly is hard work. First you must find a good school not too far away, you must save up some money and you must be prepared to devote a lot of concentrated time. It is possible to learn to fly by turning up every week or so, but this will soon be found to be a slow and frustrating process. It is far better to take a four day course and to follow this by flying every weekend for a few months. If during this period a further full week, or even two, can be included, it will be so much the better. By concentrated learning in this way you will achieve solid experience, not only of flying a hang glider but of flying in different winds and weather, and you will have become very fit. If you just go for a few short flights very occasionally you will not progress much, because each time you fly you will be trying to remember what you learnt last time; and you will discover that you have forgotten most of it. Also you will find it tiring because your muscles are not organized either for the quick reactions needed to control the aircraft or for carrying it back up the hill again!

On the first day at hang gliding school you may not even take to the air, particularly if the weather is rough. Instead you will probably spend an hour or so in a simulator. This is a control frame and harness strung from the ceiling, and in this you can practise the weight shift movements necessary to maintain flying speed, to make turns and to flare for the landing. You will be shown films of people running to take off and getting back on the ground again, so that you can see what you are supposed to try to do. You will also be given talks on why a hang glider flies, how the air flows past the wing so that it provides lift, and what happens to the airflow and the wing if you fly too slowly – or too fast. On a more down-to-earth level you may find yourself buying some new clothes. Starting from the top you will have to have a helmet. For school flying they are provided, but you will soon prefer one of your own. Good-quality motorcycle helmets without visors or peaks are fine, and there are also special hang gliding helmets which have holes for the ears so that the sound of the air can be heard more easily. The chin strap should be under, and never on, the chin. At the other end you will need some good boots; these should support the ankles but should also be flexible enough for comfortable hill walking. Boots are not essential, and when flying from soft sand dunes some pilots even risk bare feet. In Britain where most flying is done from rocky or gorse-

Figure 1.2. A hang glider is constructed from aluminium tube and Terylene (Dacron) sail fabric. Battens help the sail retain a smooth shape in flight, and the deflexer wires prevent the leading edge tubes from bending under load.

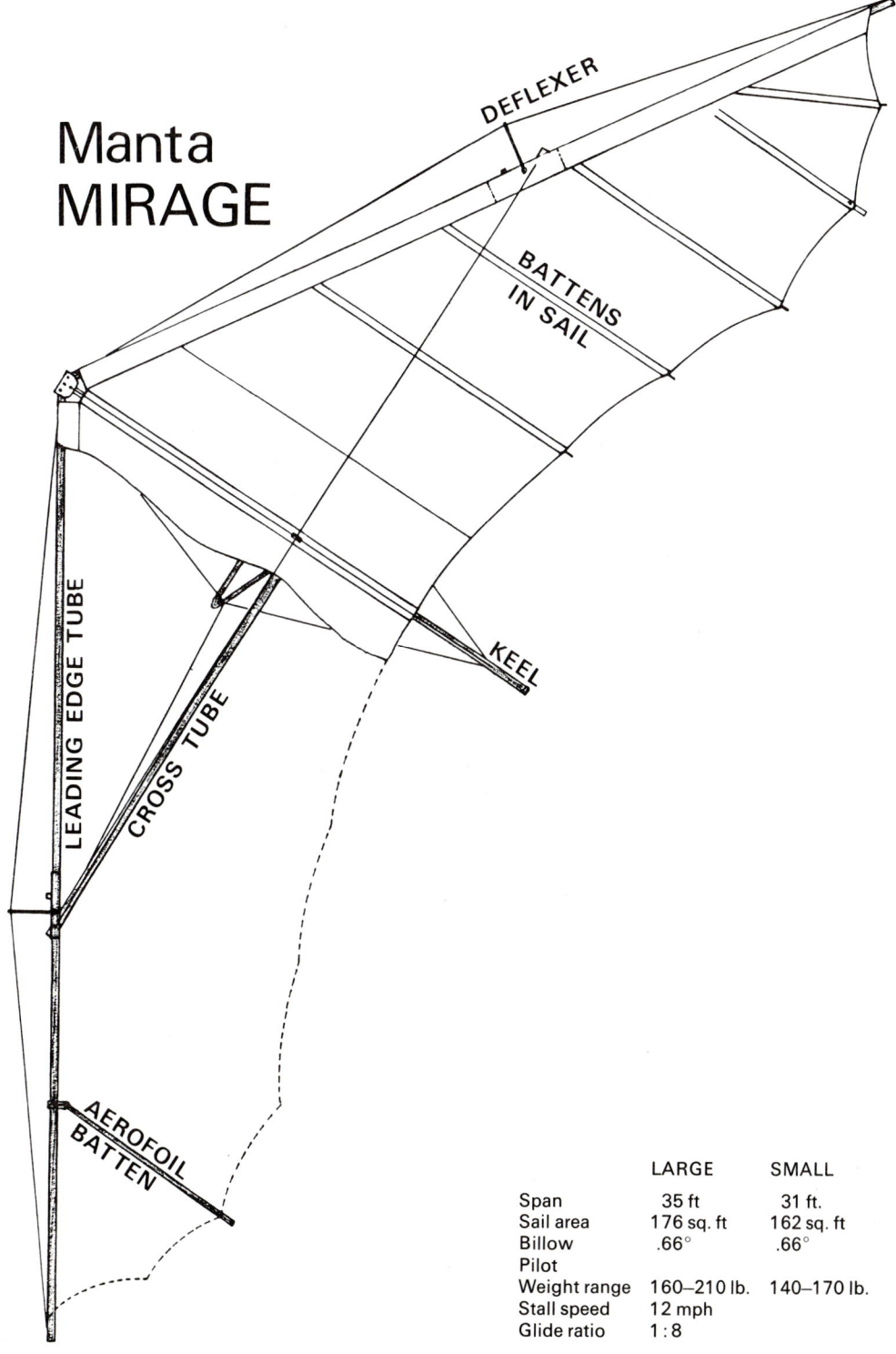

	LARGE	SMALL
Span	35 ft	31 ft.
Sail area	176 sq. ft	162 sq. ft
Billow	.66°	.66°
Pilot		
Weight range	160–210 lb.	140–170 lb.
Stall speed	12 mph	
Glide ratio	1 : 8	

Figure 1.3. Instructor and passenger about to take off on a windy day. A helper holds the front wires to prevent the sail from filling until the pilot is ready to go.

bush hills good boots will spare a lot of worries. In between there is a need to be warm, but not too hot on the ground, and also to be windproof. To start with jeans, a couple of sweaters – which can be shed if necessary – and an anorak are perfectly suitable, but soon you will probably want to get yourself a hardwearing and wind-resistant jump suit. To complete the outfit, find some tough old gloves, even if it is summer. To begin with at any rate the control frame and your hands will sometimes arrive on the ground together, and chipped knuckles feel sore.

First flights

There are various methods of learning to fly a hang glider, and they are exemplified by 'low' and 'slow': 'low' means you do not go casting yourself from great heights too soon, and 'slow' means that you should consolidate each lesson properly before progressing to the next. It may be, of course, that, although you want to fly very much, you have doubts as to whether you will like it. You may also feel somewhat apprehensive, without realizing that this is a perfectly normal reaction when starting something quite new. The best answer in these cases is to have a flight, two-up, with an instructor. Some schools give two-seater flights as a matter of course. Although your hands will be on the control frame so that you can feel and see what is happening, the instructor will do the actual controlling. There will be time to look around, down at the ground and up at the great wing above. The instructor can explain things in the air, and, if it is possible to soar and if there is time, he may encourage you to try some of the flying for yourself. Two-seater flying is also useful at later stages in training, when learning to soar in hill lift, for example.

To start the new pilot flying on his own, schools are increasingly using tether flying. This is a very simple system in which the hang glider has a long line attached to its nose, with the other end held by the instructor, and a long line from each wing tip, usually held by fellow pupils. Tether flying can also be carried out in stronger winds than would be safe for free flying by an inexperienced pilot. The first lesson is to teach you how to control your airspeed. A hang glider, like any other heavier-than-air aircraft, cannot fly unless there is air flowing past the wing at sufficient

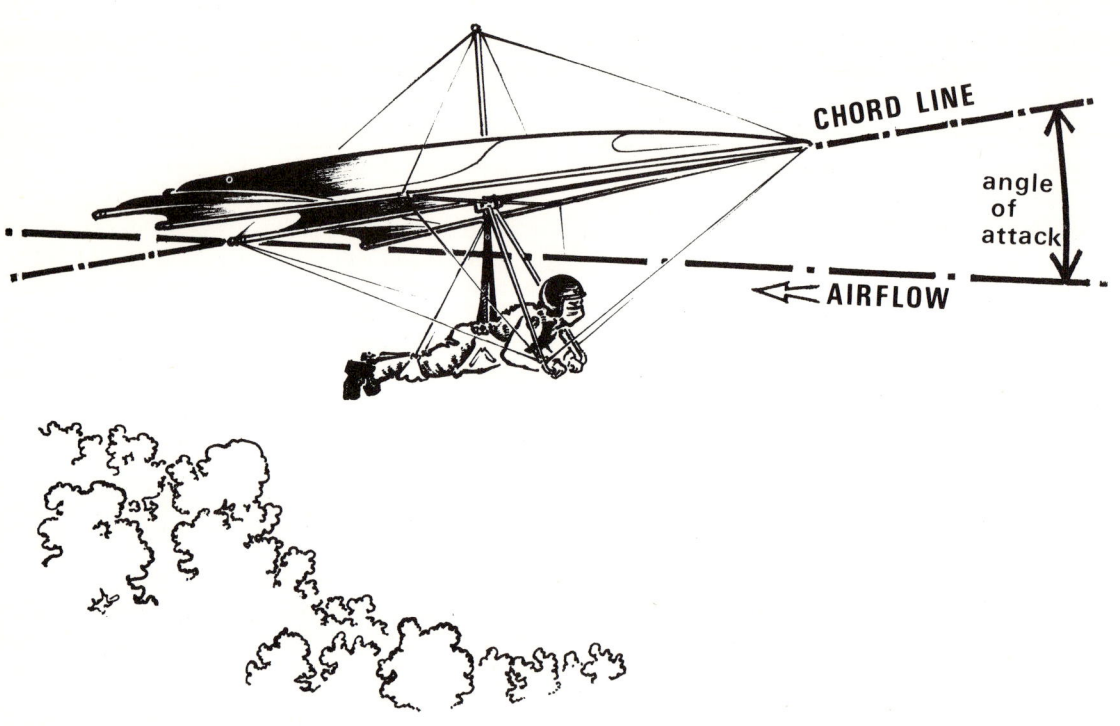

Figure 1.4. A hang glider wing, like that of any other aircraft, flies when at a positive angle to the airflow — called the angle of attack. If the angle of attack is increased too much, the wing will stall.

speed to enable it to provide lift. The best lift is achieved when the wing is flying at an angle to the airflow; this angle is called the angle of attack. The optimum angle of attack is when the wing is providing good lift with minimum drag. If the angle of attack is increased somewhat, the lift provided remains good, but the drag increases. This begins to affect the performance by increasing the rate at which the aircraft sinks. If the angle of attack is increased further, the lift produced will lessen, but the drag continues to increase. Eventually, the wing will stall. The nose of the aircraft will drop, and control will be lost until speed is regained. If the angle of attack is reduced too much on a flexible-wing hang glider, the air will begin to flow more equally over both the top and bottom surface of the wing, and in effect it will blow the sail flat. If this happens, the wing will provide little or no further lift and will dive uncontrollably. A properly designed hang glider prevents you from shifting your weight so far forwards that this can happen; this is one of the reasons why you should not adjust or modify your hang glider without really knowing what you are doing.

If you are starting to learn by the tether method, you will find yourself standing on the top of the hill underneath your hang glider, convinced that the wind is much too strong to be safe. The nose of the hang glider will be on the ground while you clip yourself in the harness onto the hang glider and get a good grip of the control frame. The instructor will be at the nose and will help you raise it, as you stand up, until the sail is flapping noisily. It is providing no lift because the angle of attack is too small. The instructor will now move away into wind, keeping the tether line taut and telling you to push out gently on the control bar to raise the nose and to increase the angle of attack. Quite suddenly you will find the noisy flapping has stopped and that the weight of the hang glider is disappearing. Your feet leave the ground, and you are flying. You now have to keep adjusting the angle of attack by pushing out or pulling in on the control bar so that you remain about the same height off the ground. If you find you are getting too high you pull in a little on the control bar, and, if you find you are back again on the hard earth, you push out. The instructor will prevent you from getting too high or out of control with the nose tether line. The wing lines are just held steady so that the hang glider is kept level.

When you have mastered control in pitch so that you are able to fly at the angle of attack and airspeed that are correct, you can start to learn about lateral control and turning. Now the wing lines will be held slack. If a wing goes up, you have to shift your weight to that side to bring it down again, and then you shift it back again, so that the wing does not go down too far. If you want to turn, you will have to bank the hang glider in the direction you want to go. So you shift your weight that way and then back again as before. The people holding the wing tethers will prevent things from getting out of hand, while you are working at how much to move or how quickly to do it. The next stage is to have both nose and wing tethers slack so that you have to control the hang glider in pitch and in roll at the same time. If you have progressed too quickly, you will find that you are concentrating on speed and are failing to keep the wings level, or that you are concentrating just on keeping the wings level, only to find that you are back on the ground because you forgot about the angle of attack and the airspeed.

If you are learning without tethers, you will have to fly in less strong winds, which means that you will have to run to obtain enough airspeed to take off. You will not be able to fly from the top of the hill either but from part of the way down it, so that you will be back on the ground again before mistakes have had a chance to develop into anything serious. Learning this way is perfectly feasible, and this is how most hang glider pilots start, but you have more things to do at the same time. You need to make a determined run, carrying what seems to be a totally unwieldly weight. You have to push out to get the sail to fill and fly and then to pull in again so that you do not just shoot up into the sky and stall, and you also have to remember to keep the wings level. If you run and fail to push out, the hang glider nose will hit the ground, and you will arrive on your tummy. You also have to remember to land only a few seconds after getting airborne. Many schools use the VHF radio, on 129.9 MHz, to talk to the solo beginner in flight, via a small radio receiver installed in his helmet. This system works well. Most beginners soon get to the stage where simple straight flights ending with a stand-up landing happen every time – or almost. Flying feels great, you feel orientated and there is time to look around. The top of the large hill beckons, and that dream of soaring with the birds begins to nag.

This is the moment when the risk is perhaps greatest. You know what you can do, but you cannot know all you have to know. It is absolutely fundamental in any sort of flying that you do only one new thing at a time, and you go on doing that until you have got it absolutely right.

When you can make those short straight flights, the next step is either to take off from a little higher up the hill in the same wind and weather or to fly from the same place in a slightly stronger wind, but *not* both together.

Turns
When you are able to take off from higher up the hill, pick a point about 45 degrees to the left or to the right of your into-wind line. In the air turn towards it and then turn back again, so that you land precisely into wind. Do this both ways and go on doing it until you are all the time in control of the situation. It may be tiring keeping on carrying your wing back up the hill, but, if you are learning to fly solo, there is no other way of doing it with any degree of certainty or safety. After a 45 degree change of direction has been achieved, the turn can be increased so as to fly along parallel to the hill, before you go out into the valley for an into-wind landing.

Drift
A problem that now begins to show itself is the effect of wind drift. So far, with all flying being carried out substantially into wind, there has not been any apparent drift, and the speed over the ground has been slow. If the hang glider is now turned so that it is pointing parallel to the hill, its path over the ground will not be parallel, because the wind is drifting it steadily back into the slope. It is easy to come to grief this way. You have turned along the hill and are now looking out towards your landing place, working out how to get there; the next thing you know is that your wing has caught in the bushes and that the ground is harder than you expected.

Airspeed and groundspeed
The matter of airspeed and groundspeed demands concentration when you start flying downwind, as indeed you must if making a 360 degree turn. The

Figure 1.6. To obtain the best performance from a hang glider the pilot flies prone to reduce the drag of his body – vertical this would be about 10 square feet and horizontal about 2 square feet.

normal airspeed of the hang glider is, say, 20 miles per hour, and, when flying into a wind of 12 miles per hour, its speed *over the ground* will be only a slow 8 miles per hour. However, if the hang glider, still flying at an airspeed of 20 miles per hour, is turned and flies downwind, its speed *over the ground* will be (20 + 12) = 32 miles per hour. If the wind is 25 miles per hour, the groundspeed will be 45 miles per hour. If you have so far only flown more or less into wind, the sudden change from flying over the ground always at a mere 8 to 10 miles per hour to rushing over it at 40 to 50 miles per hour can be very frightening. If you do not appreciate what is happening, you find yourself flying towards the hill and trying to slow down the headlong rush by pushing out on the control bar and by reducing the *airspeed*. All this does is to cause the hang glider to stall. If you are to fly safely, you need not only to understand the problems that can arise – by talking to your instructor and by reading books – but to work at each problem slowly and thoroughly, until you fully understand it and can keep control over any situation in which you may find yourself.

Pilot proficiency standards and badges

The British Hang Gliding Association (BHGA), and indeed the national associations of other countries, issue a series of pilot proficiency badges which can be gained as progress is made. Not only does it help you to know how far you have progressed, but it also helps you to know what to work for next. Most clubs give their hills a 'difficulty' rating, according to the weather on the day, so that both local flier and visitor

Figure 1.5. The hang glider landing into the wind has a speed over the ground of only 1 or 2 miles per hour, although its airspeed is still about 18 miles per hour. The hang glider flying with the wind is travelling over the ground at his airspeed *plus* the speed of the wind – at about 33 to 35 miles per hour.

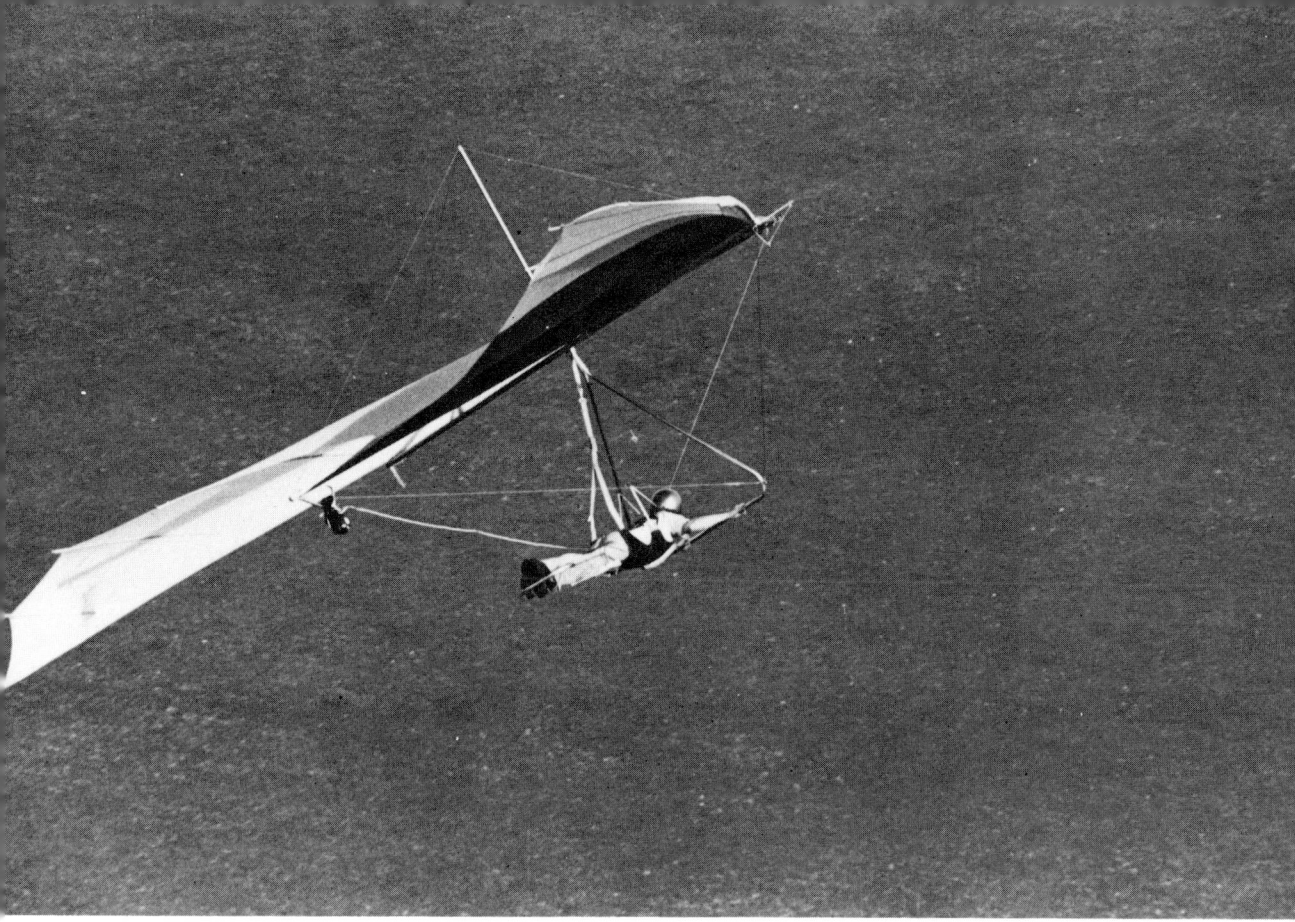

know whether or not they have reached the standard at which it is safe and sensible for them to fly. Competition organizers usually specify a minimum grade of pilot proficiency before a flier may enter. The proficiency standards are not only for beginners, the advanced go only to the top pilots. There is also the Fédération Aéronautique Internationale (FAI) international Delta Silver badge for which a distance of 50 kilometres must be soared, a height of 1,000 metres reached, as well as a duration flight of 5 hours. No one in the world has yet gained this coveted badge.

Owning a hang glider

After flying on school hang gliders for a while, you will become increasingly enthusiastic about having one of your own. What you get will depend on your pocket, on how much hang gliding you have done and on what sort of flying you expect to do in the future. It is a matter which should not be rushed. For a start you will need an aircraft to match your own weight. If you are too heavy for the one you obtain, it will sink faster and will have a slightly higher stalling speed. It may also be insufficiently strong. If you get one that is too big, the stalling speed will be slow, but it will be unwieldy and difficult to control. It is worth reading advertisements to see what is on offer, talking to the owners of hang gliders that attract you, and above all getting the advice of your instructor. There really is some merit in buying a good second-hand aircraft initially and in keeping some money until, at the end of a season's flying, you know more what you really want.

Although, at the school, you were taught how to put the hang glider together, to inspect it to see that it was airworthy, to stop it being blown over on the hilltop and to put it away in its bag, there was always the instructor or someone else to see that it was all done properly. Now, as the proud owner, there is only you. If you take off with one of the rigging wires lying in the grass or forget to clip your harness onto the hang glider, there is no one to blame but you. Most pilots realize this for the first few flights, but, as the new toy becomes familiar, some get careless. A hang glider may be simple and no executive jet when it comes to cost, but it is still an aircraft. It has to be correctly assembled, be complete, and in good condition *on every flight*. If you feel that your memory is not all it might be, make a pocket check list and use it. If you find something wrong, or odd, on the aircraft, ask the advice of someone with more experience *before* you fly it. Never be afraid to ask questions that may sound silly – it is cheap at the price.

Figure 1.7. To turn, the pilot moves his weight towards the side to which he wants to go. Once steadily in the turn he centralizes his weight until he wishes to come out of the turn.

Hang gliders are surprisingly rugged. They can take quite a beating from bushes and rough ground without damage. They can be battered in their bags on roof racks and can be left out in the rain, but their strength and toughness should never be taken for granted. Dents and deep scratches in aluminium tubes make them weaker, and so does straightening a bent tube. A small tear in the fabric can become a big one in a sharp gust. Attachment bolts may be bent if they hit rocks, and the harness can be cut on stones. If these things go unnoticed or unrepaired, it is inviting trouble. If a hang glider has to be put in its bag wet, it should be shaken out and dried on reaching home. If it has been flying in sea air and has landed on the beach, it should be washed in fresh water. Looking after the aircraft is an integral part of flying, and just as important.

Slope soaring
With a good aircraft and some solid flying experience under your belt you will be ready for soaring. Flying from the hill you will have felt the buoyant air which has carried other hang gliders high above you, before flying out from the hill to concentrate on a good stand-up landing in the field below.

Most soaring is done in the air which rises over a hill when the wind is blowing towards it. The air does not flow tidily along the valley floor and then up the face of the slope. Apart from the fact that the air near the ground is slowed up by obstructions such as trees, it tends to start to take off some distance out ahead of the hill. This means that the true wind is blowing only near and above the top of the hill, and low down near the foot there will be less wind, even dead air (Fig. 7.6).

The best shaped hills for soaring are those which are fairly steep, such as the Downs, which have a smooth rounded crest and a fairly flat top for some distance back. It is also better if the hill is long so that air will be forced up over the top for some distance and will not be able to escape around the ends. If the ground falls away behind the crest of the ridge, there will probably be severe turbulence in this region, particularly in strong winds. When landing on top of the hill you may have a real problem; if you try to get down close to the windward edge, you may find yourself still in lift, and simply going up again, but, if you get too far behind the crest, you are likely to be dumped ignominiously in the bushes or to be cartwheeled into a gulley. Sharp-edged cliffs are also only for the more expert, as the air is not able to flow smoothly up and over the top. Vicious eddies develop near the top of the vertical face, and also on the top just back from the edge.

The smoothest slope lift is often found over large round hills near the sea and in winter, because the air is untroubled either by obstructions up wind or by thermals.

Thermal soaring
In summer hill lift is often augmented by thermals. These warm air upcurrents usually form over a village, ploughed fields or sunny sheltered hollows out in the valley, and they drift, rising as they go, towards the hill. As they reach the influence of the slope lift, they continue up with it. On reaching the top they go on rising freely, drifting with the wind, until they cool to the same temperature as the surrounding air. As well as providing a supplement to the slope lift, the passing thermal bubble affects the local wind direction as air moves in from all around to replace that which has risen in the thermal. This has the effect of reducing the slope lift temporarily on

either side of the thermal, so pilots in this air will sink down, while the lucky ones who have got caught in the thermal rise up even faster. If you are observant when slope soaring and watch for little changes in the wind direction way out ahead of the hill, it is possible to anticipate the arrival of a thermal and to position yourself to be in the right place at the right moment.

Having got yourself in a thermal over the hill, the difficulty is to stay in its confines, because it cannot expand and grow large until it has risen much higher. You are unable to circle, because you have not enough height, and in any case this would probably result in flying out of it inadvertently and into the sinking air behind the hill. The best way is to fly slowly and to make an S-turn into the wind, trying to stay in the strongest parts of the lift. If it is possible to stay with the thermal and to reach several hundred feet above the hill, then it may be practicable to circle – provided that you know whether the centre of the upcurrent is to the right or left of you. If the thermal tries to tip you out of it, the centre of the thermal is more likely to be on the side of the wing that was pushed up. Push it down, and turn towards it.

Cumulus clouds

Unless the air is very dry, a cumulus cloud will form at the top of each thermal. So a growing cloud is a sure sign that there is a thermal underneath. When the thermal bubble has completely reached the cloud base, there will be no more rising air to feed the cloud, and it will decay and evaporate. A summer day's cumulus only has a life of about 20 minutes, so you will need to teach yourself by observation to distinguish between the new and the old, if you want to use their energy. Thermals are sometimes marked by circling seagulls or rooks. Swallows and swifts mark thermals, not because they are soaring but when chasing insects that have been swept up from the thermal source (Fig. 7.3).

Cold and fatigue

When you start soaring and making longer flights, instead of humping your hang glider back up the hill, you will discover two things: that the air is cold, even in summer, and that flying can be even more tiring than hill climbing. It is important to realize this because in the air you cannot pull on another sweater or stop and rest. The effect of cold is insidious. It slows down brain as well as muscle, and you will fly less competently. If you continue to fly when you are tired as well as cold, the chance of messing up the landing is great. In any case three flights of 1 hour in a day is more fun and better experience than one flight of 3 hours; and you can warm up and have a hot drink in between.

Instruments

It is entirely practicable to fly a hang glider without an air-speed indicator or any instruments at all. The aircraft is stable, and the pilot can sense tiny changes in sound and in the feel of the air because he is as near a part of it as it is possible to get. An altimeter is not necessary, certainly for local flying, as it is soon possible to learn to judge height in terms of where the hang glider will land. The one instrument which is of real value is the variometer, which indicates whether the aircraft is gaining or losing height. It works on the basis of the difference in pressure between the free air and that in a flask. When the hang glider goes up, it moves into air of lower pressure than that in the flask, which flows out in an effort to equalize. When the hang glider sinks, the pressure of the air outside the flask is greater than that within, and air flows in the other direction. There are various ways in which this flow can be made to register either on a dial or as varying sound. Audio variometers are popular because the information is fed to the pilot without his having to keep looking at an instrument face.

The future

Hang gliding has a great future because the era of cross-country soaring is only just beginning. As techniques for finding and using thermals in hang gliders become better known, more pilots will be able to set out on voyages of exploration along ranges of hills using thermals to jump the gaps. Some pilots in the USA have already made pure thermal flights of 150 kilometres, and in Britain, where conditions are much more difficult, the longest cross-country distance is already 30 kilometres, For the hang glider there are still large enough areas of uncontrolled airspace to provide good soaring for many years to come.

Figure 1.8. A hang glider is usually flown without instruments, but for soaring and cross-country flying a variometer is essential. Most varios are audio as well as having a dial presentation.

This pilot's helmet has ear holes so that he can listen to the sound of the airflow as well as hear the audio indications.

ASSOCIATIONS

British Hang Gliding Association
Address: Monksilver, Taunton, Somerset
No. of members: 4,000
No. of hang gliders: 2,400
No. of clubs and schools: 40
   No. of flights annually: 100,000
   Minimum age for flying solo: 16 years

The BHGA is responsible for pilot proficiency standards, training and qualification of instructors, registration of schools and hang glider airworthiness in the UK. It is the national contact with the Civil Aviation Authority (CAA), local authorities and landowners.

Members of the BHGA are individuals and affiliated clubs. The annual subscription is £7.50 which includes the monthly magazine *Wings!* and insurance.

Pilot licences and certificates
No pilot licences are required for hang gliding. A series of pilot proficiency certificates of increasing standard of difficulty are available, except that a manufacturer will not sell a hang glider to a pilot who has not yet obtained the Elementary Certificate, and a pilot may not train as an instructor, may not fly across country or may not enter major championships until he has gained a higher rating.

Training Courses
Beginners' training courses of 4 days' duration are available at all schools. Training is also given in clubs. List and dates may be obtained from the BHGA.

Figure 1.10. The Wills Wing Cross Country. Both the Moonraker and the Cross Country have a glide ratio approaching 1:10.

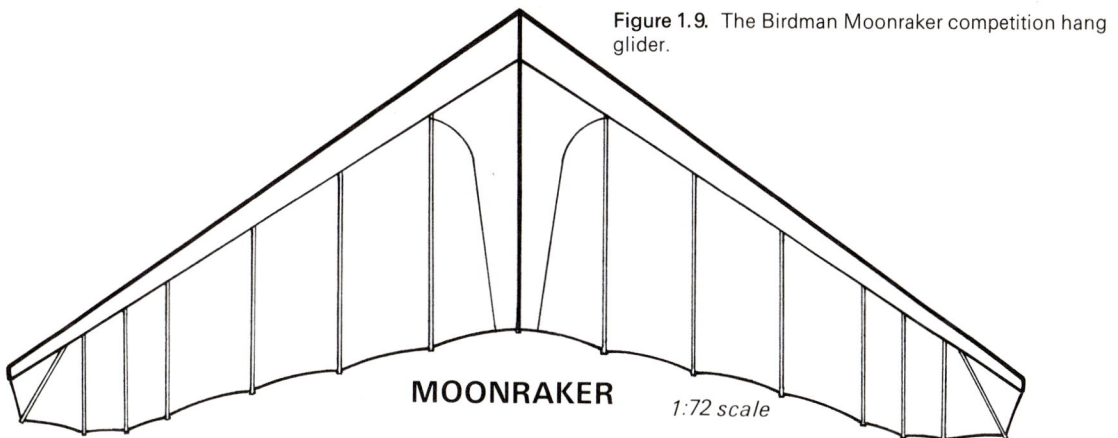

Figure 1.9. The Birdman Moonraker competition hang glider.

MOONRAKER *1:72 scale*

Span	32 ft
Nose angle	108°
Sail billow	.5°
Aspect ratio	190 sq ft
Root chord	10 ft
Leading edge tubes	20 ft

	LARGE	SMALL
Span	37.5	35.8
Leading edge	22 ft	21 ft
Keel	11 ft	10 ft
Nose angle	113°	113°
Sail area	220 sq. ft	185 sq. ft
Aspect ratio	6.4	6.6
Sail billow	.3°	.3°
Pilot weight range	160–220 lbs	130–180 lbs

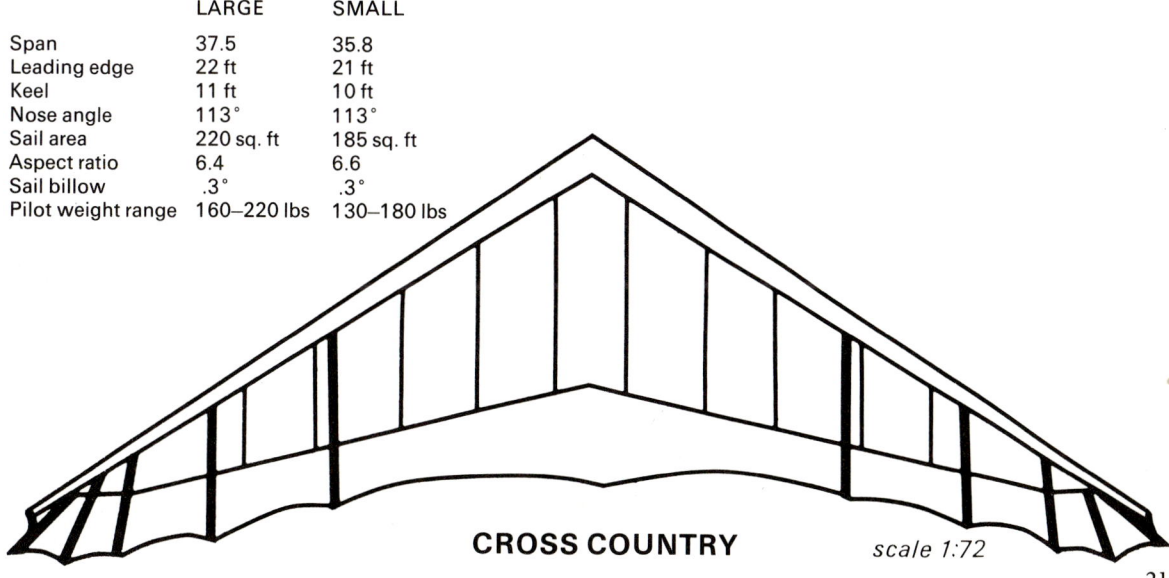

CROSS COUNTRY *scale 1:72*

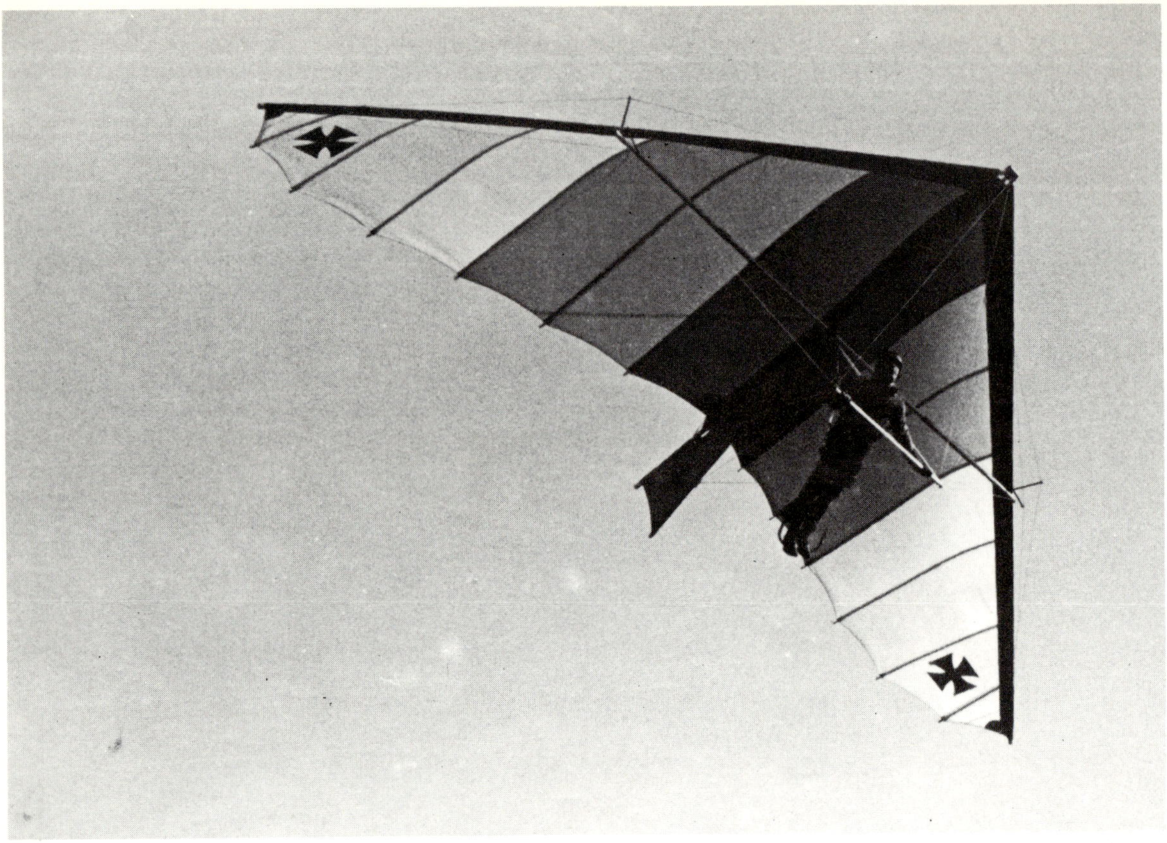

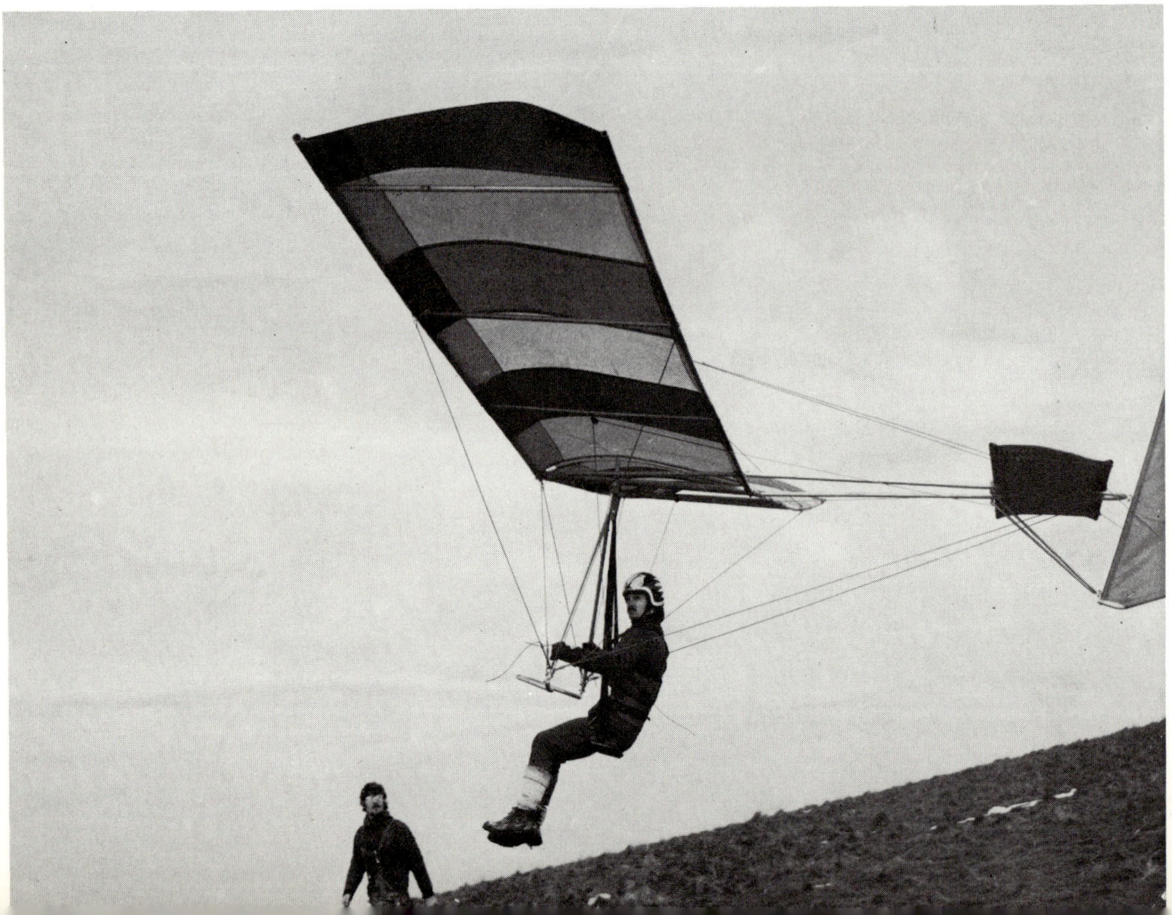

Figure 1.11. The Scorpion has a fully battened sail with almost no billow, the directional stability being assisted by a small fixed fin.

Figure 1.12. The Quicksilver. A semi-rigid wing controlled by weight shift and having a glide ratio of about 1:8. Several hundred of these are being flown.

Figure 1.13. The Breenwave. An experimental tailless with the pilot flying supine.

Figure 1.14. The Swiss C-FL Canard, designed for high performance, and built of kevlar and epoxy. The C-FL is heavier, faster and more expensive than most hang gliders.

Figure 1.15. The Icarus V rigid-wing swept tailless hang glider soaring over Californian cliffs.

The requirements are a distance of 50 kilometres, a height gain of 1,000 metres and a duration of 5 hours. The FAI is introducing in 1978 the Delta Gold. For this the pilot has to fly a distance of 300 km and a closed circuit goal flight of 200 km.

CODE OF GOOD PRACTICE

Never go flying on your own.

Ensure that permission of the landowner or controlling authority has been obtained before using a site, and when seeking permission present your BHGA and club membership cards. State exactly where you wish to fly and to land.

When visiting other club sites contact them in advance and observe their local rules.

Do not fly from any site where livestock may be disturbed or about to bear their young – usually March to May. Check with the farmer.

Use only recognized gates and paths. Do not climb over walls and fences. Close gates. Do not let animals escape when using a gate. Do not take dogs without permission, and keep them under control.

Avoid standing crops. If you do land in them, minimize your movements and keep spectators out. Report any damage, however small, to the landowner.

Do not leave litter.

If flying is likely to cause traffic congestion, inform the local police. Designate take-off and landing areas, and keep them free from spectators.

Rig clear of the take-off area, and enter it only when you are ready to fly. Do not leave a rigged hang glider unattended.

Park your car with consideration for others especially when loading or unloading. Find a proper parking place. Drive considerately.

Wear a well-fitting crash helmet on every flight.

Figure 1.16. The FAI Delta Bronze and Silver badge for hang glider pilots.

2 Gliding

Lilienthal was the great-grandfather of gliding, just as he was for hang gliding. There was the same lack of interest in flying without power following the invention of the aeroplane, until the end of the First World War, when the Germans returned to the Rhön Mountains to fly without the engines forbidden by the treaty of Versailles. At first these early gliders were a mixture of simple rigid-wing biplane hang gliders and very lightweight aircraft of aeroplane appearance, such as the Blaue Maus, but in 1922 Arthur Martens brought along his newly designed Vampyr, the forerunner of the modern glider. From then on the development of gliding was a relentless pursuit of performance so that every scrap of available energy in the air could be utilised. This has produced the most elegant, beautiful and efficient aircraft the world has ever seen. In 1922 the glide ratio of the Vampyr was 1:8 – about the same as a good hang glider. Now the glide ratio of a top competition glider is approaching 1:50. This means that from a height of 1 mile (5,280 feet) it will fly a theoretical distance of 50 miles. The actual distance may, of course, be different from this; it will be greater if lift is encountered or there is a helping tail wind, or it will be less if some of the height has to be devoted to making a safe approach and landing. This pursuit of ever-better performance has resulted in engineless flights of 1,000 miles distance in a day, speeds of 100 miles per hour around a triangular course and an altitude record of over 46,000 feet. Gliding is high-technology flying, and as a result, at the top end of the scale, it is expensive.

Clubs

All gliding in Britain, and in most other countries, is organized in clubs. This is because a glider cannot launch itself or cannot retrieve itself after a field landing. In a club everyone helps each other. As a member you learn not only to fly but to look after the gliders, to drive the winch or tow-car to launch them, to keep the flying logsheet and to put everything back into the hangar at night. At club level, gliding is not only fun, and not too expensive, but a fine way of making new friends. Most gliding clubs have residential accommodation, and some people spend the whole of the weekend and every holiday at their club. Even if you run out of money for flying, you are still involved with gliders out on the field, or you can crew on a retrieve to collect a glider from some remote village. Some people think that, if they are not actually flying, they are not learning anything of value to themselves. This is certainly not so, and many of today's top pilots are only as good as they are because of the days and weeks spent hanging around a gliding club in their early days. Even unconsciously, while perhaps pushing gliders about at the launch point, they were absorbing an understanding of the weather, what the sky looked like when gliders were able to soar and what changes in the clouds took place to kill the upcurrents. In winter, in non-soaring weather, when owners worked on their gliders to prepare them for the coming season, they helped and learnt a great deal about both the aircraft and its instruments. Club gliding can be a total involvement, and to many it is a complete way of life.

Soaring cross-country

However much a pilot enjoys just being at his club, the greatest delight of all is cross-country flying. To fly a glider, without any helpful engine, to some distant point and then back home again is a great challenge, and every flight, even over the same route, will be different. There will be moments of exhilaration, when the glider is romping upwards in a strong thermal towards a growing cumulus cloud. The view is tremendous in the clear air – and maybe far below there is another glider not climbing as fast as you are. Then, suddenly almost, there is despair. The thermal dies; you fly on expecting to find another, but the air now has a dead feeling. Your precious height begins to disappear as the altimeter needle relentlessly unwinds. You look ahead for a good cumulus; they are there but too far away to reach. You look back, not wanting to throw away hard-won distance, but you have to stay up somehow. The afternoon is still young, and it is of no interest to spend it sitting in a stubble field looking up at the sky. Yes, about half a mile back along the route a new cumulus cloud is just forming. There is not much wind so the thermal will be more or less underneath. You turn round with a feeling of mixed reluctance and hope and soon fly into the shadow of the cloud. You do not notice the sudden coolness as you search around for the invisible elusive

Figure 2.1. The Grunau Baby was one of the best known gliders of the 1930s and was made of spruce and birch plywood: span 44 feet; weight, 260 lb; glide ratio, 1:18; cost about £100.

lift. Then the variometer needle flickers upwards to indicate climb, and the audio squeaks. You throw the glider into a turn to circle in the lift, but you were too quick. The vario needle subsides to sink, and the audio goes quiet. Cursing yourself for impatience you fly more warily, trying to sense the thermal by minute changes in the feel of the air. The left wing bumps up a little: maybe the thermal is that way. You look at the vario, but the needle is still showing sink. Well, it is worth a try. Carefully you turn to the left, watching the vario like a hawk. Very slowly the needle moves upwards; it is still showing sink, but not so much. Then, quite suddenly you are in the lift. There is a surge, the vario needle shoots upwards to 4 knots climb, and the audio comes to life. You begin to circle, cautiously at first and then with increasing confidence as the vario tells you that the lift is strengthening and that you are now on your way up again at 6 knots. This time you stay with the thermal right up to cloud base and, while climbing, attend to your navigation. Your turning point of a big motorway junction should now be in sight; and it is. The grey snake with its streams of little coloured dots is converging from the right 3,000 feet below, and about 4 miles ahead is the straight line of trees which mark the ancient Roman road that crosses under the new one. You will be able to reach it easily and to photograph it with the Instamatic camera fixed on the left side of the canopy, and be able to reach that good looking cloud just ahead, to start you home. You leave the thermal just as the wisps of cloud begin to form a straggly curtain around the glider and speed on your way to the turn point junction. By arriving just to the right of it, the photograph can be taken as you make a left turn around the point, and you will waste almost no time at all. Flying steadily you start the turn, finger on the camera button when – bang! With a great surge the glider hits a new strong thermal, and your finger is jerked off the button before you can press it. What should you do? Use the new thermal, or throw it away and concentrate on the photograph. You decide to use it, but, just as you start circling, it mysteriously disappears; and another couple of circles fails to relocate it. Now you have drifted away from the photograph position, and lost a couple of hundred feet as well. What a fool; you would have been better to have just got that photograph; or would you?

Figure 2.2. Slope soaring. Although hill lift will often support a glider at a height of two to three times the height of the hill (see Chapter 7), as the wind dies away in the evening the glider may be able to continue to soar only by very careful flying. This glider is too low to land back on the top of the hill, so the pilot will almost certainly have to land at the bottom.

Figure 2.3. Soaring in mountains is one of the most delightful ways of flying, but the upcurrents – and downcurrents – are not always where they might be expected.

soon as it is possible to reach home with just a few hundred feet in hand for the landing. This final glide needs both careful calculation and navigation. With a glide ratio of, say, 1:40 and with the wind behind you, the final glide will sometimes have to be started long before the destination can be seen. When racing, this last glide will need to be made as fast as possible, with the glider being flown near its maximum speed, even though this will increase drag and will reduce the glide angle. Often, when you finally see your goal airfield, it looks so far away that you are sure that you will never be able to reach it. You do your calculations again which confirm that you will get there; then you fly into lift, and there is a great temptation to use it; to make sure. But you decide not to and instantly regret it as you fly into sink. You calculate again, and it is still all right. You will reach the airfield, in spite of the ground beginning to look far too close. As the field gets nearer, and you realize your sums were correct you speed up, diving over the finish line at 20 feet and 120 knots' airspeed, and pull up into a climb. The clean glider slips so easily through the air that from this speed you will gain 600 to 700 feet, more than enough to make a leisurely circuit of the field and land near friends who are already back. The glider rumbles gently to a stop, and you open the canopy to the scent of warm grass – and a smug feeling of satisfaction.

Cross-country soaring is full of the need for decisions – your decisions, each one of which interacts with the next and contributes to the success or failure of the flight. Even when planning a flight, you have to try to decide which will be the best part of the day in which to cover the most difficult part of the route or arrange it so that your return to base will be downwind. Then, if you are later than you expected and if the thermals are beginning to die away as the warmth of the sun weakens, you will have the wind to drift you gently home.

Soaring the glider all the way back to where you started from is both exciting and satisfying, particularly if you are in a competition race. But, if you go on looking for, and using, thermals until you have arrived home, not only will you have much more height than is necessary, but you will have wasted time. What is necessary is to stop using thermals as

The glider
Most gliders are now made of fibre-glass and epoxy resin. This is a magnificent material because the most efficient aerodynamic shape can be designed into the mould, and the finish is incredibly smooth. To achieve a glide ratio approaching 1:50, drag has to be reduced to the absolute minimum – supersonic fighters and Concorde produce more drag than a good fibre-glass glider. In a big competition the pilot will keep the wing surface absolutely clean, because even greasy finger marks will pick up dust and will spoil the laminar flow. Fibre-glass gliders are also immensely strong, even more so than they need be in order to make the long thin wings stiff enough. A top competition glider has a span of some 21 metres and an aspect ratio (the ratio of span to chord or width) of perhaps 25, and this wing is entirely unsupported by drag-producing struts or wires; even the control

surface hinges are inside so as to avoid drag. The undercarriage is retractable, and the pilot sits in a reclining position so that the cross-section of the fuselage can be as small as possible. The problem with such clean and slippery aircraft is not one of going places but of stopping. With such high performance no airfield would be large enough for ordinary landings; unless the glider had means of producing plenty of drag on demand. To this end some gliders have airbrakes, flaps and a tail parachute as well. Airbrakes simply produce drag, in the form of plates which can be made to protrude from the wings. Some airbrakes are very powerful and reduce the glide ratio to about 1:10. Such considerable drag, of course, slows the glider, so in order to maintain plenty of flying speed the nose has to be lowered. This steeper approach path also helps the pilot to obtain a better view ahead. Flaps provide drag, but they also increase lift, when lowered slightly, so that the wing section is effectively altered from a fast to a slower high-lift one. At this small angle, flaps improve lift with only a small increase in drag, but, if lowered to 85 or 90 degrees, they will produce almost as much drag as airbrakes with no improvement in lift. Because flaps reduce the stall speed, the glider will probably stall if the flaps are suddenly closed when it is coming in to land. Airbrakes do not effectively alter the stall speed and so can be safely closed at any time on the approach if the glider seems to be getting low.

Tail parachutes are 'one-shot' drag producers and are more useful as an emergency aid, particularly as they have to be repacked after each landing. If used, however, they are very effective and rapidly slow the glider down.

Club and school gliders are not so exotic as competition aircraft. They are not only less expensive

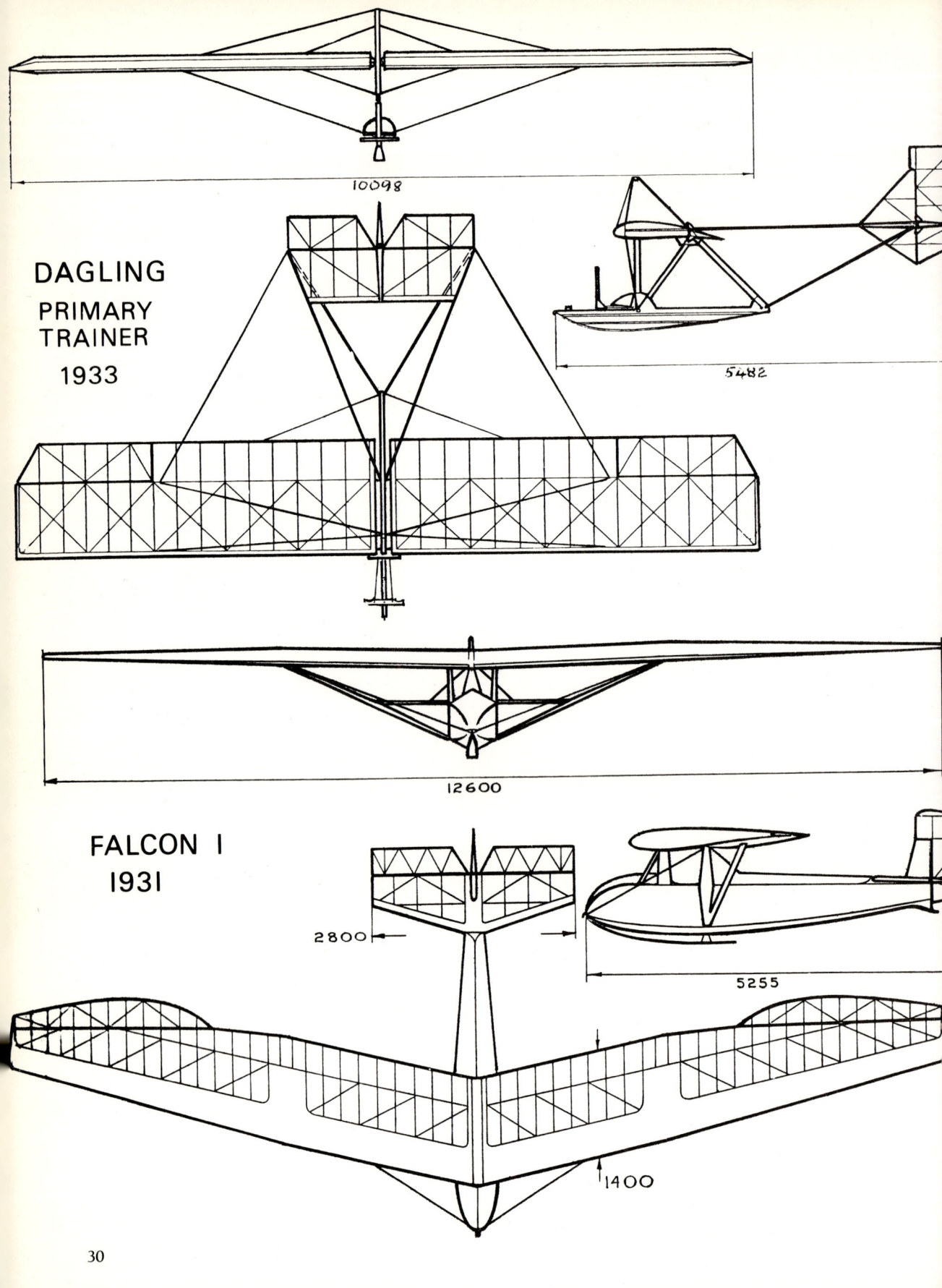

Figure 2.4. Three British gliders of 40 years ago made by Slingsby Sailplanes. The Dagling on which beginners learnt to fly solo was usually launched by catapult. The Falcon was used for early hill soaring, although a few cross-country flights of around 50 miles were made. The pilot had no upward view at all. The Kirby Kite was the popular cross-country glider of the day with a glide ratio of about 1 : 20. Several flights of over 140 miles were made. The Kite was the last Slingsby single-seater sailplane to be made with an open cockpit. A few Kites and Grunaus are now being restored and flown again.

scale 1:72

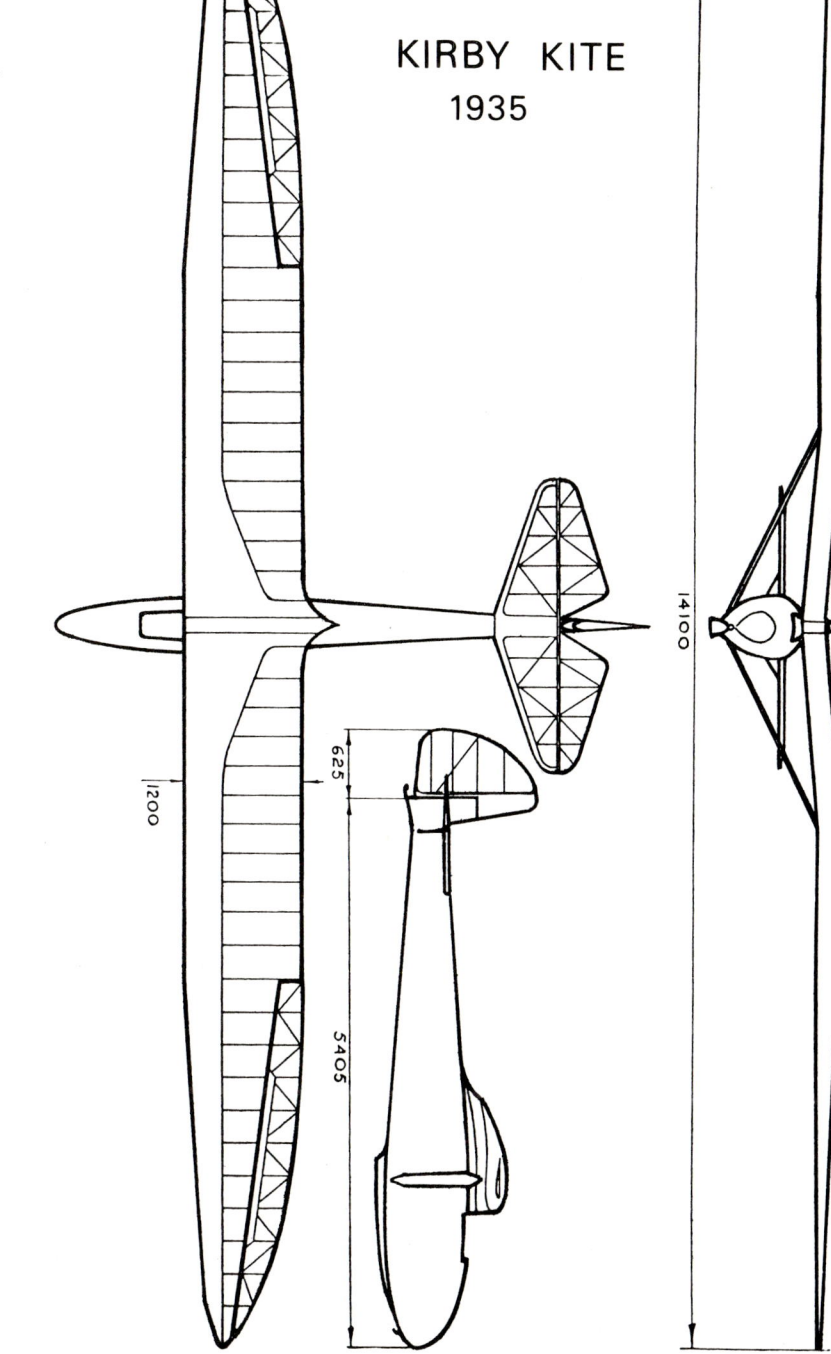

KIRBY KITE
1935

DAGLING

Span	33 ft
Length	17 ft 10 in.
Weight empty	180 lb

FALCON 1

Span	43 ft
Length	17 ft 5 in.
Weight empty	265 lb
Stall speed	28 mph

KIRBY KITE

Span	47 ft
Length	20 ft 4 in.
Weight empty	260 lb

Figure 2.5. To provide evidence that he has reached the turning points on an out-and-return or triangular course flight, the pilot takes pictures of the turning point feature. Instamatic cameras are used and fixed to the side of the cockpit just inside the canopy Perspex.

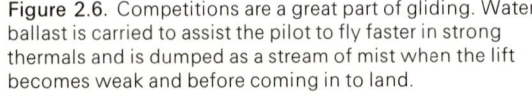

Figure 2.6. Competitions are a great part of gliding. Water ballast is carried to assist the pilot to fly faster in strong thermals and is dumped as a stream of mist when the lift becomes weak and before coming in to land.

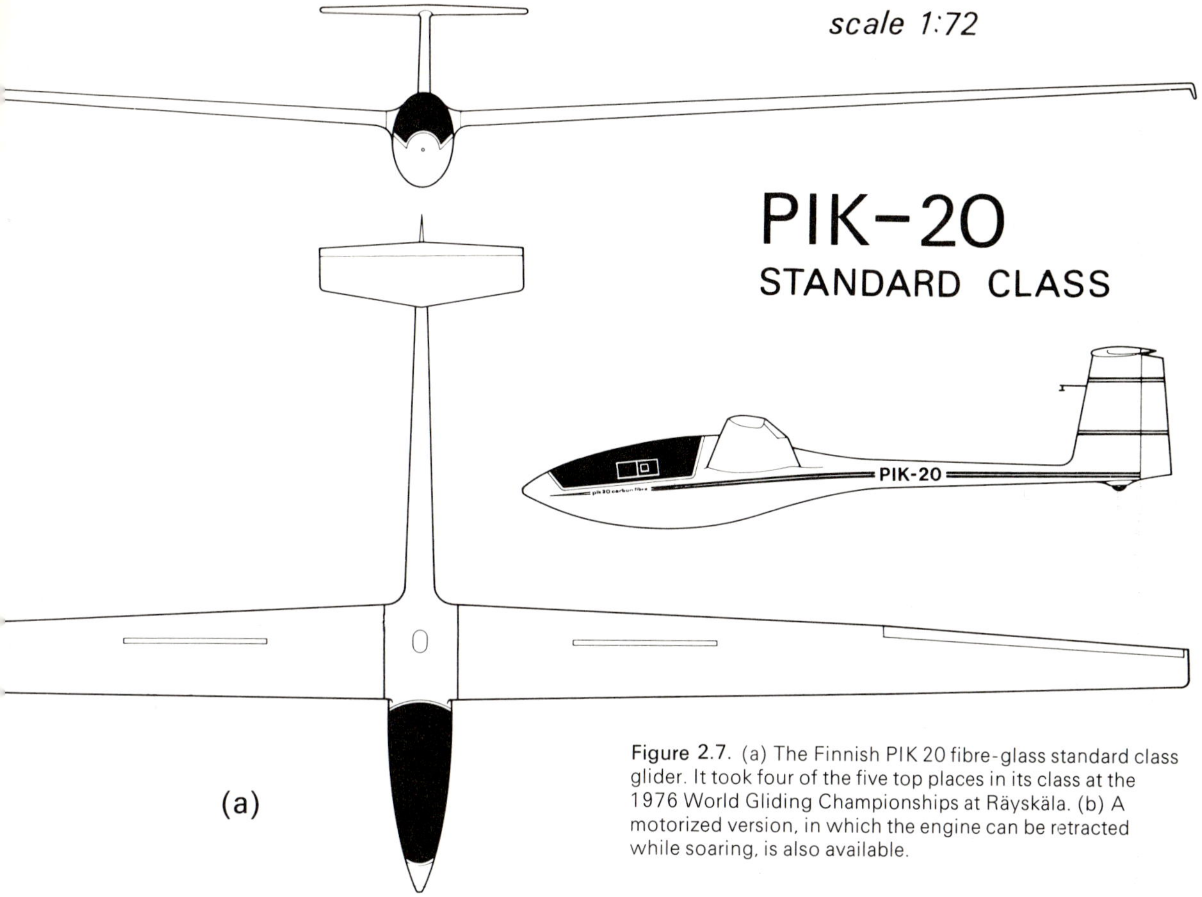

scale 1:72

PIK-20
STANDARD CLASS

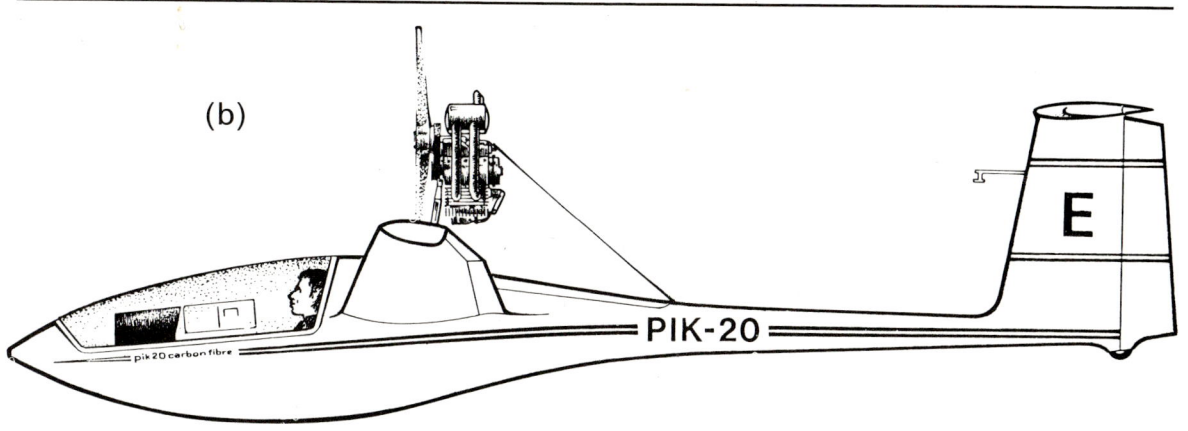

Figure 2.7. (a) The Finnish PIK 20 fibre-glass standard class glider. It took four of the five top places in its class at the 1976 World Gliding Championships at Räyskälä. (b) A motorized version, in which the engine can be retracted while soaring, is also available.

DIMENSIONS		
Wing span	15.0 m	49.2 ft
Aspect ratio	22.5	
Wing profile	Wortman	
Tail profile	Wortman	
Flaps movement	−18°	+20°

WEIGHTS AND LOADINGS		
Empty weight	220 kg	484 lb
Max flying weight	450 kg	990 lb
Max water ballast	140 kg	308 lb
Wing loading	30–45 kg/m²	6.1–8.2 lb/sq. ft
Max load factor at manoeuvring speed	185 km/h +5.3 −2.65	
in rough air	240 km/h +2.7 −5.1	
in calm air	270 km/h +4.5 −2.5	

PERFORMANCE		
Flying weight	450 kg	990 lbs.
Best L/D at 108 km/h	42	
Min sink at 85 km/h	0.63 m/s	130 ft/min
Stalling speed at 300 kg	60 km/h	37 mph

OPERATIONAL DATA		
Max aero tow speed	185 km/h	115 mph
Max winch launch speed	125 km/h	77 mph
Manoeuvring speed	185 km/h	115 mph
Max flying speed	262 km/h	163 mph

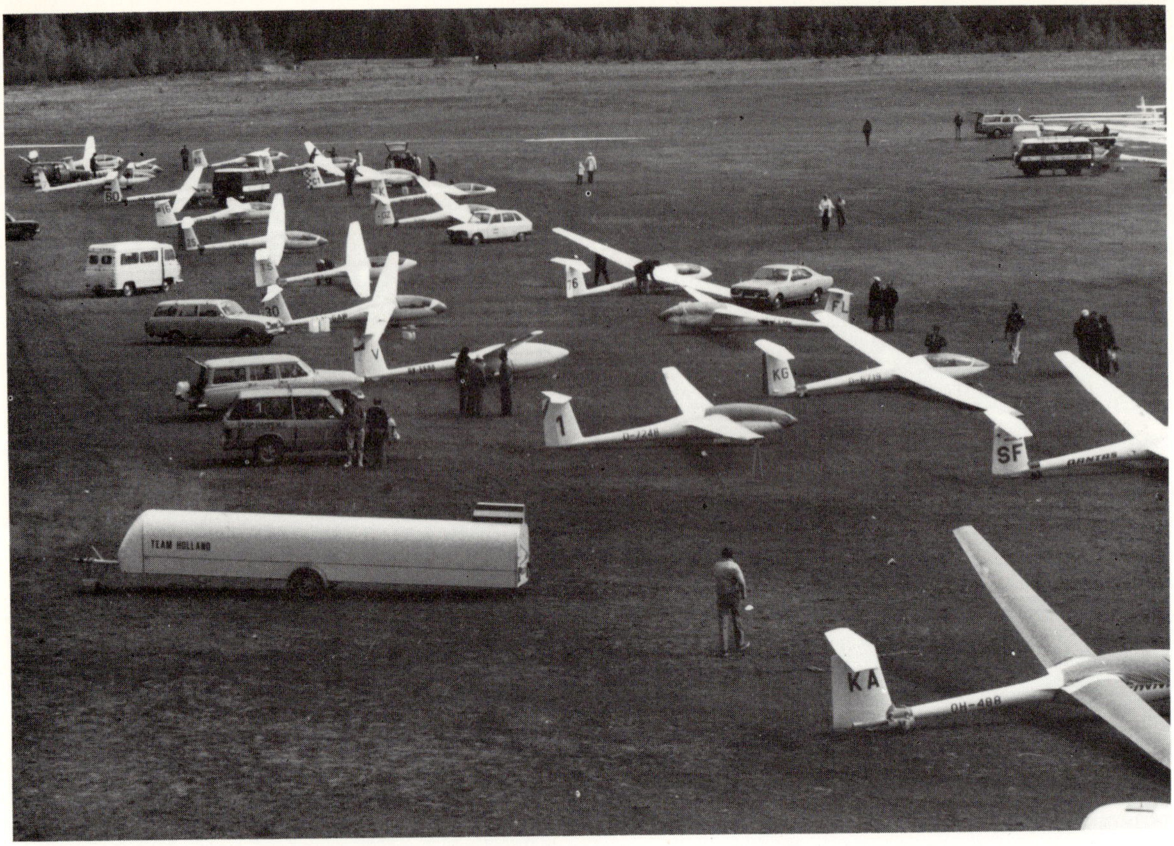
TEAM HOLLAND
KA
OH-498
SF
KG
FL
1

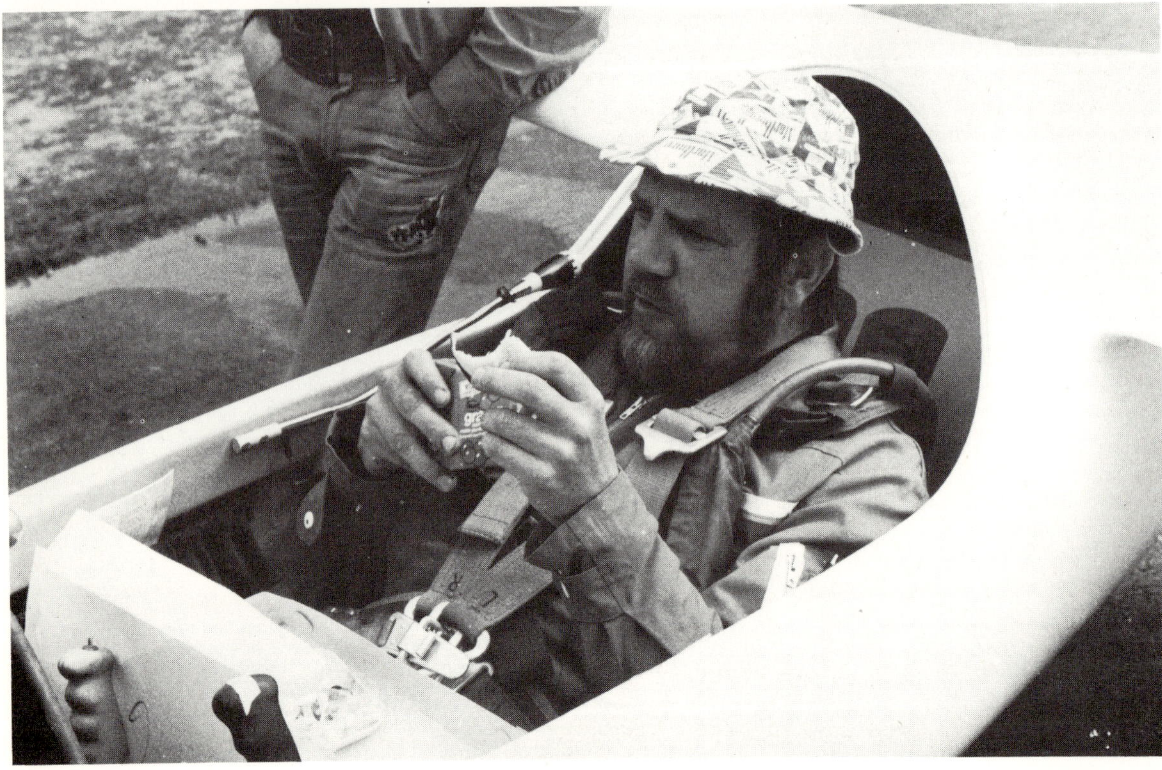

Figure 2.8. One of the problems of competition flying is waiting to get started, usually for the thermals to become good enough. (*Bottom*) It is a time for lunch.

Figure 2.9. Rebuilding a Vintage Olympia fuselage. Wooden gliders are not too difficult but very time consuming to repair.

but also easier for the less experienced pilot to fly. More often they are made of wood or have wood wings and a welded steel tube fuselage, or they may be made of aluminium. These materials do not, in general, give such a low drag shape and finish as fibre-glass, but they are easier and cheaper to repair. The glide ratio, as would be expected, is less, about 1:28 to 1:35, but this is enough for training and for extensive cross-country soaring, where speed is not the primary objective. Most club gliders are fitted with airbrakes only, without flaps or tail parachutes, and they normally have fixed landing gear.

Owning a glider

Some pilots fly club gliders and never own one themselves, but it is often frustrating when a beautiful soaring day comes along and everyone else is flying. This is why most pilots join a syndicate when they have got through their training and have put in enough flying time to be able to look after themselves. The average syndicate has three to four members, who jointly own and look after their glider, flying it in turn. However, in many clubs the new pilot is likely to find one or two large syndicates owning an old, although properly airworthy, glider. Its performance may not be all that great, but a share in it and its trailer will be cheap, perhaps a few hundred pounds. Buying in to such a syndicate will provide the opportunity to get plenty of flying; but, as such syndicates work on a self-help basis to keep down costs, you will also be expected to do plenty of work. Keeping the glider clean, doing repair work on the trailer and during the winter turning up every weekend to help with the annual certificate of airworthiness overhaul are all part of the deal. It is often not too difficult to obtain a share in these larger syndicates, because there are always pilots who, having had a couple of years flying with the group, are now ready to go on to something more advanced.

When considering buying a glider or joining a syndicate, it should not be forgotten that there is more equipment than just a glider. Apart from the trailer, there is usually an impressive array of instruments, parachute and barograph.

Instruments
Although gliders, like hang gliders, can be flown safely without instruments, the glider is usually well equipped in this respect because of the precision calculations needed to soar across country. To work out the point from which he can commence the final glide, for example, the pilot needs to know his actual height, exact speed and precise rate of climb in thermals: it is not enough to be 'about' 10 knots above the stall or 'over 4,000 feet': as an insurance, most gliders are equipped with two variometers in case one should go wrong.

Cloud flying is a skill helpful to the cross-country soaring pilot, because the thermal lift not only continues in the cloud but becomes stronger. Sometimes, if clouds are widely separated, the only way to obtain enough height to reach the next area of lift is to climb up inside them. The instruments used to cope with cloud flying are either a turn-and-slip indicator or an artificial horizon, or both. These instruments run off batteries and will not do so if these have been allowed to go flat!

Parachutes
Because gliding is a safe form of flying, some people wonder why glider pilots wear parachutes: the seats are even designed so that it is not practicable to fly without a 'chute, unless the space is filled with cushions. The origin of parachutes in gliders goes back to the early days when not only were gliders weak, but the only known way of getting high was to climb inside thunderstorms. The combination of the two problems was sometimes disastrous. Now, gliders are very strong, and very little thunderstorm flying is done, but parachutes are still worn. Apart from the natural disinclination to change established habits, the parachute provides a means of escape in the event of a collision. Gliders fly close to each other in thermals, and in a big competition there may be fifteen or twenty gliders circling together. Even though collisions are rare, there is sense in wearing a parachute.

Figure 2.10. The Astir single-seater glass fibre glider built by Grob of Germany. It has a span of 15 metres and a glide ratio of 1:37, and is in general use by private owner syndicates and clubs.

Figure 2.11. (a) The cockpit of a Swiss Pilatus B4 single-seater all-metal club glider and (b) a typical glider instrument panel. The variometer indicates in knots' rise and sink. 1 knot approximates to 100 feet per minute.

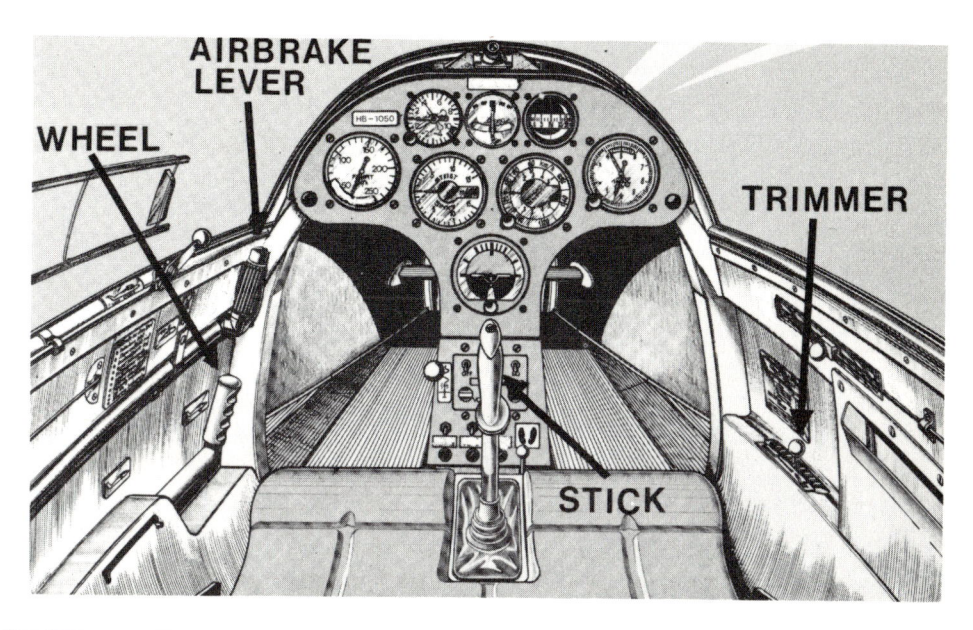

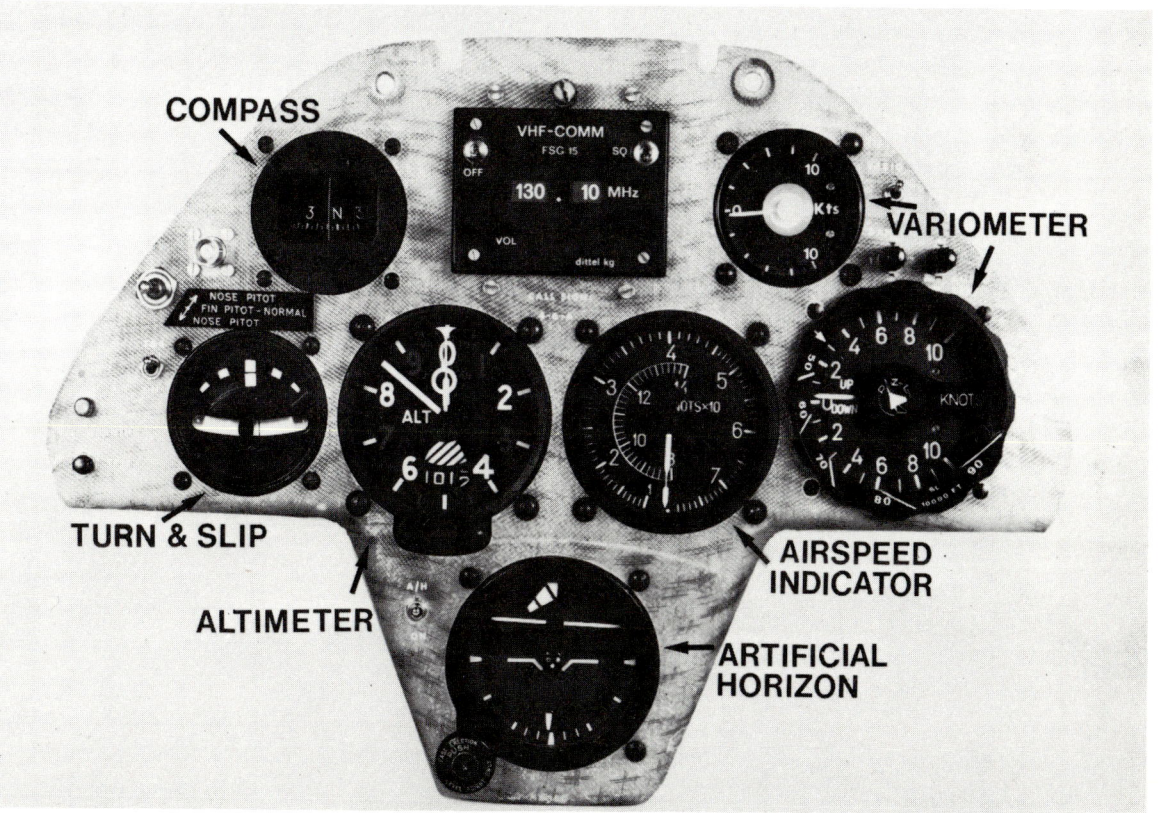

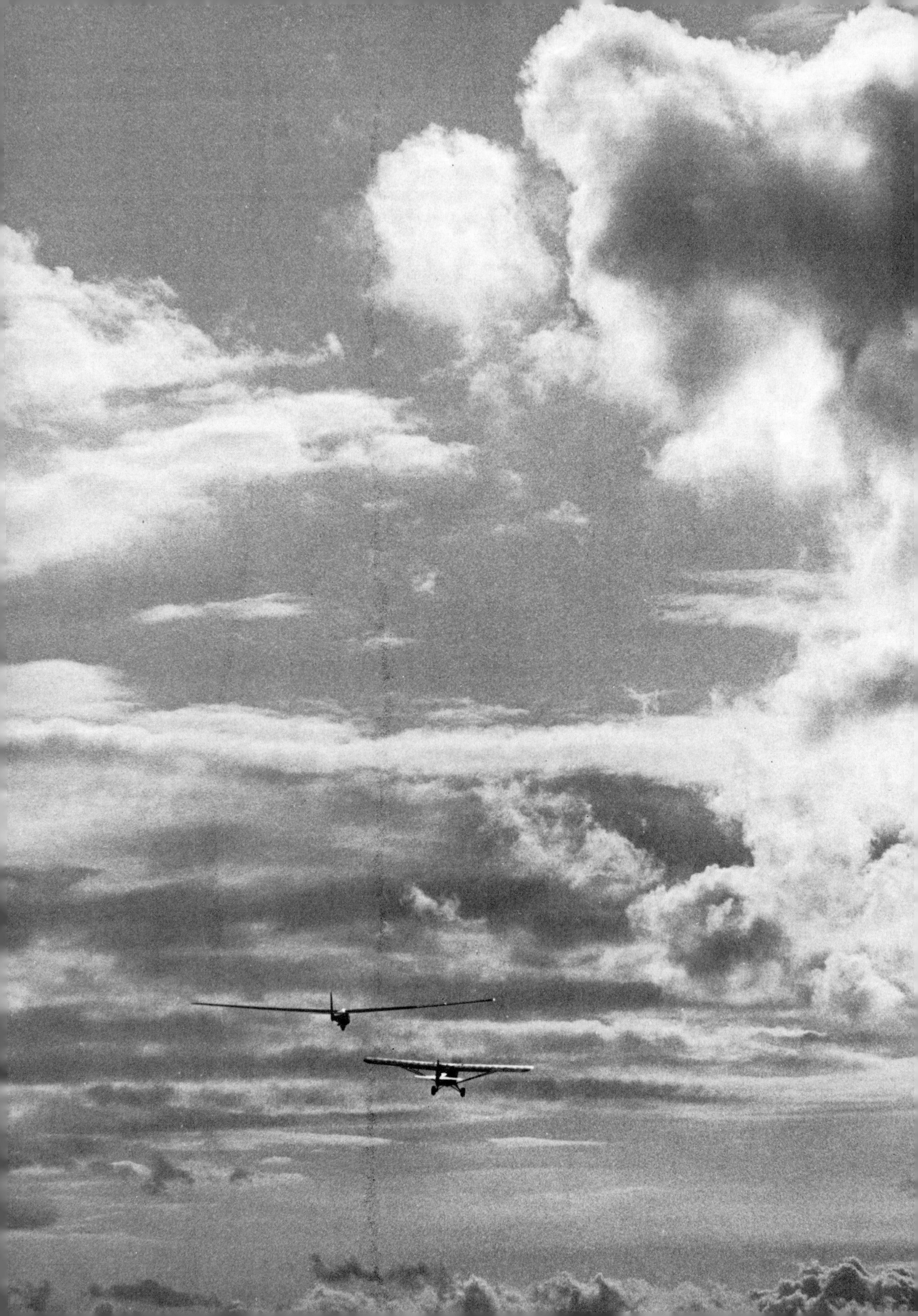

Figure 2.12. Aerotowing is a satisfactory means of launching because the glider can be taken to a suitable area of sky to start soaring. The tow rope is usually nylon, 120 feet long and with a breaking load of 1,000 lb.

Figure 2.13. An Olympia single-seater launched by a hand-stretched bungey catapult from a hill top. Now in the vintage category, the Elliott Olympia was the mainstay of gliding in Britain in the 1950s.

Barographs

When flying high, and often out of sight and sound of people on the ground, one needs a barograph as evidence of the height gained and the length of the flight. It is merely a recording altimeter, leaving a track of progress made on a revolving drum. As well as substantiating the flight for possible record purposes, the barograph trace gives the pilot a faithful story of what happened. It will show heart-stopping low points where a field landing was only averted by the timely arrival of an unexpected thermal, and it will be possible for him to work out the rate of climb achieved in each thermal.

Launching

Gliders are launched by tow car or winch, or by aeroplane tow, and occasionally from hilltops with a rubber shock cord catapult. The usual way, and the cheapest, is by tow car or winch, using a powerful engine on the ground to provide the necessary power. The long, and usually steel, launching cable is attached to the tow car or stationary winch at one end, with the other connected to the release hook of the glider – when the pilot is ready. Signals are given, slack is carefully taken up and then the cable is pulled fast enough to give the glider flying speed. The glider will take off quickly, but it should not at first be climbed steeply, in case the cable breaks or the engine fails. As a safe height of around 100 feet is gained, the nose can be raised and the glider will go up at an angle of 40 or 45 degrees. When the maximum height, usually around 1,000 feet, is reached, the pilot releases his end of the cable and flies away. This free end is then retrieved and is taken to the next glider to be launched.

Aerotowing is the best method of launching for the

Figure 2.14. The Eagle training two-seater soaring over Hampshire. The instructor sits in the rear seat.

pilot wanting to soar, because the aeroplane can tow him to a suitable cloud and can sometimes even leave him in good lift. The tow rope between the two aircraft is usually nylon, as thick as a pencil and about 20 metres long. It can be released from either end. Acceleration at take-off is slow, so that the glider pilot may initially have some difficulty in keeping straight, but thereafter the glider is flying level at a normal altitude. The tug pilot endeavours to avoid making sharp turns, and the glider pilot does his best to formate on the aeroplane. It is perhaps the most enjoyable way of getting into the air. Aerotowing is also useful for test flying new gliders, since they can be towed up to 10,000 feet without difficulty, and also for retrieving gliders at the end of a cross-country flight. But, if the glider pilot thinks he would like an aerotow back home, it is no good his ending up in any small meadow. He has to choose either an airstrip or a really big field and must obtain the permission of the owner before telephoning the club to ask for the tug.

Rubber rope, or bungey, launching is now rare, although in the early days it was the main means of getting gliders into the air. It does not provide any altitude, only flying speed, so it needs to be done from a hilltop. It is rare because most present-day gliders are too fast and too heavy to be shot into the air by half a dozen people pulling on the Y-shaped length of shock cord. There are, however, some club gliders which are still slow and light enough, and it is a good way of launching the increasingly large number of vintage gliders that are being rebuilt so lovingly. It is fun being launched by bungey. You sit, ready in the glider, on the crest of the ridge while the crew run full-tilt down the face stretching the rope. Then suddenly you shoot forward and straight out over the valley, with the speed up to 50 miles per hour in a few seconds. Quickly, you turn to stay in the hill lift and to gain enough height to find some thermals – or just to look at the view.

Learning to fly
The need in learning to fly a glider is not just to be able to go up, to fly around the airfield and to come in and land again but to be able to use the energy in the air fully. This means that you have to learn to fly really accurately and neatly, because every carelessly executed turn adds drag and brings you back to earth more quickly – and it is the launch which costs the money. You also need to learn to judge your approaches and landings really well, because there is no engine to carry you over that last field or hedge; if you undershoot, that is where you will land. It is not really any more difficult to fly accurately than to slop around the sky, but it takes practice and a determination to do it all properly. The satisfaction comes with the end result, the successful completion of an exciting cross-country flight.

The first lesson is usually a simple flight with the instructor doing all the flying, telling you how the controls work and pointing out landmarks and the location of the landing field. The two-seater may be a glider with tandem or side-by-side seating, or it may be a motor glider, powered by a 50 horsepower Volkswagen engine. The advantage of the motor glider is that, although it is not as quiet as a glider, you can take off when you are ready to go instead of waiting for a launching cable. If time is a problem, the motor glider will see you through the basic training more quickly.

Training follows a well-established pattern, starting with learning to control attitude (angle of attack) and speed, and followed by turns. Then come landings. On a motor glider the instructor will still be doing the actual take-off, but you will not be missing much. Take-off in a glider on a winch or tow car launch is a very simple process; it is what happens in the air that is important.

It does not take long for the average learner to master the handling and co-ordination of the controls; what is more difficult, however, is to develop the necessary judgement: it may be more important where you land than how you do it. So a lot of time will be devoted to teaching you how to judge whether you are too high or too low when coming in to land and how to use the airbrakes to adjust your height. The instructor will expend considerable effort in teaching you how to keep a good look-out for other aircraft and, at a later stage, how to join a thermal full of gliders without scattering them in fear.

During the course of pre-solo training you will be taught to cope with possible emergencies: what to do if the launching cable breaks just as you have started

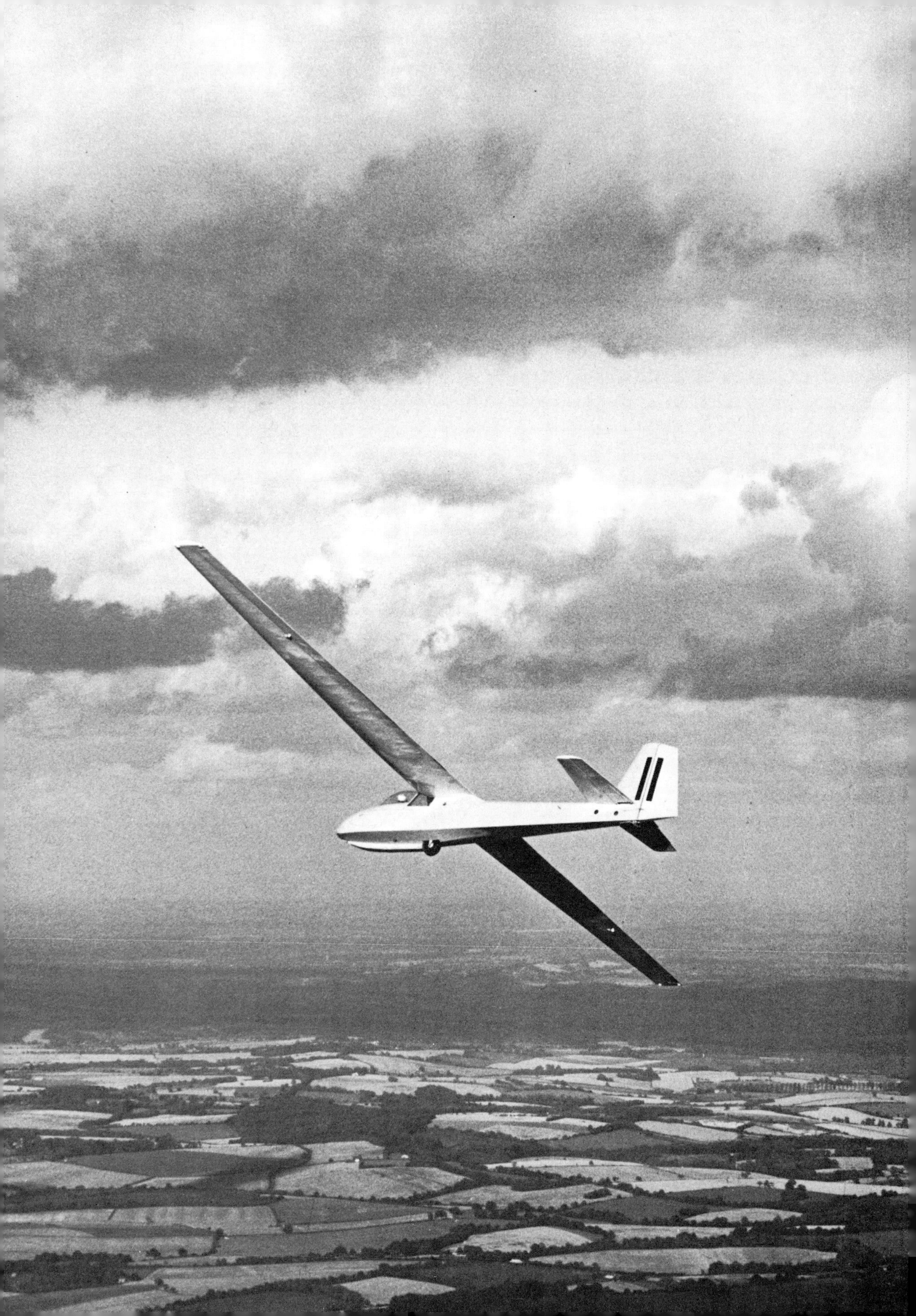

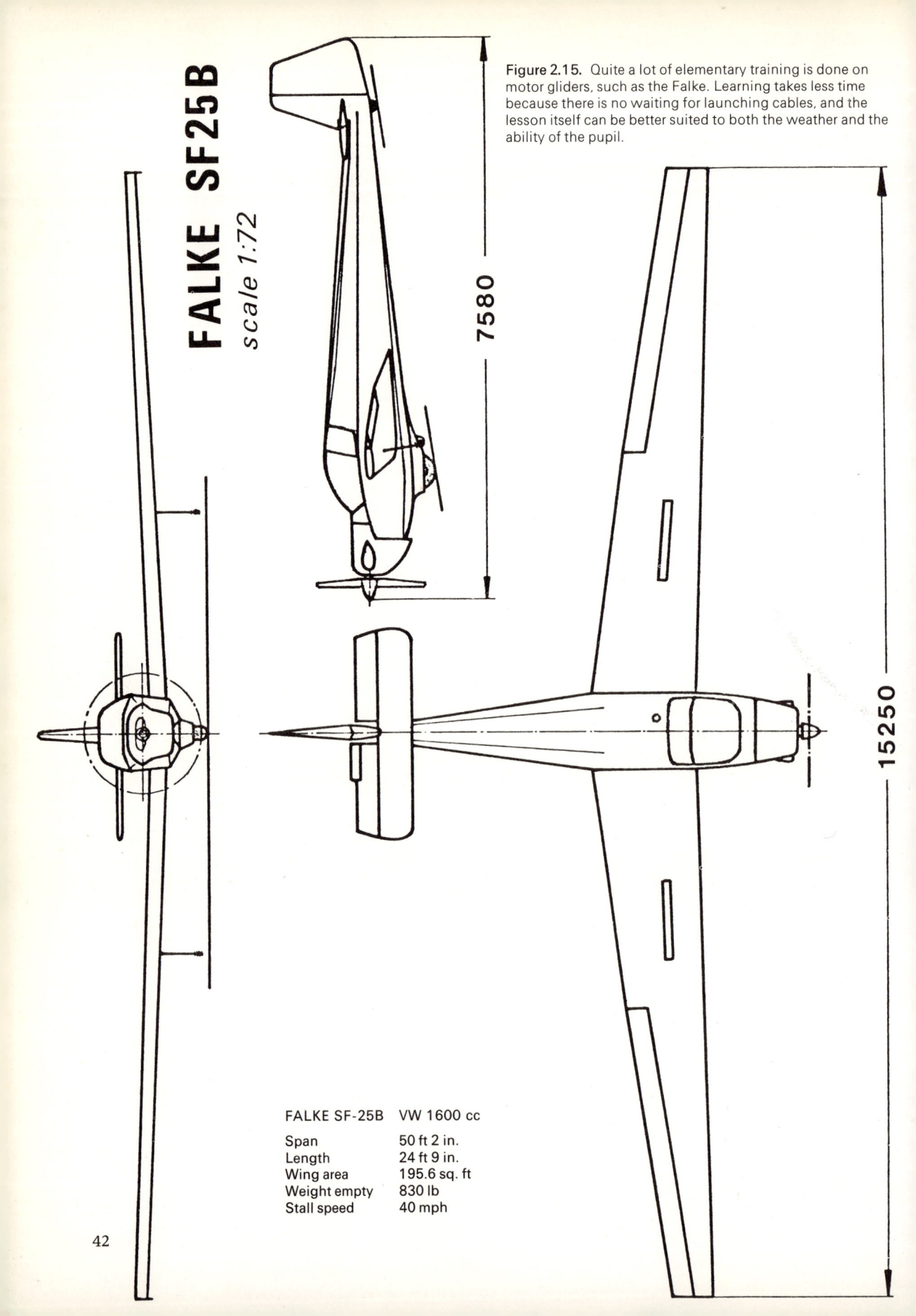

Figure 2.15. Quite a lot of elementary training is done on motor gliders, such as the Falke. Learning takes less time because there is no waiting for launching cables, and the lesson itself can be better suited to both the weather and the ability of the pupil.

FALKE SF25B
scale 1:72

FALKE SF-25B	VW 1600 cc
Span	50 ft 2 in.
Length	24 ft 9 in.
Wing area	195.6 sq. ft
Weight empty	830 lb
Stall speed	40 mph

to climb steeply at 150 feet; how to regain flying speed quickly, and release the broken end of the cable so that it will not catch in anything; how to land safely without running through the far hedge. It is also necessary to learn what to do if you inadvertently stall the glider but even more important to learn what it feels like if you are beginning to fly it too slowly. You will be shown that if you do let the glider stall, and fail to correct in time, it may start to spin – and you must know how to recover with the minimum loss of height.

By now you will be flying a two-seater glider, even if you began on the motor glider. The instructor will still be there, but by now doing almost none of the flying. Mostly, he will say little so as to see what mistakes you make and whether you recognize and correct them or not. He will be helping you to put a bit of polish on those turns and may occasionally congratulate you on a landing, but do not expect any praise if you fail to keep a good look-out, if you come into land without enough height to spare or if you fail to make your cockpit check properly before take-off. The time is approaching when you will be on your own, and the instructor wants to be sure that you are able to look after yourself.

First solo
Although you have a feeling that you are near solo, it always comes as a surprise when the instructor gets out, does up the loose and empty straps in his seat and says, for instance, 'That circuit was fine, do just the same again; I'm going to have some tea.' Suddenly you are in a turmoil. You know you are ready to go solo, but now you wonder if you will be able to do it correctly. You think the instructor is callous leaving you for a cup of tea, although you know it is only something he said, because you have seen him send other people solo; he will be watching you all round the circuit until you are safely on the ground again. Mechanically, you hear your voice going through the cockpit check, having the cable hooked on and saying that you are ready to launch. The glider moves, and suddenly you are flying; you have forgotten all about the instructor and your doubts. Carefully, you prevent the nose coming up too much and look out sideways. It is all familiar, the edge of the airfield and the woods beyond. Higher now you ease the nose up to gain the best height from the launch. You can feel the tautness of the cable as a quick rumbling vibration, above the sound of the air past the canopy. Now the nose of the glider begins to nod gently, and it is harder to keep the stick back, because near the top of the launch the cable-pull is more from below. You ease the back pressure on the stick to reduce the loads. Almost in level flight now, there is no more height to be gained, and you pull the yellow release knob hard – and again to make sure. The vibration and noise subsides, and as you fly free you check your speed – 40 knots, just what it ought to be. Suddenly you feel elated. Here you are, alone at last. Then you realize that it is time you got on with the circuit, and you turn cross-wind. There is the airfield, just where it ought to be. You repress the ridiculous idea of what to do if it had disappeared and scan the horizon for other aircraft. There are two gliders circling together across wind, but they show no signs of joining the circuit. You turn onto the downwind leg and check the windsock to see if there has been any change in strength and direction since you took off. It is just the same. You look at the landing area to see if it is clear of other gliders. It is, so you concentrate on planning the approach. Yes, your height and distance out from the airfield perimeter seem about right. It is nearly time to turn onto the base leg and to fly across wind about one field back from the fence. You wonder whether turning now will bring you in a bit too high, but this is better than undershooting, so you turn. You look again at the landing area, and now it has a glider right in the middle of it. How did it get there? You cannot make up your mind whether there is room to land to the right of it or whether you should open the brakes and land short. Just as indecision is becoming a major factor in your life, you see a group of people starting to push it out of the way – for you. The landing area is clear again. You consider your height. It seems about right, but you forgot to increase speed for the approach to 50 knots and to put your hand ready on the airbrake. You do these things and realize it is already time that you turned into wind for the final approach. During the turn there is just a chance to take another quick look around for other gliders, and then you find yourself automatically opening the

43

PRE-FLIGHT
CHECK LIST

Controls
Ballast
Straps
Instruments
Trim
Canopy
Brakes

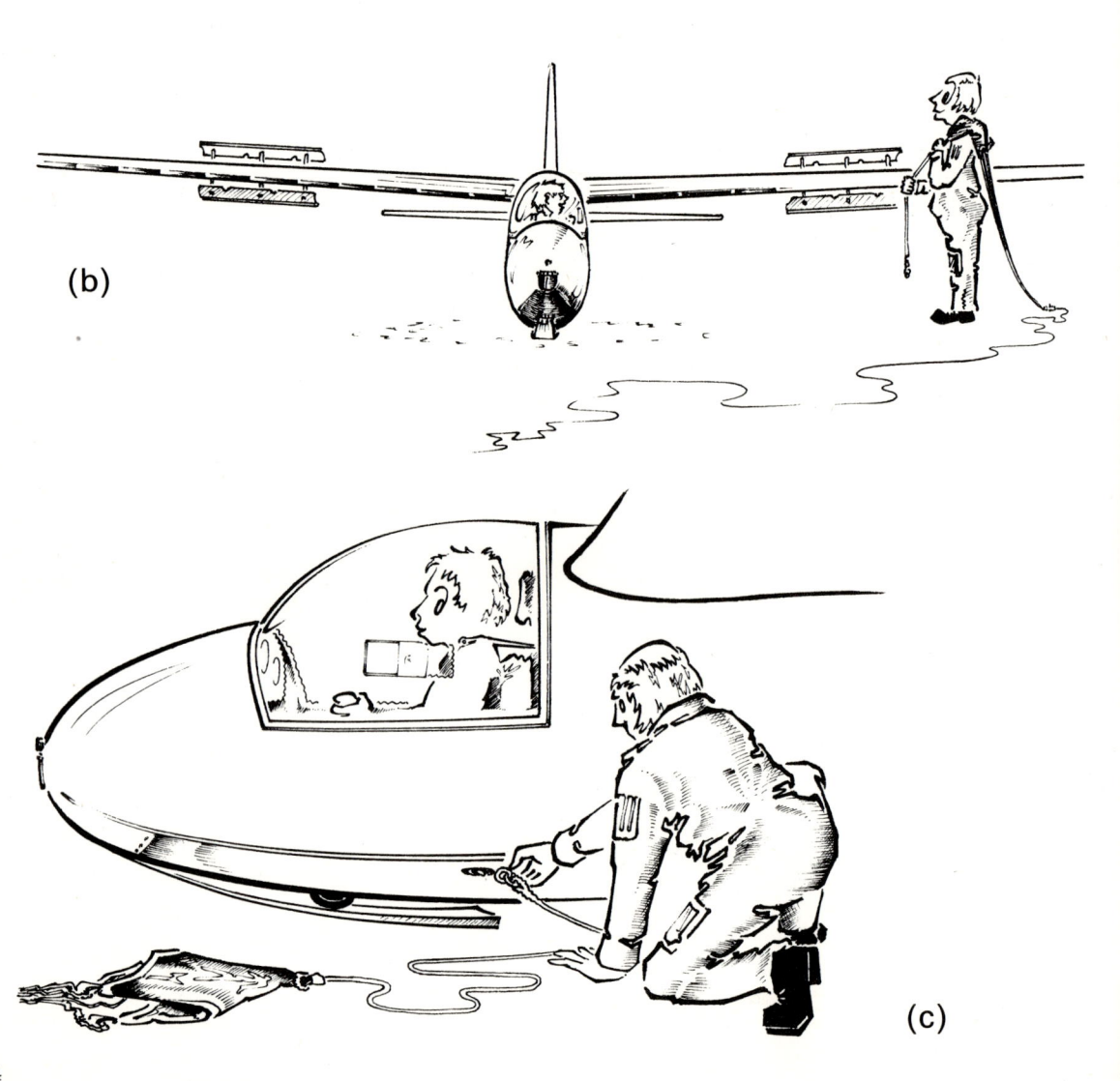

(a)

(b)

(c)

Figure 2.16. Getting into the air. (a) Before take-off the pilot carries out his cockpit check. (b) & (c) Then asks for the launching cable to be hooked on and checked. (d) When he is ready the pilot calls, 'All clear above and behind' and the batsman checks this. (e) Then he calls, 'Take up slack'. On this signal the batsman waves the bat low down. (f) Then the batsman shows the signal 'All out'. If an emergency 'stop' is needed, the bat is held up stationary.

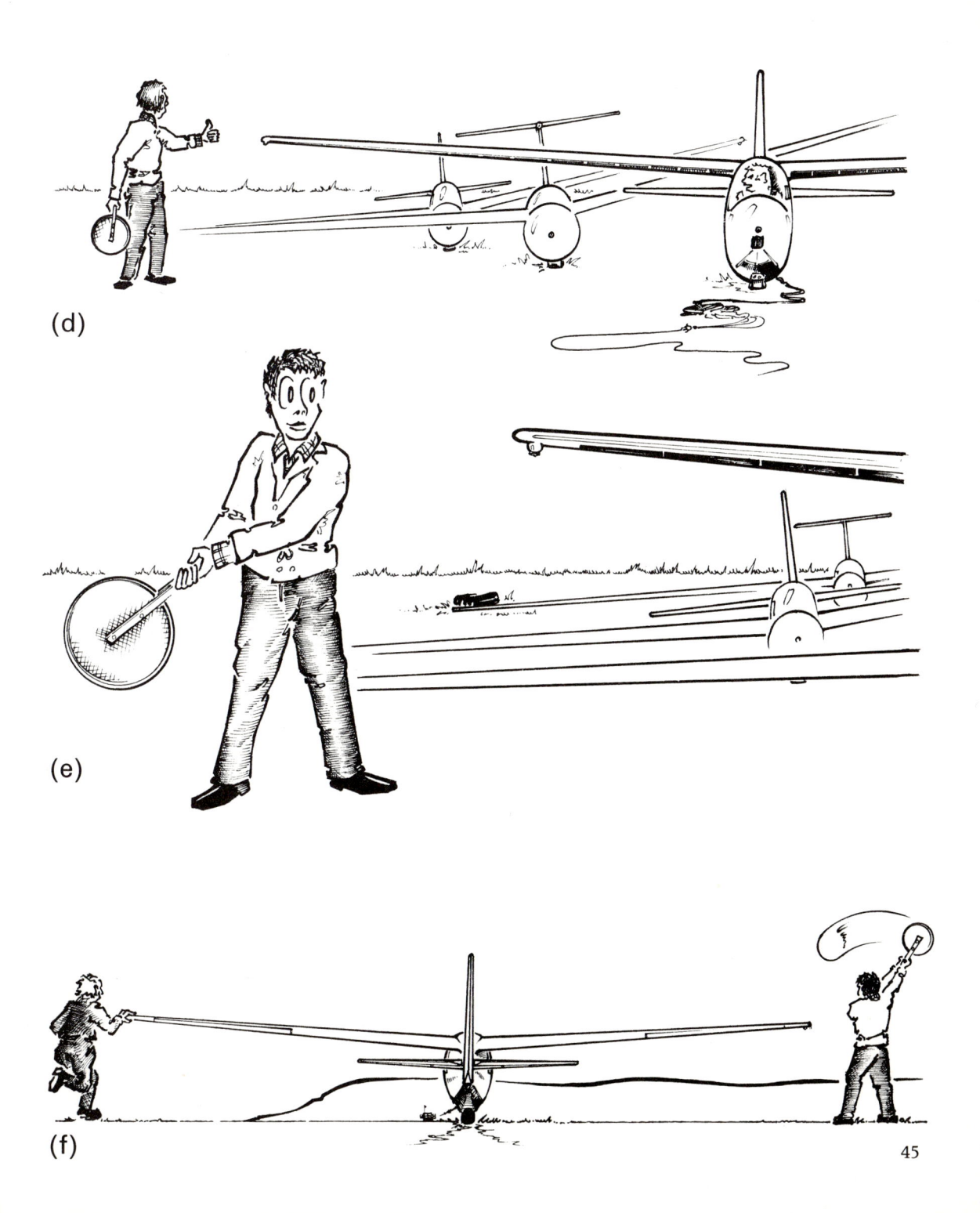

(d)

(e)

(f)

airbrakes. The glide steepens, and you check the airspeed. The ground is close now, and you begin to ease back the stick so as not to run straight into it. 'Look well ahead for the landing!' comes the ghost of the instructor's voice. You do, holding the airbrakes steady as you float over the ground. There is a small bump, then another and then the wheel is on the ground, squeaking like it has been all day. The glider slows and stops, the wing dips on to the ground, and now you can smile.

There is no time for self-congratulation, because the first solo is only a step in becoming a pilot, and you now have to do a couple more circuits to prove that the one flight was not just a fluke. But it is a good step to have reached.

ASSOCIATIONS

British Gliding Association
  Address: Kimberley House, Vaughan Way, Leicester, LE1 4SG
  Telephone No.: Leicester 51051
  No. of pilots: 10,275
  No. of gliders: 1,175
  No. of clubs: 96
  No. of hours' flying annually: 137,190
  Minimum age for flying solo: 16 years

The British Gliding Association (BGA) is the national authority for sporting gliding in the UK. It operates through an elected executive committee, specialist committees and a small professional staff. The BGA looks after pilot proficiency certificates, airworthiness and instructor standards.

Members of the BGA are clubs with a membership of twenty-five or more; associate members are clubs with less than twenty-five members and interested individuals.

Sailplane and Gliding magazine is on sale through clubs and by a direct subscription of £4.90, single copy 60p. It appears bimonthly commencing February each year.

Pilot licences and certificates

No pilot licences are required for gliding. The BGA requires a declaration of fitness before flying solo. A series of pilot proficiency certificates and badges are available but not mandatory, except that a pilot wishing to fly cross-country must hold a Bronze badge, and a Silver if wishing to enter championships.

A and B
Before attempting the test the pilots must have twenty flights in gliders. The test requirements are three solo flights, each comprising as a minimum a circuit of the landing field followed by a normal landing. He must know the rules of the air.

C
He must hold A and B. He must carry out a soaring flight of at least 5 minutes with a normal landing, and must show a reasonable knowledge of controlled airspace rules.

Bronze badge
He must hold A and B. He must have made two soaring flights each of 30 minutes when launched by car winch or bungey or of 60 minutes after release from an aerotow not exceeding 2000 feet, followed by a normal landing in a designated area. He must have made a minimum of two dual flights satisfactorily, demonstrating accurate flying, understanding of stalling and spinning and correct recovery, and two field landings into a field or a marked-off part of the airfield without use of altimeter. He must pass written papers on air law, and have completed at least fifty solo flights in gliders.

Silver badge (FAI international standard)
The requirements are a distance of 50 kilometres, a gain of height of 1,000 metres and a duration of 5 hours.

Gold badge (FAI)
The requirements are a distance of 300 kilometres and a gain of height of 3,000 metres.

Diamonds (FAI)
The requirements are a distance of 500 kilometres, a closed circuit goal of 300 kilometres and a gain of height of 5,000 metres.

1,000 km badge
A distance of 1,000 kilometres straight or over an out-and-return or triangular course.

Training courses
Beginners' courses, mostly of 5 days' duration, are run by most clubs. A list is available from the BGA.

CODE OF GOOD PRACTICE

A great deal is owed to farmers who have given help to pilots who have arrived in their fields as uninvited guests. Most glider cross-country flights are planned to end on an airfield, but a pilot failing to do so should select a field that not only is safe to land in but will cause minimum inconvenience to the farmer. Particular care should be taken to avoid landing in standing crops. Land as far from livestock as possible.

Discourage onlookers from coming into the field – avoid landing by a housing estate. Contact the farmer or his representative, and pay for any telephone calls. Keep the retrieve car out of the field unless permission has been obtained.

Ensure no animals escape while gates are open, and close them before leaving.

Figure 2.17. The B and FAI Silver badges for glider pilots.

3 Aeroplanes

Some people prefer to fly with an engine. They do not think of the power unit as something which may stop but as a means of getting where they want to go. They like to take their friends along and often use the aeroplane for business trips; but much of this sort of flying is nearer to mini-airliner operations than to sport flying. The piloting of small aeroplanes came nearest to real flying for fun in the 1930s before the days of controlled airspace, radio aids and inflationary costs. Aeroplanes, such as the Gipsy Moth, were slow with the cockpits open to the slipstream, and you navigated your way across country with a map on your knee. This had to be held onto, otherwise the rushing air would whip it away, so that it fluttered to earth irretrievably lost; as you would then soon be. Grass airfields and private meadows were ports of call, and you had to take the weather as you found it. These were the days of the great explorations, with long flights like the Mollisons' across oceans and continents, sitting between a small Gipsy engine and as many petrol tanks as could be squeezed into the back seats. Much of this sort of carefree exploratory flying is no longer practicable, and it may seem that little aeroplane flying really is no longer anything to do with sport. This is not so; the fun is just a little harder to find.

Over the years many people have learnt to fly and obtained a private pilot's licence (PPL). Maybe they started in the services, won a Cadet scholarship or just paid the bill themselves. But almost as many have allowed their licence to lapse because after a year or so it seemed too expensive to gain the much greater experience necessary to use the aeroplane in all weathers; and just making a few circuits of the airfield at weekends soon became boring. A few hours' refresher flying with an instructor would brush up the old skills, but there did not seem to be much point in persisting. In truth this lack of persistence often goes back to why the person started flying in the first place. If the reason was simply to possess a licence, then no one should be too bothered if the pilot gave up flying. But, if the enthusiasm to fly is great, there are good opportunities, provided that the pilot is prepared to put in time and energy. If he has done some gliding, as well as getting his PPL he can, for example, become a glider tug pilot.

Being a tug pilot
It demands real flying skill to tow up gliders, but it is satisfying when their pilots like to be towed by you because you manage to leave them in thermals. This type of flying will not cost you anything, except your club membership fee. When experienced as a tug pilot, you will probably be given the occasional cross-country retrieve from a field or private airstrip. The responsibility for assessing the field for a safe tow-out is yours, and the flight home in the evening sunshine with the tree shadows lengthening across the fields below gives a good feeling of independence. Some pilots enjoy towing so much that they maintain the validity of their licence this way year after year and never go near airports or controlled airspace.

Pilot Proficiency badges
As well as obtaining the mandatory PPL, the enterprising pilot has international FAI proficiency standards that are waiting to be gained. The purpose of these is to enable you to broaden your experience and to become a better pilot and, since the standards are recognized in other countries, to visit flying friends abroad and to fly with them. The badges run from Blue, through Red, Bronze, Silver and Gold. For example, the Blue requires, in addition to a PPL, a restricted radio-telephone licence, evidence of flying from both controlled and uncontrolled airfields and experience of at least three flights across mountains, such as the Alps, or at least 20 nautical miles of water.

Becoming an instructor
If you wish to continue to fly, but do not see much prospect of being able to pay indefinitely for the pleasure, it is worth starting to work to become at least an assistant instructor. Shortage of money should not, of course, be the only reason why you go in for instructing, because, unless you actually have some feeling of dedication in teaching people to fly, you will be wasting their time and money. If, through disinterest, you do not teach them well, you could also be the cause of some accident that they may have subsequently; so instructing is not something to be undertaken lightly. Initially, learning to become an instructor costs money. You need 150 hours' flying, and there are schoolwork, tests and exams. For a pilot

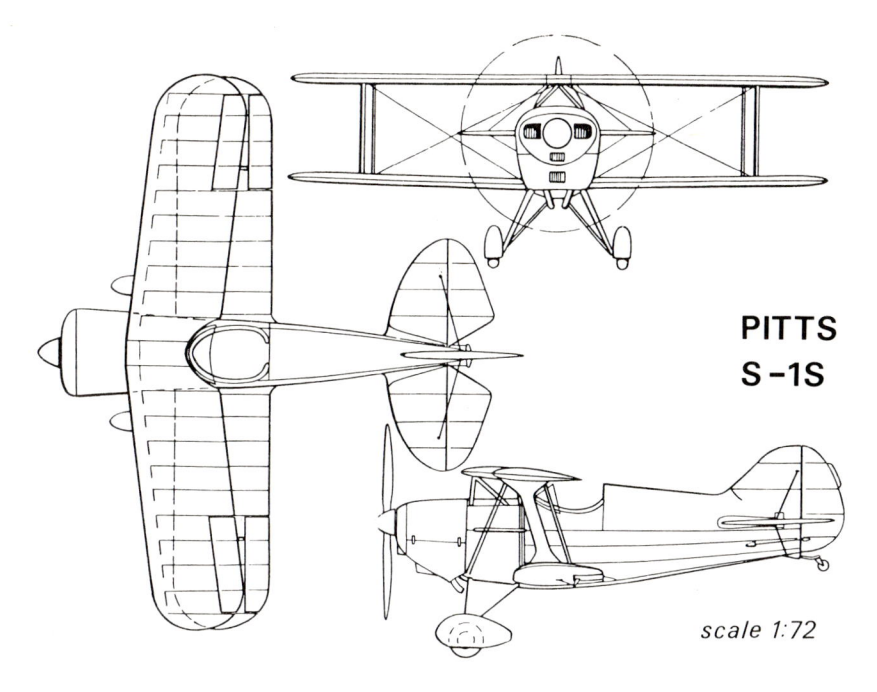

PITTS S-1S   LYCOMING 180 hp
Span   17 ft 5 in.
Length   15 ft 6 in.
Wing area   96.5 sq. ft
Weight empty   725 lb
Stall speed   64 mph

Figure 3.1. Aerobatic aircraft are small and not too fast, so that the display can be given without having to fly too far from the spectators. The American Pitts S-1S superseded the popular Zlin competition aircraft.

with just these hours, it will probably take the best part of a year, flying every weekend, to reach the standard required. But teaching others to fly can be very rewarding; it is good for improving your own skill, and once properly qualified you are able to get all the flying you could ever need.

For others, the attraction of flying a small aeroplane exists with the mastery needed to perform smooth and beautiful aerobatics.

Aerobatics

One of the advantages of enjoying aerobatics is that you do not have to go anywhere at all and so can obtain the sort of flying you like in quite short periods of time, such as a couple of hours on a spring evening. Aerobatics are most satisfying when they are practised regularly so that you are able to link loops and rolls and you know that it all feels right. To reach this standard of competence takes time, and you should start with several hours' dual under a good aerobatic instructor.

Aerobatic training is carried out at a considerable height so that there is plenty of room for correcting the mistakes which you will make. If you have so far only flown the right way up, you will find flying inverted not only initially disorientating and possibly uncomfortable as you hang in the straps, with the blood subsiding into your head, but also confusing until you get used to operating the controls the 'wrong way'. Right way up you move the stick back to make the nose go up to climb: inverted you must push it forwards. Initially, too, the noise and vibration produced when many small aeroplanes are flown fast, as when pulling up into a loop, are disconcerting. It is not in the least what might be expected, when you have only seen a beautiful display of seemingly effortless manoeuvres as a ground spectator.

Aerobatics is one of the most competitive forms of aeroplane flying, with national and world championships. Pilots are usually scored on their presentation of a compulsory programme of linked aerobatics plus a free programme chosen by the pilot himself. The aircraft used are small and strong and have fuel systems arranged to cope with inverted flight but are not very fast: too much speed requires a great deal of airspace and makes the display less interesting.

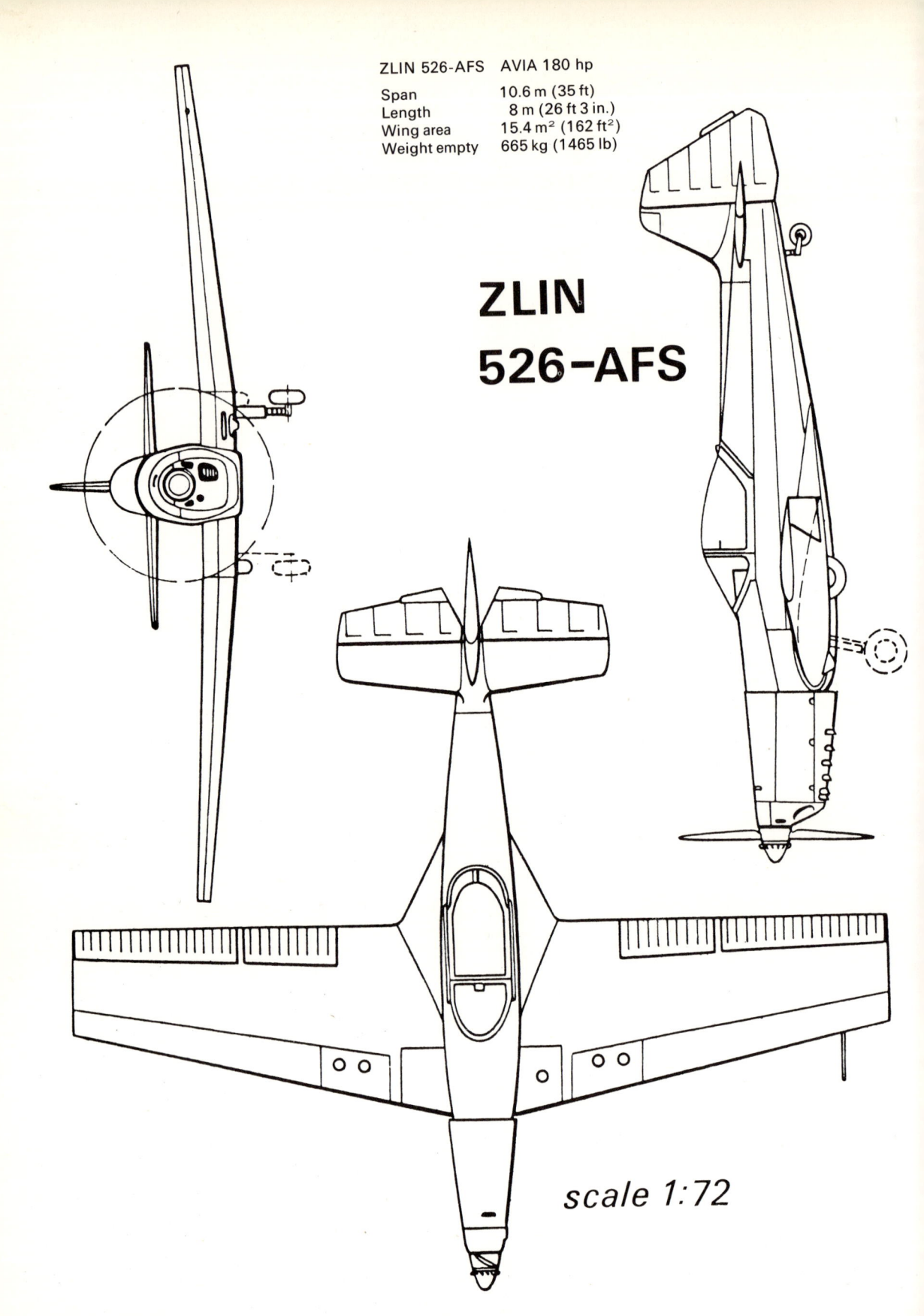

ZLIN 526-AFS   AVIA 180 hp
Span   10.6 m (35 ft)
Length   8 m (26 ft 3 in.)
Wing area   15.4 m² (162 ft²)
Weight empty   665 kg (1465 lb)

ZLIN 526-AFS

scale 1:72

Figure 3.2. Four simple aerobatic manoeuvres. In a display the pilot must link these and others in a well-presented and smoothly executed sequence.

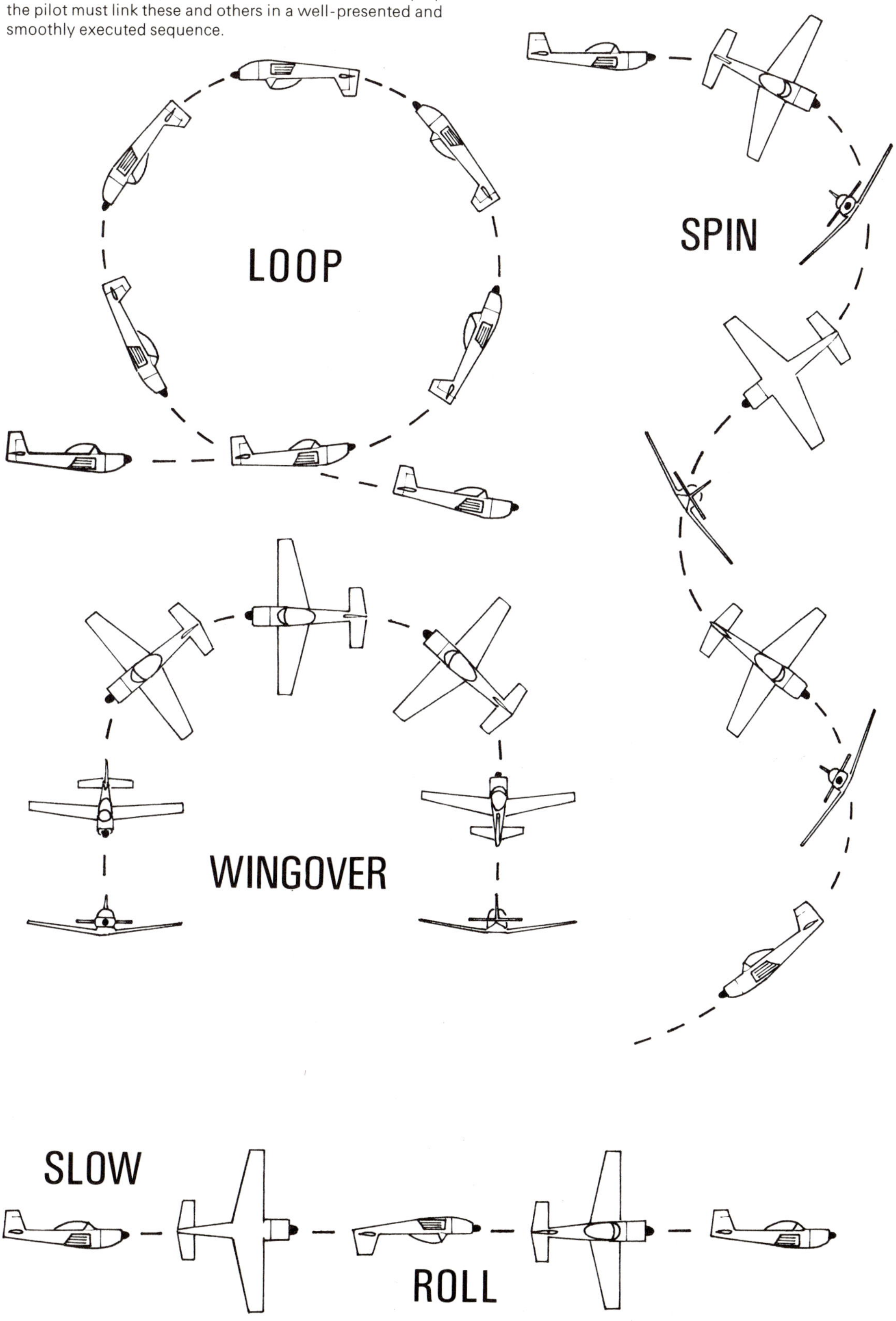

LOOP

SPIN

WINGOVER

SLOW ROLL

51

Air racing

Much nearer to motor racing, but very much in the category of flying for fun is Formula One air racing. These aeroplanes are fast but strictly limited in both size and power, so that they do not become too expensive, and racing is around pylons. It is exciting concentrated flying and also just right for the pilot who enjoys spending hours improving and tuning his equipment (Figure 3.3). But what if you do not want to do any of these things but just fly, and fly, and fly. Maybe, if you are one of these people you should think about building your own small aeroplane.

Build your own

Until you start seriously to think about it, building your own aeroplane may seem to be a remote, even impossible, concept. But aeroplanes are not difficult to construct for anyone with some space, a good set of do-it-yourself tools and the skill to use them. It is an easier job than building a glider, and not only because the aircraft is smaller. In Britain there are some 800 home-built aeroplanes flying, and in the USA no less than a staggering 5,060. Nevertheless, it is not a job to be undertaken lightly. It will take longer than you think, and the work has to be carried out with proper accuracy and thoroughness. Trying to build it in the living room during a single winter will merely produce a family revolution not an aeroplane. It may be acceptable to turn the car out of the garage for a couple of years, but it is even better if a workshop with some heating can be rented close to home.

The Popular Flying Association (PFA) looks after home-built aircraft in Britain; it will supply plans and instructions and will help you arrange for the necessary inspections to be carried out and the new creation to be finally certificated. But, before this process is set in motion, a few months of thinking will not come amiss. First of all you have to decide what you are going to do with the aeroplane when you have built it. Can you already fly as a pilot or will you have to learn to do that as well? Is there a nearby airfield with a hangar that you can operate from? Or do you want an aeroplane that can be derigged like a glider and can live on its trailer in the garden? What sort of flying do you want to do: will it be enough to visit your other home builder friends at various airfields during weekends and to go to PFA rallies? Do you want to build an aerobatic aircraft such as a Pitts or a racer such as the Cassutt? Should it be a single-seater which is cheaper or a two-seater which is a bit more expensive but which will allow you to carry family and friends. Or is the pleasure and fun just to build something and, when it is finished, to sell it and start on another one? The time not to consider all these things is when you are half-way through building a wing and have committed yourself to several hundred pounds' worth of bits and pieces. This is the fate of at least half the enthusiasts who rush into building without sufficient thought. If you do know what you want and are prepared to give up or find the space and time, the result will be immensely satisfying: but the first essential step is to study some facts and figures.

Time to build

On the assumption that you are good with your hands, can use tools properly and can read drawings, a simple single-seater will take about 1,000 hours of work. A 40 hour working week is 2,000 hours, so this would be equivalent to at least 6 months working full time. In practice it would probably not be completed in this period as there are always delays in obtaining delivery of various items from cable end-fittings to seat cushions. In terms of weekend and evening work 1,000 hours is much nearer 3 to 4 years, depending on the type of everyday job held. A person on shift work of some kind may well do better than a nine-to-fiver, simply because each aeroplane building session is longer, even if there are not so many of them.

The other factor which has a large bearing on the length of time to build is whether the work and all the tools can be left out ready for next time or have to be put away because in between the space is used for something else. The ideal is for a workshop, the size of a medium single-car garage, to be used for nothing but the aeroplane – as a minimum. In the house itself there needs to be at least a desk or table where the plans, drawings, building instructions and correspondence with suppliers and inspectors can be kept in splendid isolation and security.

Cost

The price of a home-built aeroplane can vary considerably even for the same type. It all depends on how much shopping around is done, how much discount can be obtained and how much help is given by other home aeroplane builders. It also helps to make sure that what you are ordering is exactly what

Figure 3.3. The Rollason Beta and Airmark Cassutt Formula 1 racing aircraft. The nearest aircraft was built by its pilot, Tom Storey. The general arrangement drawings to 1:72 scale show their small size (b and c).

ROLLASON BETA		AIRMARK CASSUTT IIIM	
Span	20 ft 5 in.	Span	14 ft 11 in.
Length	16 ft 8 in.	Length	16 ft
Wing area	66 sq. ft	Wing area	66 sq. ft
Weight empty	575 lb	Weight empty	516 lb
Stall speed	60 mph		

(b) ROLLASON BETA

(c) AIRMARK CASSUTT III M

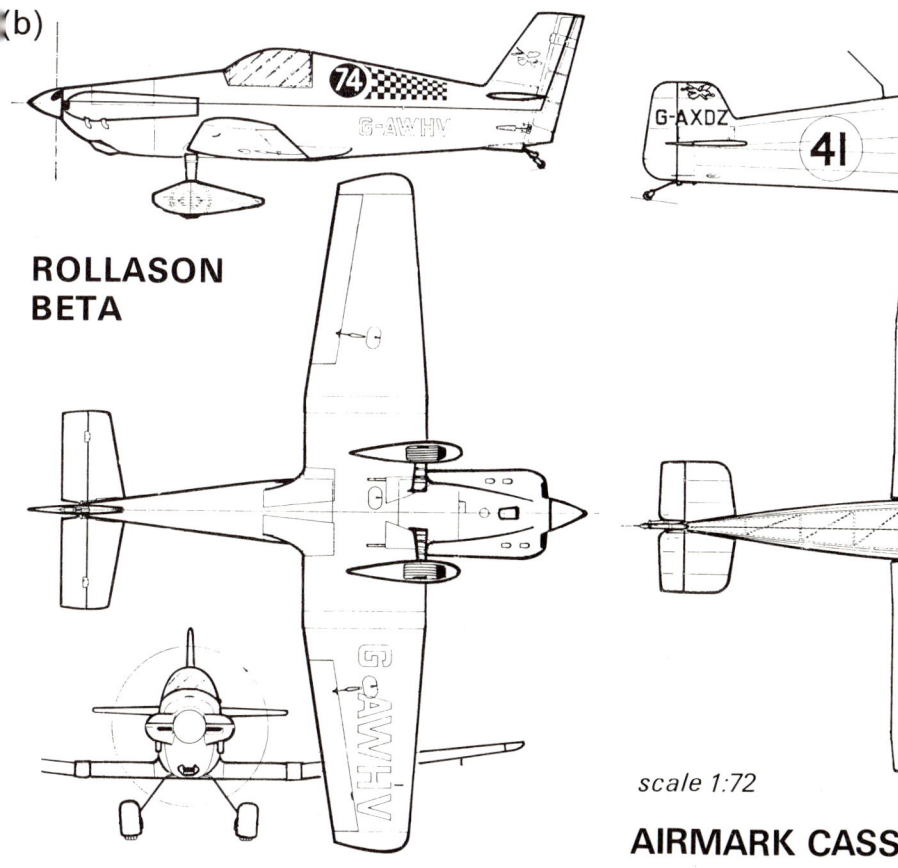

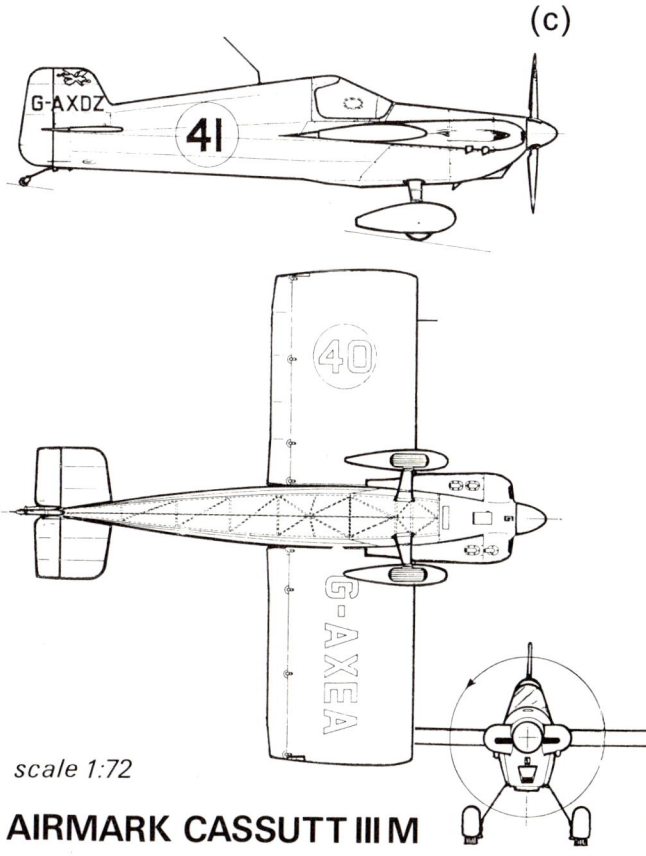

scale 1:72

53

you want and not something that has to be altered or sent back again. For a small single-seater, an Evans VP-1, which was built in Britain between the years 1973 and 1976 the actual costs were as follows.

	£
Aeroplane, all constructional materials, engine, wheels, instruments, paint	991
Plans, instructional manuals, books	34
Comprehensive insurance, including for flying	85
Registration of aircraft fee	5
Certificate of Airworthiness (1977, now £18)	24
	1,139
In addition	
Tow bar for car	40
Extra tools, saw blades, sandpaper	31
Grand total	1,210

This VP-1 was built single handed by its owner, Robert Lowe, and these were his costs. In many ways the ideal would be for two people to become partners, to share the work and eventually the flying. This, like all ideals, is easier to hope for than obtain. To achieve success the partners would need to live reasonably close to each other so that *both* can get on with the work even in short periods of spare time, and both need to be equally competent, although their skills do not need to be the same. In many ways it is better if one partner does all the constructional woodwork, and the other looks after the engine, all metal fittings and the instruments. Last, but not least, it is advisable that the flying experience of both is comparable, so that they can fly their product turn about, without either worrying himself silly that the other will break it. If this condition cannot apply, because one partner has perhaps thousands of hours flying and the other is only the recent possessor of a pilot's licence, then the junior partner must agree to stick by whatever supervisory requirements are laid down by the senior – at least for the first year. This may seem irksome to the newer pilot, but it will be even more so if he breaks the precious aeroplane in some silly incident, so that neither then has anything to fly. Like all agreements between friends, it should be in writing and should cover as many eventualities as imagination will reasonably allow.

Figure 3.4. Formula 1 air racing takes place around a pylon-marked course to strict rules to prevent it from becoming too expensive.
The rules are as follows.
(1) The *wing area* must be a minimum of 66 square feet which gives approximately a maximum of 12 lb per square foot wing loading.
(2) The *undercarriage* must be fixed, with two main wheels of a minimum size. Brakes are compulsory.
(3) The *engines* must be a maximum of 200 c.in. capacity and must be stock. This means the horizontally opposed four-cylinder air-cooled Continental engine built under licence in Britain for all types of light aircraft by Rolls Royce Motors. Modifications to the engine except balancing, polishing and minor carburettor adjustments are not allowed.
(4) The *fuel tanks* must hold a minimum of 5 gallons and standard aviation fuel must be used.
(5) The *propellers* must be fixed pitch.
(6) The *construction* must be of approved materials and must follow normal aircraft practice. The minimum empty weight must be 500 lb, and the structure must be capable of withstanding a load of 6 g and also of a maximum speed greater than the maximum speed of the machine in level flight.
(7) *Control and manoeuvrability.* The aircraft must be highly manoeuvrable, and in practice this means that they must be fully aerobatic. Racing aircraft are not noted for their stability, but they must be able to fly straight and level in turbulence without pitching and snaking.
(8) The *cockpit* must be of a minimum size to accommodate a pilot wearing a crash helmet which is compulsory and a parachute. Pilots must weigh a minimum of 160 lb, or, if lighter than this, the weight must be made up by carrying ballast in the cockpit. There are also strict field of vision requirements and pilots must be seated more or less upright.

Pilot qualifications. All competing pilots must have either 500 hours' experience or 10 hours on the racer they are flying for every 100 hours short of the 500 hours mark. They must have an absolute minimum of 100 hours. Also they must have 2 hours' recent experience on type. Pilots must also demonstrate their ability to take off in a straight line without veering more than 5 feet and they must also have flown at least five laps of the course, one of which must be at full power before competing. If they have not competed before, they must fly a minimum of ten laps of the course.

Race rules. The aircraft race round a course which is as near as possible to 3 miles long. The course is hexagonal in shape and is marked by six pylons. There are two straights of 1 mile and there are two turns at each end through half a mile.

Sometimes it is possible to reduce costs by purchasing the bits of an aeroplane that someone else has started but never finished. There are many of these advertised in the PFA journal, mostly by people who began to build before starting to think about what was involved. Before finally buying a heap of someone else's dreams, it is absolutely essential to take along a PFA inspector and to be advised by him. The seemingly beautiful pieces of shaped plywood, neat piles of ready-made ribs and the plastic bucket full of shiny nuts, bolts and miscellaneous metal fittings may fire the prospective purchaser with impatient enthusiasm; except that the inspector's eagle eye will have spotted that the ribs have been made of heavier $\frac{3}{16}$ instead of $\frac{1}{8}$ ply and that most of the bolts will be about 2 millimetres too short.

Getting started

Before obtaining the drawings to build the Evans VP-1, Robert Lowe spent 8 months thinking about building an aeroplane. Already a very experienced pilot, he would have had no problem in flying whatever exotic or speedy bird that he chose to construct; but he was realistic enough to appreciate that the object was to get into the air and not to spend more years than he need in the workshop. He decided on a single-seater also for reasons of cost and simplicity, and one with an open cockpit, because he liked flying in the fresh air. During this 8 months he gathered information, such as where he could get good welding done locally. He talked to other home builders and also found a farmer friend with a private airstrip, who agreed to let him fly from it and to use a corner of his small hangar. He considered various designs, some more seriously than others, and finally chose the VP-1, because it had the additional advantage that it could be derigged and towed with his car, either on a trailer or backwards on its own wheels. Then he sent for the plans. When they arrived he found them complete and easy to read, with some pages of instruction at the end of the book. The first requirement was to make a long narrow worktable, which then acted as a jig for both fuselage and wings. This worktable was the only thing he did not think was satisfactory in the plans, as it did not seem strong or stiff enough, so he remedied this. The first real item to be built was the square box-like fuselage, from the engine firewall back to the tail. It was a straightforward carpentry and glue job which did not take very long and produced an encouraging

VP-1

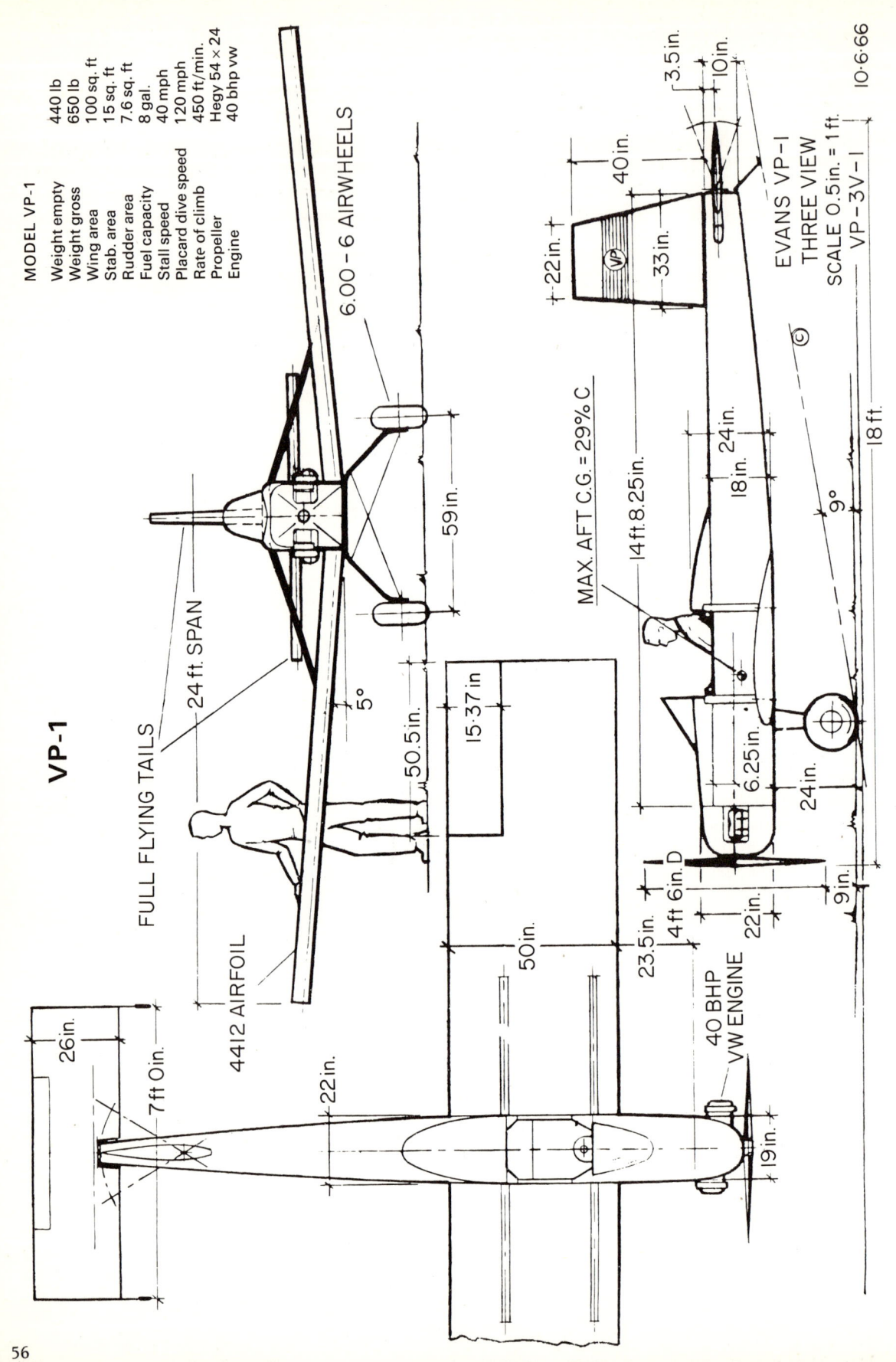

MODEL VP-1

Weight empty	440 lb
Weight gross	650 lb
Wing area	100 sq. ft
Stab. area	15 sq. ft
Rudder area	7.6 sq. ft
Fuel capacity	8 gal.
Stall speed	40 mph
Placard dive speed	120 mph
Rate of climb	450 ft/min.
Propeller	Hegy 54 × 24
Engine	40 bhp vw

EVANS VP-1 THREE VIEW
SCALE 0.5 in. = 1 ft.
VP-3V-1
10·6·66

Figure 3.5. The VP-1 is a simple aeroplane intended for home-building by pilots without aeronautical experience. This is an example of the first drawing in the comprehensive instruction manual. It was the choice of Robert Lowe after several months of thinking what to build.

sense of achievement. As soon as possible he made and fitted the undercarriage, for the very practical reason that this made the fuselage mobile, so it could be easily pushed into spare corners of the garage.

Robert Lowe worked on his aeroplane most evenings and weekends for the next 3 years. He had a two-car garage next to his house, and, although his car had to live out for long spells, there was room for the narrow jig worktable to be permanently installed down the middle, between the two doors. He was lucky in that a PFA inspector lived nearby and gave him considerable advisory help, as well as making nineteen formal inspections at different stages during construction.

At times work went easily and results showed up quickly, as in mass producing the BS 1088 mahogany marine plywood wing ribs. At other times progress seemed to slow right down, even to the extent of his wondering about abandoning the whole project. The difficult bits mainly involved small metal fittings, firstly in getting the correct specification steel and then in making up the parts or getting them made – one firm took 6 months to say that a particular bit could not be manufactured. In despair, he talked to an engineering friend at work about the problem. He offered to try without making promises, and the next day telephoned to say it was all done. Despair disappeared, and the work went on again.

Three parts of the VP-1 are fibre-glass; the cowlings, the fairing behind the pilot, and the combined petrol tank and top fuselage fairing. The latter two he decided to make on a simple plaster male mould, instead of the other way round, and to sand the surface smooth.

The cowlings were a very simple shape to make, except that the best mould to use was undoubtedly the actual cowlings from another VP-1. Robert Lowe asked to borrow some for this purpose, but the owner was not prepared to lend; instead he made a set himself and presented them.

The engine
The VP-1 is fitted with a converted 1,600cc Volkswagen engine fitted with dual ignition and driving a wooden propeller. There was not much difficulty in getting hold of an engine, but a great deal of time was saved when a fellow PFA member, used to working with this particular conversion, offered to overhaul and tune it.

Assembly
While this was going on Robert Lowe's collection of components was beginning at last to look like an aeroplane. The rudder and all-flying tailplane were covered with cotton and were doped. Then the wings were covered with Dacron, which he had not been able to obtain earlier. The inspector had studied the skeletal aeroplane with minute care and had later examined and passed the smooth taut fabric. The VP-1 was now ready to paint. Two-part polyurethane was used, which covered fabric, plywood, the aluminium leading edge and fibre-glass equally well. Finally in resplendent blue and white the VP-1 stood out in the garden under the summer sun. The engine, cowlings, final inspection, various bits of paperwork and a host of minor adjustments still needed to be fitted or completed, but flying would soon now be a reality.

Test Flying
Robert Lowe test flew his own VP-1. The first flight was intended to be a circuit of the airfield, but it became only a straight hop, because on getting airborne there was a curious vibration. Thinking that in spite of all his care and attention something had come loose, he immediately landed straight ahead. Another careful inspection revealed nothing amiss, but someone said that one of the wheels might not be balanced and was perhaps rumbling while rotating in the air. On the second take-off Robert Lowe stopped the rotation with the wheel brakes as soon as he was airborne, and there was no vibration. This VP-1 has now flown for over 20 hours, behaves itself perfectly and in the eyes of its owner is more than worth all the time and effort.

More usually the home builder does not have the background flying experience to do the test flying himself, and this is where the PFA comes to the rescue again. It is not a question of an aeroplane coming apart in the air or of anything dramatic happening but of checking that it actually works as it is intended to. Will it fly hands off, in trim, or does it want to go nose high? Does it remain level laterally, or is constant attention needed to prevent the left wing going gently

Figure 3.6. (a) The instrument panel set up on the bulkhead. A comprehensive panel is not required as this sort of aeroplane is not likely to be used for all-weather flying. It could, in fact, be flown perfectly safely by an experienced pilot without any instruments at all. (b) The bulkhead built into the fuselage. (c) The fuselage complete with fibre-glass fuel tank and fairings, but with the tail surfaces yet to be covered. The windscreen surround is strong, so as to act also as a roll bar, should the aeroplane end up upside down. The next stage was to build and fit the undercarriage so that the fuselage could be moved into convenient corners of the workshop while work continued on the wings.

Figure 3.7. (a) The wing attached showing the position of the struts. (b) The tail surfaces covered with cotton fabric and the first coat of dope. Putting the aeroplane out in the garden always slowed things down because so many friends came to see how it was getting on.

(a)

(b)

down? Is the length of the take-off run as expected; if the propeller is of too fine a pitch the take-off and climb will be good, but the top and cruising speeds will be down; and vice versa if the propeller pitch is too coarse. Test flying should be carried out in quiet weather so that turbulence and gusts will not upset the assessment, and it should not be rushed, however impatient you may feel. What you want is an aeroplane that is absolutely right, and it is worth that little extra wait to get it.

Using your aeroplane
Finally you have it in your hands, and you are ready to go. To start with you should only fly your beautiful aeroplane locally, in order to get to know it well. Its handling characteristics will probably feel quite different from the school Cessna or Cherokee on which you recently put in those hours of refresher flying. Your aeroplane is smaller and lighter, and the controls may even have a fidgety sort of feel, which will take getting used to. You will want to teach yourself at what speed you obtain the best angle of climb, how sloppy the controls begin to feel when you fly slowly – so as to avoid flying too slowly – and how to make neat landings. You will also want to evaluate the aeroplane's performance and behaviour, including how long is the landing run in no wind and how it behaves when landed with some cross-wind component. Light winds and good visibility are advisable until you feel that you are properly in control of your new toy *all the time*. At least 10 hours of this sort of assessment and familiarization should be flown locally, before setting off for anywhere else.

Finding your way
For many pilots of home-built aircraft the first real problem turns up soon on an early cross-country flight, because he gets lost.

In the flying club aeroplanes there was radio, and navigation was mostly flying on a compass heading from beacon to beacon. If lost, you could be found by radar, and you could be set off again in the right direction. Certainly you were taught about dead reckoning navigation and map reading in class, but now you have no radio and no aids, and your memory of the lessons may seem to have become somewhat vague. *You* have to teach yourself practical do-it-yourself navigation. Not only is it infuriating and disorientating to be lost in the air, but authority views with absolutely no enthusiasm small aeroplanes which stray into controlled airspace.

59

Map reading

Most small aeroplanes do not fly very fast, and they do not always have either very good or accurate compasses: so like gliders the mainstay of practical cross-country navigation is the map. This should be an up-to-date aeronautical chart marked with controlled airspace. As far as the aeroplane pilot is concerned, charts come in two scales: half-million and quarter-million. The half-million (1:500,000) scale is approximately 8 miles to the inch, and the quarter-million (1:250,000) approximately 4 miles to the inch. The half-million map is better for long flights and route planning, and the quarter-million for short distances and getting to know the locality, because there is space on it for smaller villages and other features of a more minor, though often interesting, nature.

There is only one way to navigate by map reading in a small aeroplane, and that is to know where you are all the time. This does not mean that you must know the name of the town or village underneath, but that you have something in sight at all times which has been positively identified, however distant, and you know your relationship to it. If you know that the headland near the horizon is Portland Bill or the mountain away to the north is definitely Snowdon, then you can work out your *precise* location anytime you want. The way most people get lost in fine weather is that they forget to locate and identify a new prominent feature before losing sight of the earlier one that they have now passed.

If you discover that this is exactly what you have done, the next thing not to do is to blunder on in the hope that something recognizable will turn up. It may do, but, what is more likely, because of the disorientating feeling of being lost, you will fail to recognize some prominent feature for what it is and become even more lost.

Instead, look around for some near and clear feature, such as a town with a river and railway, or a motorway junction, and fly around it until you have identified it on the map. Also be certain; it is very easy to convince yourself that the town must be Worcester, or Appleby, or Royston, because you feel it ought to be. If it is not and if you depart from it as though it were, you will go even more astray.

The second difficulty that besets the lost pilot is that, because of his total concentration on finding himself, he forgets to check on how much petrol he has left. If the engine now suddenly stops, he really does have a problem.

Figure 3.8. (a) & (b) After 3 years and 2 months, Robert Lowe has his aeroplane and as soon as possible gets himself into the air.

Planning a flight and setting off

However good the weather, and however well you think you know the way, you should never fly without a map, and you should draw a route line – the track – on it in soft pencil. Some pilots cover their maps with plastic film and use felt tips or chinagraph pencils, but these may make such a thick or heavy line that it is possible for information, such as a television mast obstruction mark, to be obscured. A protractor should be used to find the true heading, and the magnetic variation should be added. This is at present about 7 degrees west of north in Britain. The magnetic heading is what should be set on the compass – if this is accurate. But few compasses in small aeroplanes or gliders read accurately, because they are affected by metal or magnetic objects, including camera light metres, in the cockpits. This inaccuracy, or deviation, can be corrected and allowed for, and this should be done. Nevertheless, such compasses should never be relied on for absolute accuracy.

The important thing is to fly in the right direction, and the simplest way to do this is to note one or two landmarks more or less en route which will be visible before you set course. You take off, climb up to 1,500 to 2,000 feet and look for the landmarks. Say that one of these is a prominent hill on the Downs about 8 miles ahead and a little to the left of your track line. You will need to pass this hill with it about a mile away, and go over a small village that you cannot see from this distance. A little closer, and to the right of the track, is a town with a housing estate running out from it like an arm. The tip of this arm almost touches your pencil line. So, over the centre of the home field you set off along your line, aiming to pass close to the tip of the housing estate and pointing a bit to the right of the distant hill. Note the time you depart. As the tip of the housing estate passes under the wing look at your compass and remember the heading. Continue to fly straight, and, as you approach the hill and fly over the centre of the village that you could not see earlier, read your compass again. It should read the same as before, and this is the heading which should take you reliably to your destination, unless the wind changes or you wander away to look at something on the ground. This simple method has built in for you variation, deviation and any cross-wind component. Although you have now got an accurate compass bearing, you should still continue to work on a landmark chain.

THE KITTIWAKE

Figure 3.9. Another home-built, the frontispiece scene did not remain a mere drawing in the sand. Aeronautical engineer, Roy Procter, wanted to design and build a metal aeroplane specially for towing gliders. After many years' work it flew and now tows gliders at the Lasham Gliding Centre.

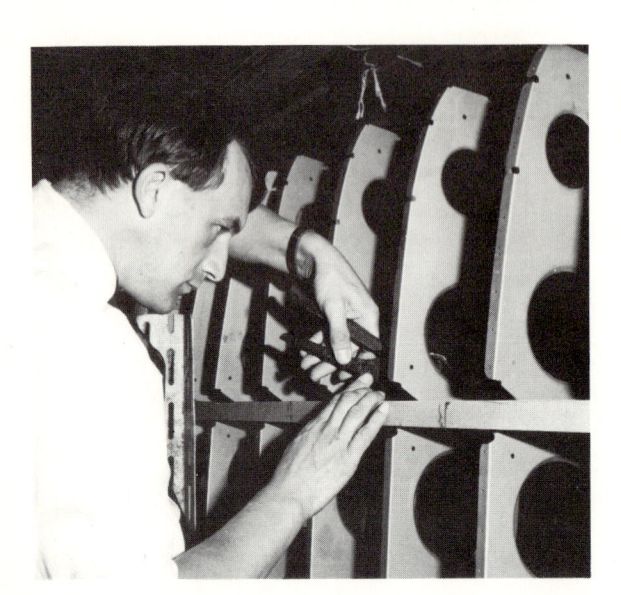

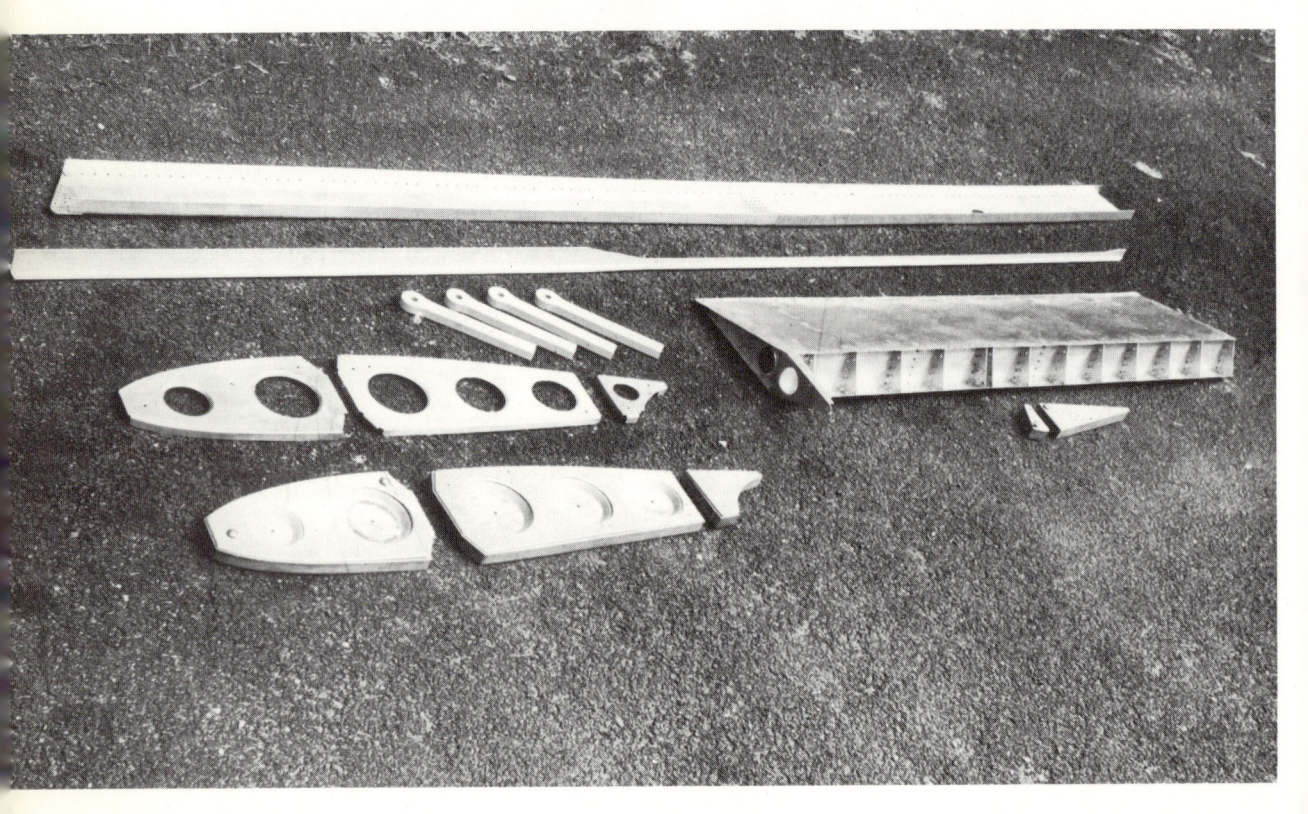

63

Before the hill on the Downs disappears behind you, look ahead and identify the next feature.

So far the weather has been clear, and, although it is not sensible to go flying about in small aeroplanes in bad weather and poor visibility until considerable experience has been gained, it is not always possible to avoid getting caught out in conditions where so little can be seen that map and compass navigation becomes chancy. In such conditions it is even more essential to avoid getting lost. The most sensible thing to do is to follow those roads and railways that will arrive at, or very close to, your destination, preferably, of course, having anticipated such a situation, and having made a plan. A careful check should be made for obstructions such as radio masts, because it is most practical to do this sort of cross-country flying at only 700 to 1,000 feet. It is also a rule that such ground features are followed by keeping to the right of them – the opposite of the English rule of the road. Following roads and railways without too much height demands concentration, it also requires the pilot to remember that he may not be alone and that there is maybe another aeroplane around somewhere, with its pilot also not keeping a good look-out.

Weather
Unless it is apparent that the weather at the destination is good, it is imprudent to set off without obtaining information on how the weather is likely to behave. If it could deteriorate at some stage, then considerable thought must be devoted to alternative plans and diversions. Probably the most common aeroplane pilot killer is the approaching warm front – and, if you are flying towards it, its arrival may be surprisingly rapid! The problems are many: cloud base steadily lowers until it is on the ground at the front itself; the base itself is amorphous and indistinct and reduces visibility; the very moist air will form even lower cloud around hills; drizzle falls, and this may be as snow near cloud base, or even down to the ground in cold weather, making visibility almost nil. As if this were not enough, the lowering air-pressure towards the front causes the altimeter to overread, showing the pilot height that he has not got. There is only one thing to do in a small aeroplane in this sort of weather and that is to turn back before it is too late. If you get lost as well, the chances of flying into hidden hills is great, and you certainly would not have been the first pilot to do so. Small and home-built aeroplanes are for the pleasures of flying, and the greatest pleasure is when the weather is warm and fine, particularly in an open cockpit.

Most cross-country flights will probably be made to PFA rallies to get together with other home aeroplane-builders and restorers of vintage aircraft; although not many have the persistence and determination to fly from Australia to Britain, a distance of 14,000 miles, for a weekend meet, as one pilot did in 1976. It took him a flying time of 98 hours over 16 days; he flew at a speed of 130 knots. Life was quite exciting on the way as Calcutta radar missed him and told him he was not there, even as he was landing, and over the Middle East he was shot at and forced down by Migs. But he made it!

Figure 3.10. The FAI proficiency badge for aeroplane pilots.

Popular Flying Association

ASSOCIATIONS

Aircraft Owners' and Pilots' Association
Address: 50A Cambridge Street,
London, SW1V 4QQ
Telephone No.: 01-834 5631-32

Popular Flying Association
Address: Terminal Building, Shoreham Airport,
Shoreham-by-Sea, Sussex BN4 5FF
Telephone No.: Shoreham-by-Sea 61616

British Aerobatic Association
Address: 62 Ennerdale Road, Kew, Richmond,
Surrey TW9 2DL

Formula 1 Air Racing Association
Address: 50A Cambridge Street,
London SW1V 4QQ
Telephone No.: 01-834 5631

No. of pilots: 19,817
No. of aeroplanes: 2,987
No of hours' flying annually: (All General Aviation) 800,000
No of clubs and schools: 150
Minimum age for flying solo: 17 years

Aircraft Owner's and Pilot's Association

The Aircraft Owners' and Pilots' Association (AOPA) looks after private and sporting aeroplane flying in the UK in conjunction with the CAA except in the special areas covered by the PFA (amateur construction), the Aerobatic and the Formula 1 Racing Associations. The AOPA (UK) is the controlling body for aeroplane and man-powered aircraft record attempts.

The PFA is responsible to the CAA for the recommendation of special category certificates of airworthiness for ultra-light aircraft. Its engineering executive vets new aircraft designs and suggests and approves modifications. It has a national network of inspectors for home-built projects. PFA groups look after instruction and aircraft construction and preservation. The aim of the PFA is to get the would-be aviator into the air as cheaply as possible.

Pilot licences and certificates
All aeroplane pilots in the UK have to hold at least a PPL, or a restricted PPL for motor gliders, issued by the CAA. A medical examination by an approved CAA doctor is required. In addition pilot proficiency certificates are being introduced by the FAI.

Training courses
The standard training course for a PPL, consisting of flying for 35 to 40 hours, are run by school and clubs registered with the AOPA (UK). Most are non-residential, but there is wide national coverage

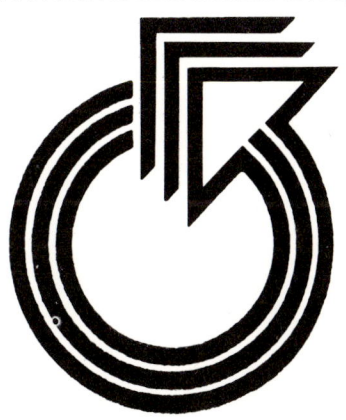

Formula 1 Air Racing

4 Man-powered Aircraft

To anyone who has built, has finally finished and has flown his own strong small aeroplane, creating a flimsy lightweight to pedal into the air may seem quite easy, like playing with toys. But it is quite the opposite. Designing and building an aircraft which can take off and fly under muscle power alone, even for a few hundred yards, is perhaps the most difficult challenge in aviation.

Ever since man first got his feet off the ground, he has dreamed of floating through the sky flapping his wings like a bird or pedalling a great slowly revolving propeller. Sometimes he has thought about launching off a hilltop by rubber catapult or running, and then pedalling, or soaring in slope or thermal lift, and pedalling or flapping his way to the next upcurrent. But these things do not happen, or have not yet, because concentration becomes so entirely devoted to solving the first problem; that of making an aircraft light enough so that the tiny 0.5 horsepower that man is able to develop can be utilized effectively. You cannot get something for nothing. If man cannot develop any more power, then the aircraft has to be designed to fly within this limitation. Perhaps the first serious attempt to fly by muscle power was in 1929 when the German glider designer, Alexander Lippisch, built the Schwinguin. This was small, with a span of a little under 10 metres, and the wings were designed to flap. At that time the complex movements of a bird's wing in flight had not been revealed by the present plethora of slow-motion films, and the mechanical arrangements did not do much more than allow the wings to move more or less vertically up and down. A young pilot athlete flew Schwinguin, launched from flat ground, by a rubber catapult. It soon became obvious that the performance of the aircraft was no better with the wings flapping than when they were still and that, when the flapping was stopped with the wings drooping, there was not much lateral stability either. Later, various modifications were made to increase the area of the trailing edge to allow the wing to be more flexible – like a bird's soft wing – and this helped, but as the mechanism to move the wings became more complicated, the aircraft merely became heavier – and more muscle was needed. On one flight, after the bungey launch, a distance of 200 metres was flown with flapping all the way, but the effort was considerable. The pilot, clearly dreaming of practical solutions such as putting a small engine in it, lost interest and ceased to work hard enough, needing to be bribed with leave to visit his girl friend, in order to achieve the effort and success Lippisch was hoping for. The last flight achieved nearly 300 metres in distance. After this, experiments ceased because Lippisch realized that his aircraft was too heavy, and

Figure 4.1. In 1922 the idea of propelling oneself into the air achieved reality but not success. G. W. Cain hoped in vain to pedal himself into the slope lift over Itford Hill in Sussex and soar.

Figure 4.2. Many man-powered aircraft start life in notebook pages and on the backs of envelopes, with ideas for overcoming the incredibly difficult problem of successfully using man's meagre 0.5 horsepower to the best advantage.

then the pilot was killed in an accident elsewhere.

In 1933 the first prize ever for man-powered flight was offered in Germany. It was not won, but in 1935 a consolation prize was given to the designer of the Mufli. This was a 44 feet span conventional glider-shape aircraft with the pilot pedalling a propeller mounted above the wing. It was the design forerunner of most of the man-powered experiments to come. It was also launched by a catapult from flat ground and flew a distance approaching 800 metres. After this, interest seemed to die away. In 1967 the prize which had been offered by Henry Kremer in 1957 was doubled in value to £10,000, and the competition was opened to all nationalities. This sparked off no less than six designs, mainly from universities, polytechnics and apprentice schools, who saw the challenge as a worthy project for bright new brains.

The first of these to fly was the Sumpac, designed

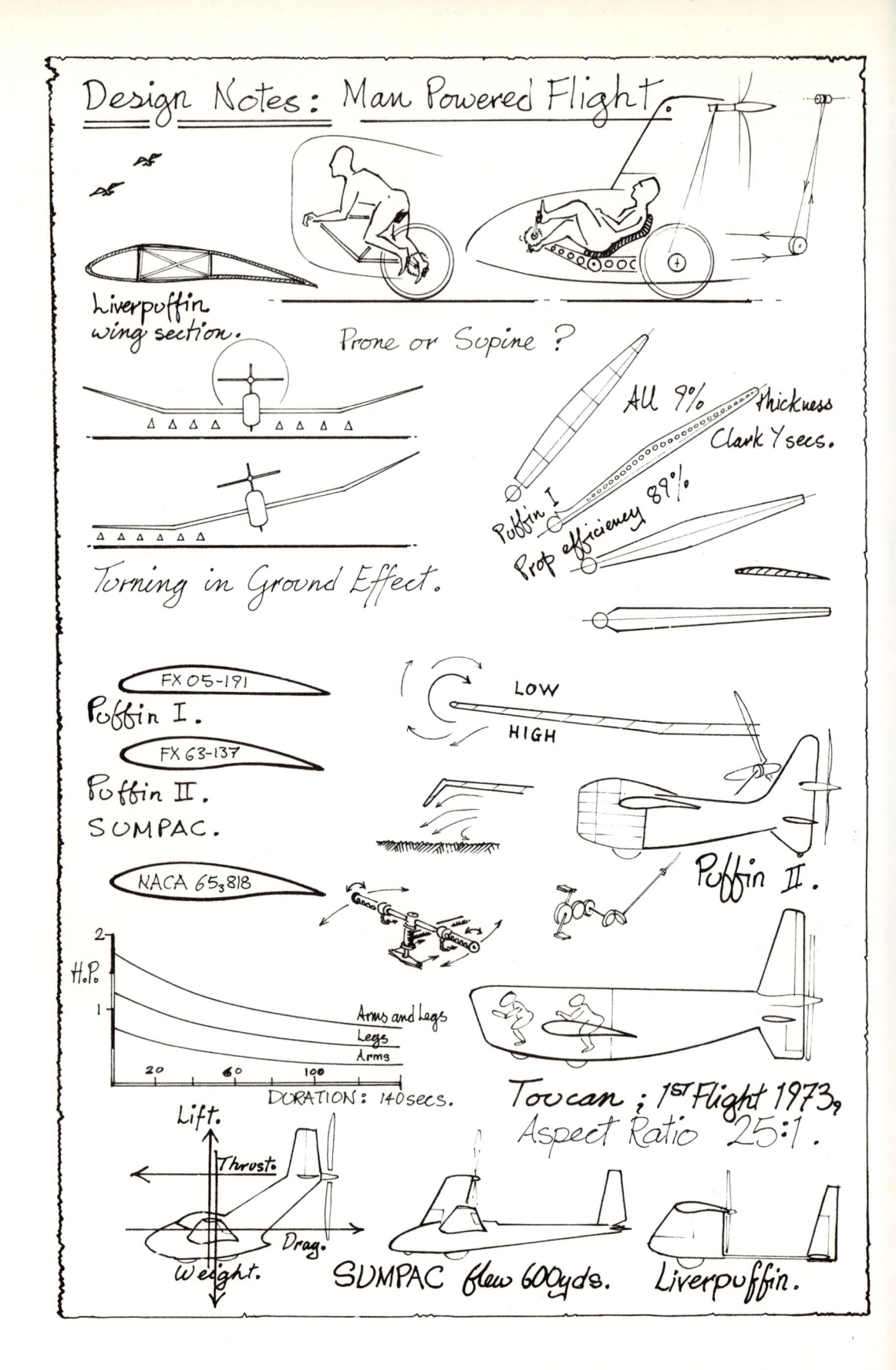

Design Notes: Man Powered Flight

Liverpuffin wing section.

Prone or Supine?

All 9% thickness Clark Y secs.
Puffin I
Prop efficiency 89%

Turning in Ground Effect.

FX 05-191 — Puffin I.
FX 63-137 — Puffin II. SUMPAC.
NACA 65₃818

LOW / HIGH

Puffin II.

H.P.
Arms and Legs
Legs
Arms
DURATION: 140 secs.

Toucan; 1ˢᵗ Flight 1973, Aspect Ratio 25:1.

Lift. Thrust. Drag. Weight.

SUMPAC flew 600 yds.   Liverpuffin.

Flying prone. A German-built UP Dragonfly competing in the WHGC at Kossen Austria, 1976

Hang gliding is flying like the birds, unless you prefer to feel like a moth or a butterfly

Cumulus clouds are signposts to thermals to this 15-metre-span standard Libelle glider

But out on the starting grid in a World Championship there may be long waits for the thermals to begin. Standard Libelle at Marfa, Texas

Figure 4.3. The de Havilland Hatfield Group Puffin, which was awarded a special prize of £50 for the first man-powered aircraft to fly over half a mile piloted by J. Wimpenny in May 1962.

and built by three postgraduate students at Southampton University, aided by financial assistance from the Royal Aeronautical Society. Sumpac had a span of 80 feet against Mufli's 44 feet and weighed 128 lb against 81 lb. Although the extra weight increased the energy and effort required from the pedaller pilot, the actual wing loading of Sumpac was much less, only 0.9 lb per square foot against 2.37 lb per square foot, which meant that it would be able to take off at a slower speed. It is the balance of the various characteristics of an aircraft to achieve maximum possible performance that is the intriguing – and everlasting – problem with man-powered flight. If the span is increased, the wing can be made more efficient, but this has to be balanced against greater weight. If the weight can be reduced, so can the wing loading, which enables the aircraft to become airborne at a slower speed; but a really low loading makes it very vulnerable to wind and gusts. This leads to aircraft which can be flown only in absolutely calm air; otherwise they blow away like feathers, and test flying becomes a highly protracted process. It also virtually eliminates car towing, and certainly bungey launching, in order to give the pilot some practice in flying his aircraft. This is perhaps not appreciated enough when considering some of the failures with man-powered aircraft. How can a pilot be expected to get the most out of an aircraft that he has never, or almost never, flown before?

Sumpac first flew in 1961 and within the year was making flights, including take-off, 300 metres long with turns of up to 80 degrees change of direction. It was able to fly in gentle breezes and could even be landed with some cross-wind. It was eventually broken with basically a cyclist, rather than a pilot, at the controls, when it floated up to about 30 feet in a

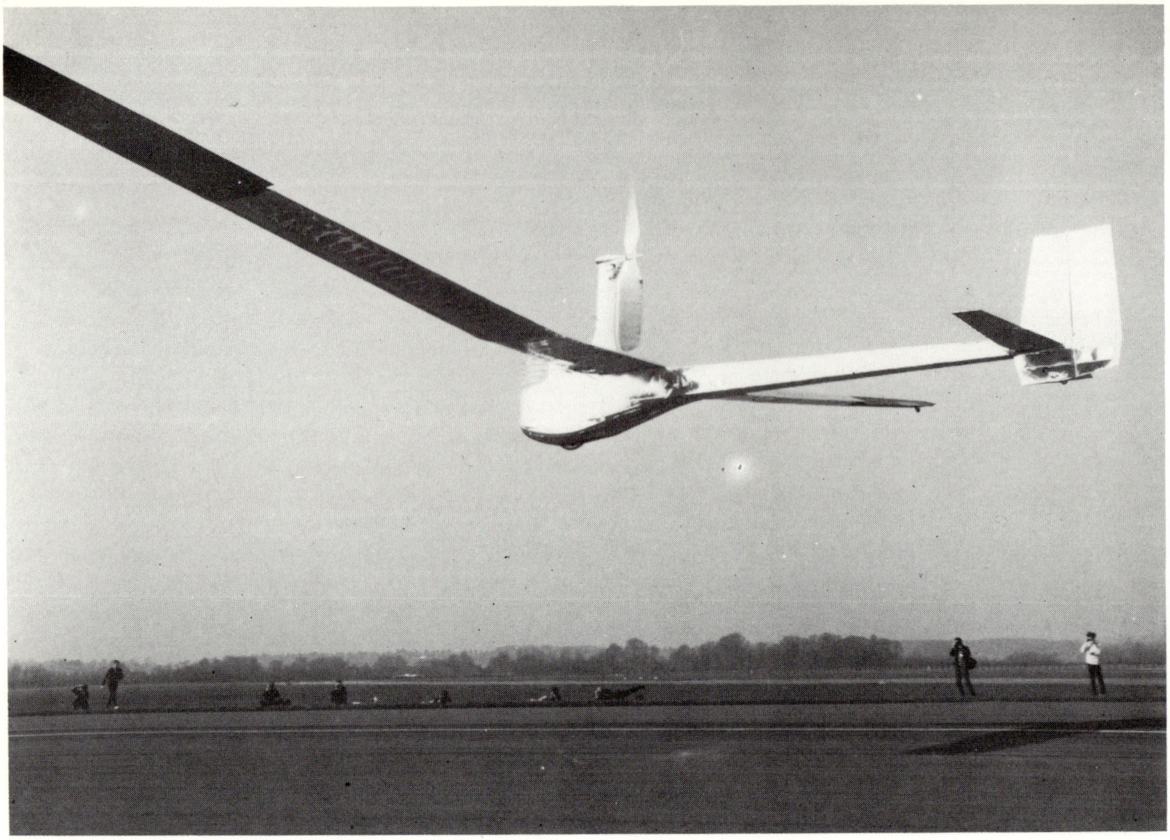

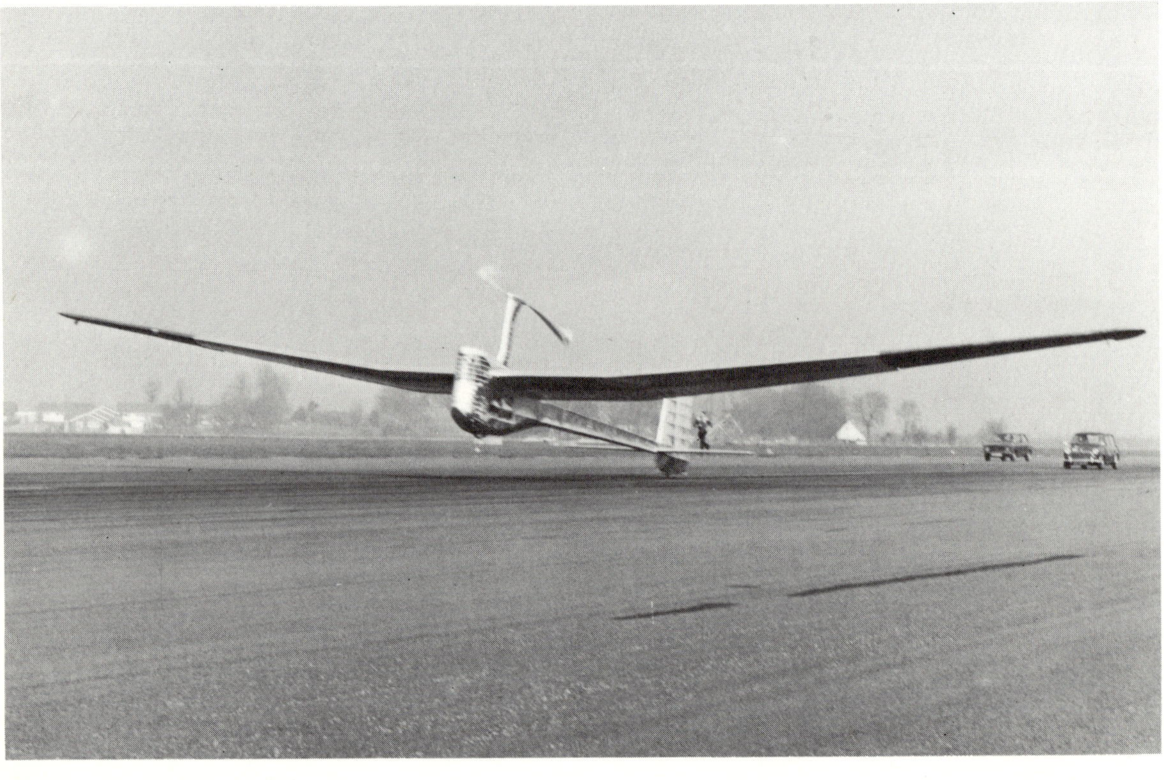

Figure 4.4. Jupiter, built by the Halton Group. The span was 80 feet, and it weighed 146 lb. It flew 1.23 kilometres piloted and pedalled by Sqn Ldr John Potter, who is shown in the cyclist's position with the nose fairing removed.

gust and stalled. The next aircraft to fly was Puffin I, the creation of the Hatfield Group at the de Havilland Aircraft Company. Puffin was not much bigger than Sumpac, with a span of 84 feet, but had a slightly lower wing loading of 0.81 lb per square foot. It was therefore even more critical as regards wind. Puffin I managed 330 metres and some turns and was awarded a special prize of £50 for the first man-powered aircraft to fly over half a mile. After more than ninety flights Puffin was also caught out by a puff of changing wind and was broken.

While repairing Puffin the wing was redesigned, and the aircraft became Puffin II. Span was now up to 93 feet, the weight was also up to 140 lb, as against 118 lb for Puffin I, but the wing loading was down. It was now a mere 0.74 lb per square foot. Both Puffins had the pilot in a good cycling position so that not only could he use his leg muscles efficiently but he could see where he was going. By 1969 Puffin II had also completed about ninety flights before she too was damaged as a result of turbulent air. One conflict which had to be resolved by the designers was whether the pilot should be basically a pilot and should exercise to strengthen his muscles or whether he should be primarily an athlete and should learn to fly. In 1971 the Hertfordshire Group Toucan bypassed the problem by being a two-seater (the Two-can!). The span was necessarily larger, at 123 feet, but the empty weight was low for such a huge aircraft, at 145 lb, so that the wing loading was also low; 0.74 lb per square foot, the same as Puffin II. In 1973, on its second flight, it travelled a distance of 220 metres. Also at this time the Weybridge Group was producing a single-seater with a span of 120 feet, with a wing loading of only 0.57 lb per square foot. This was generally similar in shape to the Puffins and the Toucan but with a very low wing to make the most of the ground effect. It too was eventually damaged.

The problem with this line of development was that, in spite of care in design and the excellence of the intricate construction, these aircraft, like the dinosaur, found themselves operating in conditions which made them often unworkable. They had considerable value as challenging technical training projects but were incredibly weather sensitive and expensive and took thousands of hours to build, and almost as many to mend.

A more practicable approach was that of an RAF group led by Sqn Ldr John Potter with the Halton Jupiter. This had a span of 80 feet like Sumpac, a quite high empty weight of 146 lb and a wing loading of 1 lb per square foot, similar to that of a hang glider. It was less sensitive to weather and less delicate, and it also made the longest flight of this era of man-powered aircraft, 1.23 kilometres.

The Kremer prize

In spite of all this expenditure of effort no one had so far come even remotely close to winning the Kremer prize. The big problem was not taking off, flying more or less straight and landing, but making turns.

The task for the prize, which had now been raised to £50,000, required the aircraft to fly a figure of eight, as follows:

Figure 4.5. The Japanese Stork of Nihon University. It has completed turns of 180 degrees and a straight distance of 2,094 metres. It is relatively small in span, 68 feet 9 inches, and weighs 79 lb. The propeller diameter is 8 ft and it will fly at an airspeed of 19 mph.

(1) The course shall be a figure of eight with two turning points not less than half a mile apart.

(2) The starting line, which is also the finishing line, shall be between the turning points and approximately at right angles to the line joining the turning points.

(3) The height, or ground clearance, shall be not less than 10 feet above the ground at both start and finish lines.

(4) No stored energy or lighter-than-air gas may be used, nor may the pilot(s) jettison anything during take-off or during the flight.

(5) No one outside the aircraft may assist in take-off, the ground crew being permitted to stabilize the wings only.

(6) The ground over which the flight is made has to be substantially flat and level, with no slope exceeding 1 in 200.

This means that the aircraft had to be turning for a substantial part of the flight, and this is where the difficulties really began. Flying straight, the pilot can pedal his aircraft along just clear of the ground, so that he is helped by the ground effect, or the cushion of air squeezed between the wing and the ground. But to do a turn he has to bank. An aircraft can, of course, be yawed around a corner without being banked, but it will be skidding and flying somewhat sideways. This increases the drag and lowers the performance – and the pilot is already pedalling as hard as he can. If the pilot banks in order to do a clean low-drag turn, he has to fly higher; otherwise the wing will hit the ground. As soon as he does this, he no longer has any ground effect benefit; so again he will have to pedal harder to achieve the same performance. By now he is likely to be running out of puff. Until 1977 no one achieved even a quarter of the Kremer course, let alone got within striking distance of the prize. A great deal about lightweight structures, and the amount of energy that a fit man can produce, had been learnt, but continued lack of success had dampened enthusiasm.

Recently, there has been a resurgence of effort. The Japanese produced a new aircraft, the Stork. The lightweight hang glider has encouraged a less conventional approach to the shape, Henry Kremer added a further prize of £1,000 for a duration of 3 minutes, and the FAI has introduced two additional man-powered aircraft records.

The £50,000 Kremer Prize is won

A completely new approach to muscle-powered aviation was made in USA by Paul MacCready, an ex-world gliding champion. He departed completely

Figure 4.6 (a) The Goodhart Manflyer, with two cyclists producing the power and also controlling the rate of turn by one pedalling harder than the other. (b) One of the special bicycles weighing only 10 lb.

(a)

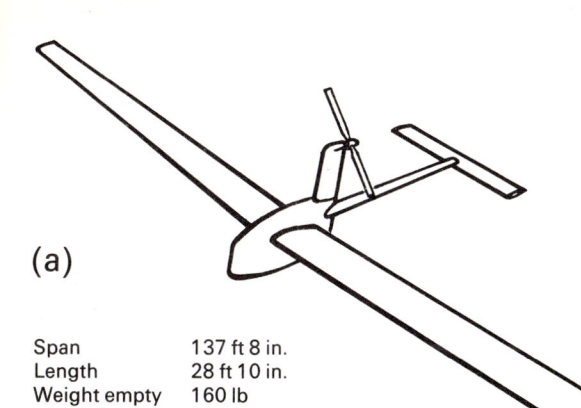

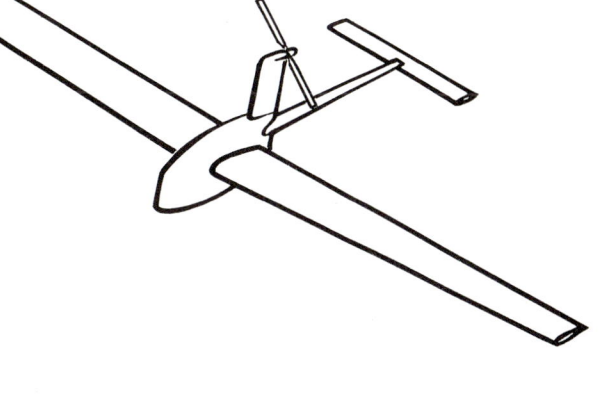

Span 137 ft 8 in.
Length 28 ft 10 in.
Weight empty 160 lb
Cruising speed 17 mph

(b)

Figure 4.7. The construction of one of the Goodhart fuselage pods and tail boom.

from the aeroplane configuration and methods of construction to a construction that is much nearer that of a hang glider. The Gossamer Condor has a span of 97 feet, but a wing loading of only 3 ounces per square foot, so it has the greatest possible weather sensitivity. This problem was, however, taken into consideration by its designer, who is also a meteorologist! Test flying and many of the other early flights, some of which lasted over a minute were made by Paul MacCready's younger son, Tyler, aged 14 years. Being already an experienced hang glider pilot, his skill, as well as his light weight was a valuable asset. California is fortunate in having fairly stable weather with calm dawns and evenings, and this of course has helped with an aircraft that will fly at a mere 8 miles per hour: it is possible to run alongside to encourage the pilot! One of the great advantages of the Gossamer Condor is that its construction is extremely simple. Even a bad break can be repaired in a few hours, and sometimes the application of a little PVC tape is all that is needed. The main structural members are thin-walled aluminium tube, like the hang glider, and the covering transparent plastic sheet. The pusher propeller is made up of balsa ribs on an aluminium tube spar. It is within the constructional ability, pocket and available spare time of any enthusiastic individual or family, so the MacCready approach opens up real possibilities for the future. But even such a relatively simple aircraft will be useless if the concept requirements are not very thoroughly considered, and if the aircraft is not designed with great care and skill. The demands are many and often in conflict. The aircraft has to be strong enough, but of the minimum possible weight: this alone is a problem ordinary aircraft designers have been working at since aeronautics began. It has to fly slowly and yet be able to be used without long waits for total calm. The wing has to be efficient, and this usually means it must be of considerable span, but it must also be possible to make turns without hitting a tip on the ground. The pilot must be able to exert maximum energy without the whole structure shuddering and shaking itself – and increasing the drag. Not only has the most suitable wing section to be selected, often a complex decision in itself, but the wing then has to be constructed so that the chosen section is exactly reproduced and does not distort in flight into a different shape. It has to be decided whether to leave the pilot in the open air, where he creates drag or to put him inside a cabin where the drag is less, but where he risks the canopy becoming misted up through his exertion and breath. The design criteria are many, and fascinating.

Figure 4.8. The MacCready Gossamer Condor prototype. The span is 97 feet and the wing loading a mere 3 ounces per square foot. It has made over three hundred flights and is very quick and easy to repair. It won the £50,000 Kremer prize on August 23 1977.

Figure 4.9. The mylar film cockpit and the pedalling position in the Condor.

Figure 4.10. Bryan Allen, the pilot who flew the Kremer course to win the £50,000 prize for the Gossamer Condor.

The challenge of man-powered flight is still wide open. The £50,000 prize has been won, but there are still more Kremer prizes to be won and records to be gained. The greatest challenge of all is the Kremer cross-channel competition – the first aircraft to be pedalled from England to France will bring its pilot £100,000! There is a lot of fun to be had not only on the backs of envelopes but also because the chance to be a pioneer is still there.

ASSOCIATIONS

The Man-powered Aircraft Group

Address: Royal Aeronautical Society, 4 Hamilton Place, London W1V OBQ
Telephone No.: 01–499 3515

The Man-powered Aircraft Group of the Royal Aeronautical Society (RAeS) provides advice and assistance towards the construction of man-powered aircraft. It also administers the Kremer prizes.

Kremer prize conditions

The competition shall be conducted by the AOPA (UK) of the Royal Aero Club under the regulations and conditions laid down by the RAeS and the FAI. Every attempt will be observed by officials of the AOPA (UK) or any body or persons authorized by them.

5 Hot Air Ballooning

Heavier-than-air aircraft cannot fly unless the air is flowing fast enough past their wings to provide them with lift. Whether this speed is provided by the aeroplane engine, the muscle power of the hang glider pilot or gravity is immaterial; speed through the air there must be. And where there is speed there is always a desire to go faster.

Hot air ballooning is quite different. The balloon obtains its lift simply by being lighter than the air that surrounds it, and its only speed is that over the ground imparted by the wind drifting it along. Because there is no air rushing past the balloon sounds from the earth can be heard clearly, even several hundred feet below, not only the hooters and engines of man but also the singing of birds. It is a peaceful way of flying. It is also the oldest, starting for all practical purposes in 1783, 120 years before the Wright Brothers got going in their aeroplane. The early experiments were with small paper bags held inverted over a kitchen fire by the brothers Joseph and Etienne Montgolfier. With these rising successfully to the ceiling the brothers made bigger bags of linen, and in the market place they built fires of wool and straw underneath them – a smoky fire being believed to be better than invisible heat. By September that year the brothers were demonstrating their creation in Paris, sending up a sheep and two fowls, all of which arrived back on the ground safely, and without the birds having to use their personalized flight systems. The King was delighted and promptly desired to send up a couple of criminals, but a free man, Pilâtre de Rozier, persuaded the king to let him go instead. He, with the Marquis d'Arlende, floated away and landed safely in the Bois de Boulogne 25 minutes later.

The hydrogen balloon was, in fact, invented somewhat in error by a Professor Charles. He heard of the Montgolfier experiments and assumed they had employed Cavendish's recent discovery of this gas. Thus with two sources of lighter-than-air support, ballooning became immensely popular, spreading all over Europe and soon reaching the USA. The hydrogen, and then the coal gas, balloon soon overtook the hot air device in popularity. The gas was available, and the flight could be made to last longer. With hot air balloons there was no practical way at the time of providing instant fire when required. The basic problem of the hydrogen balloon, the flammability of the gas, was not fully understood, and no one bothered too much about the hazards. Not only did some aeronauts give firework displays in flight from their gas balloons, but they did so even in thunderstorms. The famous Coxwell was engaged in this uncertain entertainment over Vauxhall Gardens when he was sucked up to 7,000 feet in a cumulonimbus cloud. The balloon burst and came hurtling down, remarkably failing to catch fire. Coolly, Coxwell cut the neckline, allowed the near-explosive mix to escape and descended by what then became more of a parachute than a balloon. Pilâtre de Rozier was also a very brave man, but this quality alone was not enough. Two years after his first momentous ascent and with many flights to his credit, he was ambitious to advance the sport. His new balloon, to get the best of everything, used a hydrogen envelope with a hot air container underneath. The take-off of this mini-atom bomb was uneventful, but minutes afterwards the inevitable happened – although probably due to static electricity. The only other balloonist who attempted a combination balloon was an Italian, Count Zambeccari. He became entangled with a tree shortly after take-off and spilled the spirits of wine intended for heating the air all over himself. Remarkably, nothing happened to the hydrogen, but the noble Count burst into flames. Obedient to the effect of the warming air, the balloon broke loose from the tree and ascended while the Count beat himself out. By the intervention of random probability he succeeded, landed safely and continued with his flying.

With the increasing number of heavier-than-air experiments, such as those of Cayley, Lilienthal, and Montgomery and the Wrights in USA, the aeronautical design energy and interest moved away from the balloon. By the end of the First World War, it was the aeroplane and the glider that possessed the immediate future. Hot air ballooning revived itself in the nineteen sixties, taking advantage of the new-technology neat-resistant synthetic fabrics and cylinders of propane gas basically designed for caravans. The envelope could be made almost impermeable, and instant fire was available. Propane

(a) 77,000 cu. ft.

(b) 65,000 cu. ft.

(c) 42,000 cu. ft.

(d) 56,000 cu. ft.

Figure 5.1. Balloons are of different sizes depending on how many people want to fly at the same time: (a) 77,000 cubic feet. Burner output of 6×10^6 British thermal units. (b) 65,000 cubic feet, long-range balloon with three crew; (c) 42,000 cubic feet, solo or two crew; (d) 56,000 cubic feet, two or three crew. For competitions and records balloons are divided into the following categories.

CATEGORY	CAPACITY (CUBIC METRES)	CAPACITY (CUBIC FEET)
AX–1	250 and less	2822 and less
AX–2	250–400	2822–14115
AX–3	400–600	14115–21172
AX–4	600–900	21172–31758
AX–5	900–1200	31758–42344
AX–6	1200–1600	42344–56459
AX–7	1600–2200	56459–77631
AX–8	2200–3000	77631–105861
AX–9	3000–4000	105861–141148
AX–10	4000 and above	141148 and above

Figure 5.2. (a) Many balloon baskets are made with great skill by the blind. (b) The basket of the Heineken 500,000 cubic feet balloon, which has a diameter of 110 feet, will lift 3.5 tons and carries thirty passengers.

produces no cool smoky fire, the urge from the burner blast being of the order of three house heating systems.

The new sport got under way slowly in Britain and elsewhere. It was a matter not only of finding the optimum shape and capacity in the design of the balloon but of learning how to use it. This was further complicated by the interlinked problems of pilots' licences and instructing – you could not fly without a licence, and you could not get one without flying. The few with licences were in great demand, until the pressure eased. Now this delightful way of flying is here to stay.

The balloon

Hot air balloons are large, about 30,000 cubic feet in capacity for a small solo racing balloon and up to 140,000 cubic feet suitable for a family of eight or friends. Most are about 65,000 cubic feet in capacity,

(a)

(b)

Figure 5.3. Getting ready to fly a two-man balloon, about 31,000 cubic feet. The burner produces heat equal to about three house central heating systems, but only for a few seconds at a time. (a) The trail rope is 150 feet long and is hung on the outside of the basket ready to throw. (b) A calm and sheltered place, as well as quiet weather, make for easy preparation and an undramatic take-off. (c) A twin-burner basket for two people.

are able to take three crew and are robust enough for operating throughout the year. In terms of measurement a 56,000 cubic feet balloon is about 70 feet high and 50 feet in diameter. The largest hot air balloon built is 525,000 cubic feet and can carry thirty people. The material is usually rip-stop nylon of 1.75 ounces per square yard weight, thin and translucent as a sail boat spinnaker. It is cut in gores or panels and is stitched together into the familiar spherical-pear shape. Because the fire blasts straight into the open mouth, this is usually surrounded by a short skirt of flameproof fabric, such as Nomex. As well as going up, a balloon has to come down, and, when it reaches the ground, it needs to collapse in order to stay there, otherwise the wind would blow the half-inflated balloon like a sail across the field, dragging the basket with it. For this purpose a rip panel is built into the balloon near the top and is kept closed with either a parachute rip or Velcro – another material not available to the pioneers.

The basket, and it is usually a genuine basket, because of its flexibility and excellent shock-absorbent qualities, is attached to the balloon by stainless steel rigging wires. Tough nylon tapes are sewn along the gore seams of the envelope, and are connected to the rigging wires by steel or aluminium Karibiners. Connecting balloon and basket together is one of the first acts before laying out the balloon, like a long sausage on the ground. The burner is attached to a framework above the basket and is connected to the propane cylinders strapped into its corners. Each cylinder holds 44 lb of liquid propane. The burner size varies with the balloon capacity, but a burner for a 65,000 cubic feet balloon is designed to produce about 850 kilowatts (1,100 horsepower). The fuel is fed via vapourizing coils which surround the flame, which can be turned on and off as required, a pilot light ensuring that power can be instantly available. The air in the balloon is not heated by a steady gentle warmed supply, but by roaring blasts of heat of a few seconds' duration about every half a minute. These blasts produce around 5,000,000 British thermal units per hour at a temperature of 1900°C. Combustion is almost complete, so that there is no risk of a build-up of explosive mixture in the canopy.

Balloon performance

Whereas the performance of a glider is expressed as its glide ratio, an aeroplane by its rate of climb or maximum speed, a hot air balloon performance is given as its endurance, carrying capacity or ceiling. The limiting factor is the maximum temperature to which the envelope will stand being heated. Somewhat oversimplified, the balloon lifts when the air inside it is warmed and lightened to less than the weight of the balloon and its crew in relation to the outside air. The heavier the balloon, the more heat has to be applied to obtain sufficient difference between the inside and ambient (outside) temperature. But the amount of heat is limited by the temperature that the fabric will withstand. This is normally about 110°C (250°F). If the temperature is allowed to rise much above this value, the fabric is weakened and has to be returned to the manufacturer for repairs – or in an extreme case it may catch fire. The balloon can be made too heavy by carrying too many people or too many propane cylinders, but an equivalent overload situation may also result from an attempt to arrest an inadvertently rapid descent. Like all aircraft, a balloon has to be operated within its design and constructional limitations. The endurance of a balloon depends on the amount of propane carried, any energy obtained from the air and the efficiency with which the pilot uses both the propane and this energy. If he has a three-man balloon with four propane cylinders and if he wishes to fly for a long distance, he can carry more propane only if he leaves one or both of his friends behind. Conversely, if he just wants to give some people a short ride he can leave, say, two of the cylinders on the ground and can take that weight in passengers. But he cannot do both at once. The ceiling

Figure 5.4. Inside the balloon the security of the rip panel has to be checked. If the helpers allow the mouth to close, it is very easy to get lost within.

Figure 5.5. Heating up the air inside the balloon. Sometimes a powerful ground burner is used to provide warmth rapidly and to save the propane stored inside the basket for the flight itself.

or the maximum height to which a balloon can fly is primarily limited by the excess amount of lift it has at sea level. As the balloon goes higher the air becomes 'thinner', and, although the necessary temperature difference can be maintained with the burner, the total mass of air which is being heated is less. In due course it will not be possible for the amount of warmed air in the envelope to support the weight. The effect is much the same as having a smaller balloon. If height gain is the object, then a large lightly loaded balloon is the answer. It may be thought that in the cold dense air of winter it would be easier to carry more passengers without overheating the balloon fabric, but this is not necessarily so. The propane bottle pressure also goes down, and the burner output is less. Handling can be improved by using bigger jets or keeping the cylinders indoors, so that they do not get cold.

Inflating the balloon

Balloons can cope with fresh breezes once they are in the air, but they need a sheltered place to start from. This is because it takes a while to inflate a balloon fully, and while it is lying on the ground or is upright but still partly flat, it is very vulnerable. Blown about on the ground it may be torn, and if it is up it behaves like a sail. The only way of getting airborne from an exposed field is to get the balloon more or less vertical and blast hot air up into it while all your friends, carrying the basket, run with the wind at as near wind speed as possible. This, of course, can be expensive if the far hedge or trees are reached before inflation has been completed, regardless of whether you still have any friends left. It is better to wait for less wind.

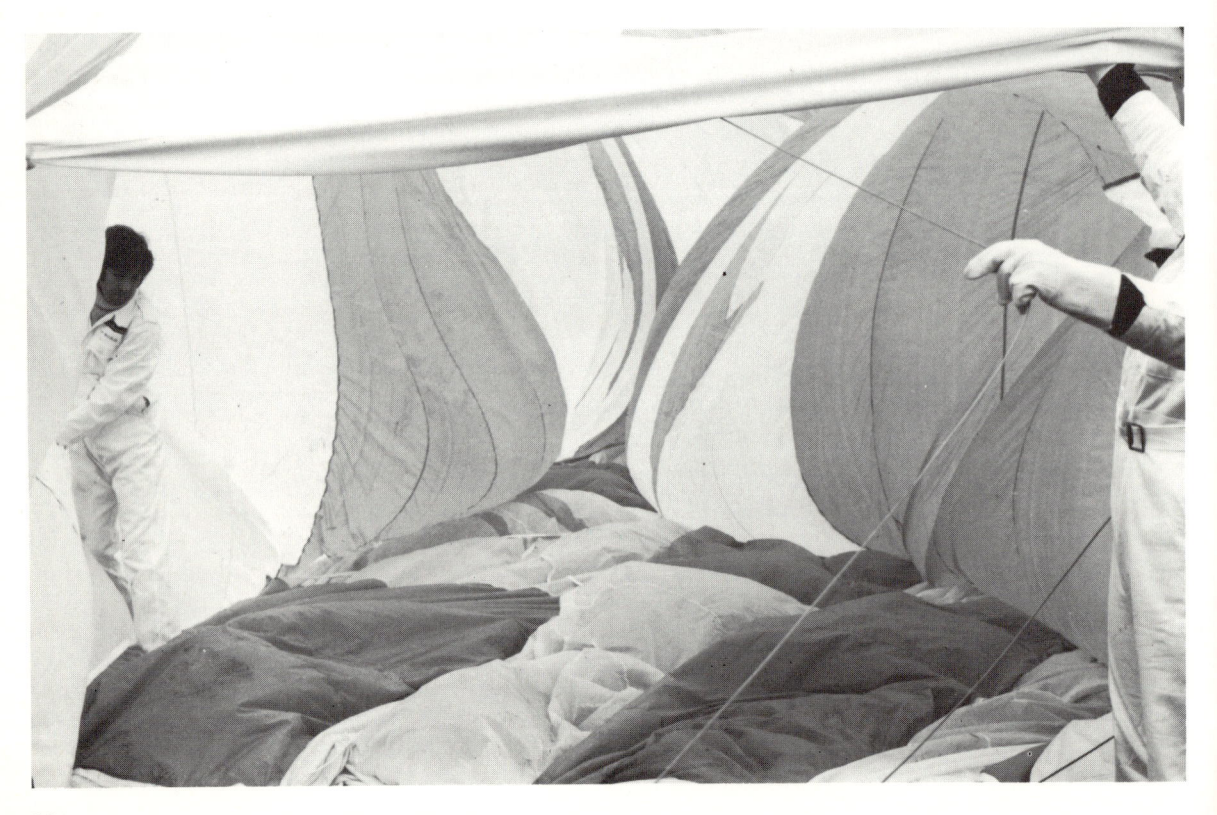

The best launching place is a field in a hollow with a good windbreak of tall trees. The balloon is unpacked and laid out full length on the ground so that nothing is twisted; and it is always surprising quite how much fabric appears from a small bag. At this stage, while it can still be reached, the rip panel is checked to see that it is securely closed. This can be done properly only from the inside, so someone has to get into the balloon and, by flailing his arms around, make his way along to the crown, have a look and then find how to come back again. This process is much more amusing to those outside than the one inside, particularly if he gets lost. The next step is to attach the basket, to connect up the propane and to try to open up the canopy so that it can eat the hot air without itself being consumed in the process. This requires a fan, or a few people to hold the neck and to try to make waves and ripples of air travel up inside the canopy, by a series of unified 'Allah-be-praised' motions. This ritual usually reduces spectators into stunned silence. Before all this hard-won air can escape again, the burner is lighted and directed into the open neck, which is being held that way by two helpers. With a massive roar the 6 feet jet of flame leaps past the helpers and into the hole. Gradually the balloon heaves up like a great breathing whale and is held horizontally by someone hanging on to the crown – on the outside. When almost fully inflated, this helper lets go and the balloon rises gently, towering massively overhead. Although not yet ready to fly, it is wise to ensure that the whole expensive edifice will not depart without the owners. One, in any case, will be inside the now upright basket still blasting off on the burner, but other helpers should contribute their weight by holding onto the basket. It is for this reason that, when changing passengers between flights, the next passenger should climb aboard, before the previous one clambers out.

When, by gently releasing their grip, the helpers find that the balloon is sitting quietly just clear of the ground it is ready to go.

Flying a balloon

The instant when the balloon actually leaves the ground is difficult to discern, particularly if there is little wind. One moment you are talking to your friends, leaning on the padded edge of the basket, like a pub bar, and then they are slowly drifting away. It seems unreal, but the sensation of other things moving, and not you, is not uncommon until you have orientated yourself. You have come to accept the intermittent roar of the burner, muffled to some extent by your crash helmet; the biggest risk is being bumped on the head by the burner as the balloon collapses on landing. Gently, in absolute calm, you rise, wave to those on the ground and look around to see where you are drifting. Straight into some trees, it seems, about level with the rooks' nests. But they slide below, and ahead is open country. From 500 feet the view is limitless but imperceptibly changing as you drift ever so slowly over the fields. Ahead is a beauty spot, solid with people sitting in their cars reading newspapers. You allow the balloon to sink lower so as to float past only 50 feet up. Then you need to burn. The sudden roar turns the car park into a crowd, and you hear the doors slamming and the cries of 'Look, mum!' Then a wood comes between you and the beauty spot. It is forgotten because the wood is more fun; you can see a wandering and puzzled fox down between the pines.

Now is the time to discover what the air is doing, so, up to 1,500 feet with a series of burns, and check the wind, which way you are going and where you are now. Visibility is very good, and the wind west northwest; you have no problem, because your drift at this height is exactly parallel to a stretch of motorway lying to the north and is clearly marked on the map. This is good, because what wind there was on the ground was northwest, so by changing your height you can have the freedom of direction in a sector, instead of a mere line. This will not matter for the flight itself, but it will allow you more choice of landing fields. You float on, talking in ordinary voices, when suddenly the smooth, smooth air is disturbed. The balloon rotates a little, putting the sun in your eyes, and you feel a momentary touch of wind; this means that the character of the air is changing. You hold your hand out over the side of the basket, flat and palm down, and the back of it feels cooler. A thermal must have caught up with the balloon, and now you are in it. A quick look at the variometer and altimeter confirms this; already you are higher, even without the burner. But you need to be experienced and very careful in thermals. The outside air is cooling with height, and, although you have a margin of warmth in the canopy while you are going up, it will be quite different coming down after the thermal dies. Now you will be sinking through air which is warming as it descends, but the air in the balloon not only is cool but is becoming increasingly relatively cooler. Suddenly you find you are dropping at a frightening rate, and you burn as hard as you can — but you go on dropping. It was exciting going up for free, but you do not get anything for nothing; you should have kept that air warm. Finally, the variometer needle creeps up to its neutral line, the altimeter stops unwinding and you breathe again.

Figure 5.6. Ready to go. The crown of the centre balloon is still being held.

Figure 5.7. To gain height the pilot has to burn for a few seconds about four times a minute to keep the temperature of the air inside the balloon warm and buoyant enough to support the weight it is carrying.

Some pilots avoid flying at all in thermal conditions.

Navigation in good weather is easy, and the simplest sum of 30 minutes flying at a wind speed of 10 miles per hour on a northwest breeze will almost pinpoint you 5 miles southeast of home. In fact ballooning is a marvellous way of learning not only to read a map but to find out about the land that so gently passes below. There is plenty of time; if there is no wind, you do not go anywhere at all, and there is so much to look at – stately homes with orderly gardens, a colourful patch of hang gliders on a hill waiting for the breeze, a pattern of cattle in a field, the private life of a small village, or just the shadows of the clouds drifting, as you are, across it all. In Britain it is not often absolutely calm, but it does happen, and then what? You find yourself poised over the middle of a lake, with only the endless cavorting of a water skier to watch and the prospect of an undesired swim. There was a balloon not long ago quite stationary over a sewage farm. An hour later it was still there – landing right in the middle of it. In no wind there is only one course of action and that is to change height, if you have the propane to spare. A thousand feet higher there may be a light drift of air to transport you to somewhere more attractive.

Eventually you will have to land. There are plenty of fields to select from because the countryside below is open downland. It is also late summer with the corn cut, but the stubble not yet burnt and dusty, so the choice is wide. About a mile ahead there is a green field of soft grass. It looks better than the prickly stubble beyond it, but it is nice to have a safe overshoot. With so little wind you have time enough on the approach to sink gently towards the green. You give little burns to prevent you from descending too fast and to keep the balloon warm enough, so that a good blast would get you back up into the sky – should the field be unsuitable on a closer look. Very slowly you creep over the hedge perhaps 20 feet up. The grass is smooth, short and striped with long shadows from the trees away to the right. You watch as it comes up to meet you, your hand still on the burner tap. Then with a slight bump you touch the ground. The balloon lurches over, half-subsiding, you rise a foot into the air, land again and stop. The balloon sits calmly above you, pleased with itself. You pull the rip panel and with a long sigh the yards of bright nylon droop rustling on to the grass. You climb out of the basket, and start to pack up.

In a wind life is exciting. Even if the take-off has been sheltered, the balloon will be quickly on its way across the landscape, and it is safer to be high. Quite apart from turbulence and gusts near the ground, there is the greater risk of power lines not seen until too late. Even at a steady 15 miles per hour, ground features come and go with some rapidity, and there is no means of turning away from whatever obstructions lie ahead.

If you are as yet inexperienced in the art of using the burner, you will almost certainly find that you are overreacting. There is in any case a lag in the operation, the blast being applied as you are starting to descend and not while you are going up. Probably, you will not appreciate that you have ceased to rise until you are firmly on the way down, particularly if you are above 1,000 feet with nothing close by to relate to. To stop the descent you burn, and almost certainly too much: up goes the balloon, faster and higher than you intended. This time you are ready, burn at about the right time, but either too little or again too much. So you progress across the landscape in a series of swoops, until you learn to get it right.

85

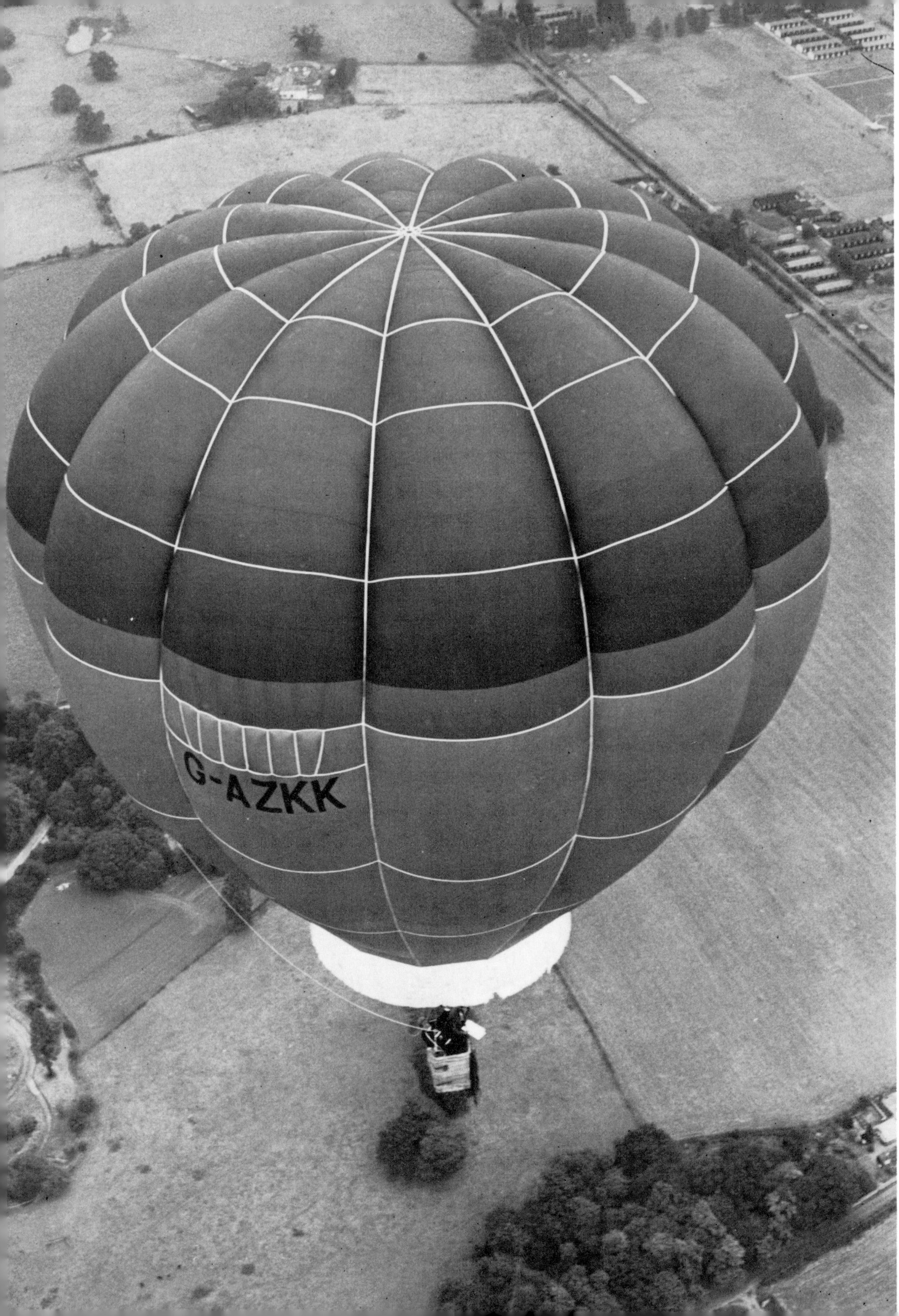
G-AZKK

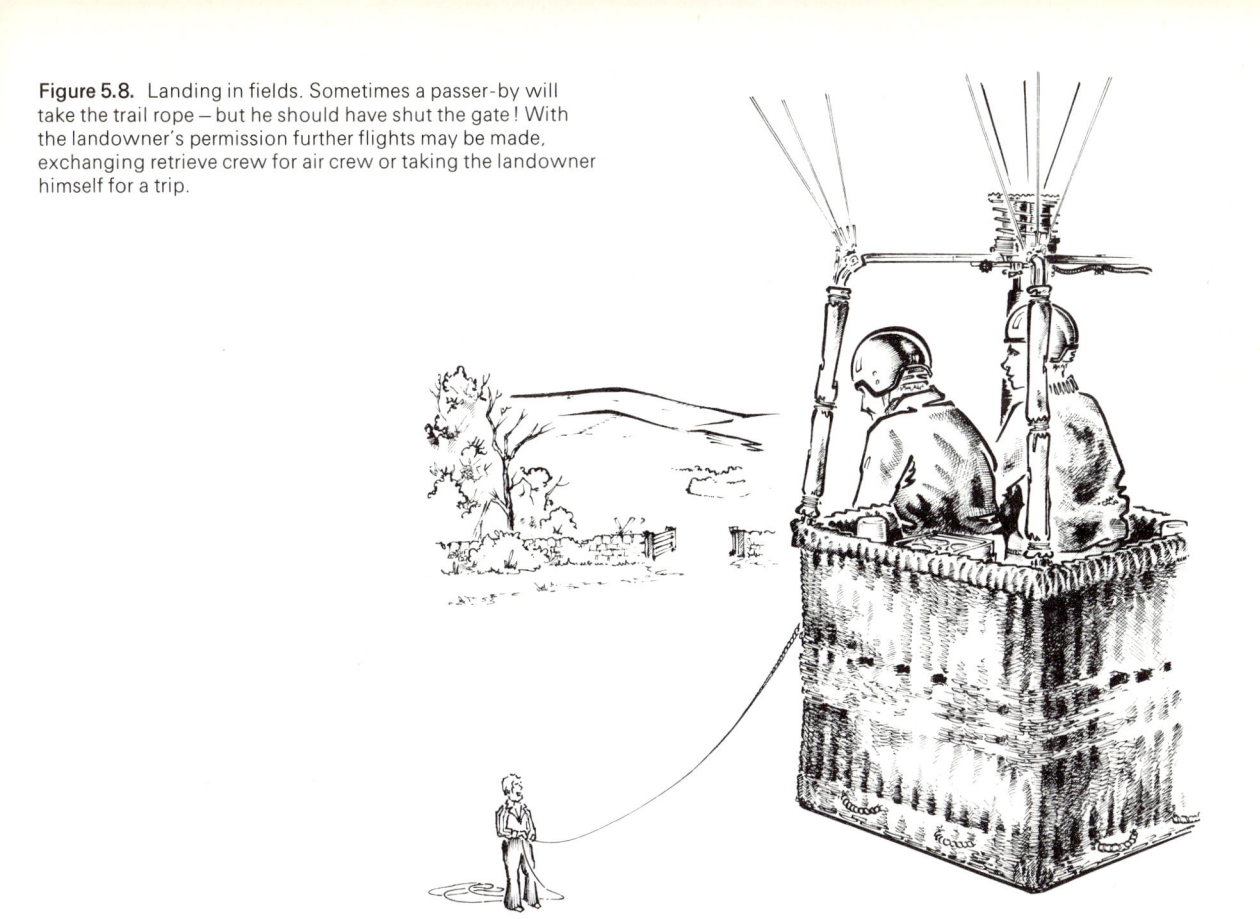

Figure 5.8. Landing in fields. Sometimes a passer-by will take the trail rope — but he should have shut the gate! With the landowner's permission further flights may be made, exchanging retrieve crew for air crew or taking the landowner himself for a trip.

Figure 5.9. Flying in company is fun although it is possible for balloons to bump into each other, particularly in the up and down sense. Two balloons setting off at the same time and from the same place may land not only at different distance from base but in slightly divergent directions because the wind at different heights need not be blowing in a constant direction.

This is why it is easier to learn in very light winds. It is safe to fly lower, where it is easier to notice whether the balloon is rising or falling.

Landing in a fresh wind may be difficult. It just happens and often too speedily for comfort, and it always happens going down wind! Some pilots have risked deliberately taking their balloon through the soft top branches of trees to slow it down. For these conditions, some balloonists throw out a trail rope. This is a rope 150 feet long which is attached to and kept in the basket on all flights. It has two functions. Any part of the trail rope arriving on the ground immediately reduces the weight of the balloon by that amount. If, therefore, the balloon is descending fast into a field, any rope that is on the ground will reduce the rate of descent because the balloon is lightened. This may not be much, but it all helps. The other function is to act as a sort of anchor. The rope end can be caught and held by people on the ground, who then pull the balloon down towards them, or it can be thrown through trees and bushes, or even across the ground to help reduce speed.

If the wind has increased during the flight, as sometimes happens, you must be prepared for a rough landing and for being dragged along the ground by the balloon. Hanging on tight in your corner of the basket is essential, but not onto the rigging wires. As soon as the basket touches, the rip should be pulled. In some situations an experienced pilot may rip just before the basket is down, but he has to be very sure of his height and what he is doing. Obviously, the best landing place is to the lee of a windbreak, but if this is composed of tall trees the next hedge may be looming up before you are down. Very few people get hurt, other than suffering bumps and bruises, even in really windy landings; the greater risk is to end up thoroughly muddy.

Learning, and a share in your own balloon

Although introductory courses are available, the best way to learn is to join a syndicate. Most balloons, like gliders, are owned by syndicates, because both have similar retrieve problems; and the best person to come and get you out of that field is the person whose turn it is to fly next. Most syndicate-owned balloons are also big enough to take three or four people at the same time so that you can learn quite a lot while flying as a passenger. The licence requirements are 12 hours' flying plus passing the necessary tests. Some balloon syndicates are quite large, although six to eight people are probably as many as are practicable if everyone is keen on flying. Obviously the more syndicate members who have cars with tow bars the better, although it is not essential. Balloon trailers are surprisingly small, like large luggage trailers.

You may decide to join a syndicate because one of your friends is already a member or because it flies from near home. In this case you have to accept the sort of balloon that already exists, and to do the sort of flying the other members enjoy, at least to begin with. If, however, you are able to become involved in the forming of a new syndicate, you can decide not only the number of people that can join and the sort of balloon you will buy but also the colours that the balloon should be. If you are a designer, or artist, the balloon can be covered with anything from pyjama stripes to a Gainsborough landscape – except that it may cost more. Some balloon manufacturers prefer you to produce your own colour scheme and send blanks to prospective customers for their ideas.

The size of the syndicate is important. It may be a matter of near-empty pockets needing a large number of members to spread the cost, or time may be the important factor, as you may want to fly every week. Whatever the requirements, it is important that everyone in the syndicate is clear as to the plan and the purpose; to keep friends, the agreement should also be in writing. The cost will, of course, need to include provision for insurance, and a fund should also be set aside for maintenance and repair. Things do go wrong with aircraft which are not anyone's fault, and acrimonious discussions can be best avoided if there is already money with which to do the mending.

Competitions

As with most other sports there are competitions and international championships. Tasks are varied, ranging from precision flying to 'hare and hound' chases. To fly a hot air balloon with the expertise necessary to go up to a given height, to stay there for so many minutes, to change height again, and so on is difficult. Almost as difficult, in fact, although more fun are the 'hare and hounds' events. In most such tasks an expert sets off in his balloon with a 10 minutes' start. He is allowed to change height so as to find and use winds blowing in slightly different directions or which are stronger or weaker. In due course, after a flight of a designated length of time, say, 30 minutes or 1 hour, he lands, and the winner is the pilot of the balloon which eventually lands closest to him. This is sometimes a difficult task to organize in a big competition. If the 'hare' lands in an unsuitable place, such as a public park, the next half hour could see anything up to a hundred balloons trying to squeeze in around him, like an aeronautical bubble bath. For this reason balloons in big competitions drop markers instead of landing.

Competitions are not only a lot of fun but also a good way of comparing your skill with that of other pilots; even as a spectator they are a fascinating introduction to the sport for the interested newcomer (see the table of competition classes, Figure 5.1).

Gas balloons and little airships

Some gas ballooning is still done, mostly in Germany and Switzerland, there are get-togethers to make grand crossings of the Alps. It is much more expensive than hot-air ballooning, and it carries a greater risk of fire and explosion, resulting from static electricity sparks. This is why nylon canopies and clothes of synthetic fabric are unsuitable. There may also be more of a problem with landing, as sudden ripping to expel hydrogen or coal gas is certainly not very safe. Helium, of course, gets rid of most of the risks, but it is even more expensive. The advantage of gas is that it can be more practicable when making longer flights. The techniques of flying a gas balloon are also different. Instead of heating the air in the balloon to go up and letting it cool to come down, the gas balloon is filled to positive buoyancy and carries the well-known sand ballast. As the flight progresses, the gas very gradually dissipates through being released in small quantities or via the envelope skin; and the air itself may be descending as well. If height is lost, a little sand is sprinkled over the side to restore equilibrium. The flight ends, unless the pilot wishes to land earlier, when there is almost no more sand to discard. Obviously, a little should be left to deal with any landing problems; otherwise the pilot may have to throw his champagne or trousers overboard to avoid hitting a tree. One of the most enterprising gas balloon flights was that of the explorer, Saloman August Andrée, in 1897. He and his friends attempted to drift across the North Pole from

Danes Island, near Spitzbergen in the gas balloon, *Eagle*, built in Paris of Chinese silk. This was no stunt but a well thought-out expedition, and Andrée intended to make his balloon travel to some extent across wind and not merely to be at its whim as regards direction. This he achieved by giving the balloon a sail. To many this seemed ridiculous as a sail will only provide drive when there is some resistance, and what resistance can a balloon produce as it drifts along? Andrée reckoned that he could obtain enough resistance by a trail rope. Its drag could cause the balloon to travel more slowly than the wind does, which would then exert some pressure over the surface of the sail and would create drive. The angle of the sail to the relative wind would impart a small off-wind component to the balloon. Unfortunately, after about 400 kilometres the balloon ran into mist which froze on the surface of the balloon and brought it down on the ice. Andrée and his friends managed to reach White Island and to set up camp for the winter where they died, probably of carbon monoxide poisoning from a heating stove. As far as the outside world was concerned, nothing was known until 1930 when the remains of the camp were accidentally found. Everything was in a remarkable state of preservation; even film that was recovered produced good photographs when developed after 30 years in the cold.

More recently, experimental hot air airships have been built. Tubby in shape, they are filled just as an ordinary hot air balloon would be, but, instead of a basket, there is a light gondola with perhaps a small Volkswagen engine and a propeller 5 feet long. Needless to say, the propeller needs a protecting ring in case it gets sat on by mother while still rotating! Fairly weather sensitive, and with a speed of about 15 miles per hour, the hot air airship is not a particularly practical vehicle. But a syndicate owning, and perhaps building, one could have a remarkably enjoyable time playing with it, provided that for a start they could afford 1,350 square yards of nylon fabric.

Figure 5.10. Hot air airship. The Cameron airship has a capacity of 96,000 cubic feet, and uses 1,350 square feet of fabric. It is powered by a Volkswagen engine driving a 5 feet long propeller.

ASSOCIATIONS

British Balloon and Airship Club
Address: Kimberley House, Vaughan Way, Leicester LE1 4SG
Telephone No.: Leicester 51051
  No. of members: 1,000
  No. of pilots: 150
  No. of aircraft: 140
  No. of clubs and schools: 40 clubs 3 schools
  No. of hours' flying annually: 4,000
  Minimum age for flying solo: 17 years

The British Balloon and Airship Club (BBAC) deals with all aspects of balloon and airship activities, including airworthiness, flying regulations, safety, competitions, etc. Each BBAC committee is in contact with the CAA on its own subject.

Members are mainly individuals. The subscription is £6 per annum which includes the bimonthly magazine *Aerostat* (published in February, April, June, August, October, December). Members, pilots and student pilots receive free circulars including safety information on special request.

Pilot licences and certificates
A PPL is required and issued by the CAA on the recommendation of the BBAC. A commercial exemption, to permit flying for aerial work, is available through the BBAC from the CAA. A simplified PPL (aeroplane) medical examination is required and should be completed by a CAA-approved doctor or local GP.

Approved instructors are appointed by the BBAC.

Training courses
Training courses are available on an organized basis only through the three balloon schools (Europa, Anglia and Aerial) and the two manufacturers (Thunder and Cameron).

CODE OF GOOD PRACTICE

The countryside is the farmers' livelihood. Grass is a crop, cattle are easily frightened and electricity supplies are depended upon. Do not fly unless you are reasonably certain that your flight path will be over country which is suitable for landing; in July and August avoid flying over the large areas of standing corn in light wind conditions.

Obtain permission before using a field. Check that the climb-out will not be at a low height over livestock. Close gates.

If you think that livestock have been disturbed, check with the farmer after landing. If the farm is not known, inform the police or the local National Farmers' Union County Secretary.

Ensure that you are covered by third party insurance.

Before landing consider possible fire risks, and before deploying the trail rope check that it will not contact livestock, telephone and power wires or buildings. After landing keep spectators out of the field, and contact the farmer without delay. Do not make tethered flights or take-off without permission.

Leave your name and address with the farmer, even if you do not think you have done any damage. If there is damage, leave the name and address of your insurers and ask the farmer to write to you.

6 Parachuting

Parachuting, and its younger cousin parascending, have come a long way since the silken canopy was invented as the only escape from a disabled aircraft. They are now sports in their own right, and they are no longer even particularly similar to each other. The parachute itself has also changed from the familiar inverted pudding-basin shape, although this classical type of 'chute is still used in its original emergency role. For sport jumping the parachute needs to be steerable, so that precise landings can be made in competitions on a disc only 10 centimetres in diameter, and there is also a need for better performance. As with gliders and hang gliders, performance is considered in terms of sink rate and glide ratio. If the parachute can be made to descend more slowly, the flight will be prolonged, and the landing will be softer. If, in addition, the parachute can be designed to possess some of the characteristics of an aerofoil and to fly *through* the air, it will no longer be at the complete mercy of any breeze that blows. It will be able to fly and make headway at an angle to, or directly against, the wind. This means that the parachutist will be able to land into wind, touching down with the least possible relative movement between himself and the ground, or even with none at all. On the classical emergency parachute, the jumper, whether airborne in fun or in anger, had to land going with the wind; otherwise he would fall flat on his back and would probably be dragged along the ground. Since the inconvenience and risk associated with a high-speed arrival – the pilot leaving a burning aeroplane might have had to do so with half a gale blowing on the ground – was invariably less than the calamity which had caused the departure, the pilot probably would not be too worried if he ended up with a broken leg. For sport parachuting this was not acceptable; either the classical parachute could be used only on days of very light winds or a new 'chute had to be developed which was less wind sensitive.

The early experiments in creating such a parachute were quite simply to make a classically shaped 'chute asymmetrical by removing one of the panels or gores. Some of the higher-pressure air inside the inflated and descending parachute escaped through this slot, causing the parachute to move, or drive, towards the opposite side. By pulling the risers, or lines from his harness up to the canopy on one side, the parachutist was able to turn it and himself to face in the desired direction. These missing panel parachutes, such as the double-L or TU, were not very efficient and were only suitable for landing into the wind if this was very light, but, with the principle of the non-symmetrical canopy shape established, development soon followed. In 1960 Pierre Lemoigne of France designed a 'chute composed of a large number of small panels with slots between. On opening, the air flowed into the canopy, and some of it went out by the rear slots, so that the 'chute wanted to fly in a constant direction. In addition the panels were arranged so that they also behaved like small aerofoils, so that the Lemoigne 'chute possessed a rudimentary glide angle. This development was a real breakthrough in sport parachuting, and in 1974 Pierre Lemoigne was awarded the FAI Leonardo da Vinci medal for his services to the sport.

Sport parachutes

For both parascending and parachuting the Para-Commander and Para-Foil types of canopy provide a flexibility and performance which give great scope to both sports, and with the Para-Foil type particularly a great future potential. The Para-Commander is basically a straightforward parachute on the Lemoigne principle. It has fixed openings at the rear of the canopy, to drive it forward, and large slots which can be inverted by the jumper on each side. If you wish to turn to the right, you invert the openings on that side, and the canopy will drive and turn to the right. You can also obtain a braking effect by inverting the slots on both sides at the same time. Most Para-Commander 'chutes are 24 feet in diameter, have a sink rate of about 13 feet per second – as against the classical rate of 16 feet per second – and weigh around 34 lb. They are controllable, and will even stall when all side openings are fully inverted, although the canopy remains fully deployed and reasonably stable.

The Para-Foil, or ram-air 'chute, was developed in the late 1960s by Domina Jalbert and was further developed by John Nicolaides of Notre Dame University in the USA. Giving the distinct impression in the air of a flying mattress, the Para-Foil is an

A bird instinctively provides itself with the necessary flight data, but a human needs instruments. Panel of a Skylark 4, at a height of 2000 feet

If you want to be an aerobatic pilot and have not got an aeroplane, just build one. Refuelling one of the Pitts Specials made by Finnish pilots

Pedalling yourself into the air needs the lightest possible aircraft The Gossamer Condor weighs only 75 lb for its 97-foot wing span *(Courtesy of Rose-Marie Licher)*

Even a light wind can make filling a balloon difficult, so tall trees are used to shelter the launch site. Start of a hot air balloon contest *(Courtesy of Peter Bish)*

Figure 6.1. The standard emergency aeroplane parachute (left) is not particularly steerable, nor can it be persuaded to make headway against the wind, so all landings will, in effect, be downward. The Para-Commander (centre) is both steerable and can make headway against light winds. The Para-Foil (right) will make headway against winds of over 20 miles per hour.

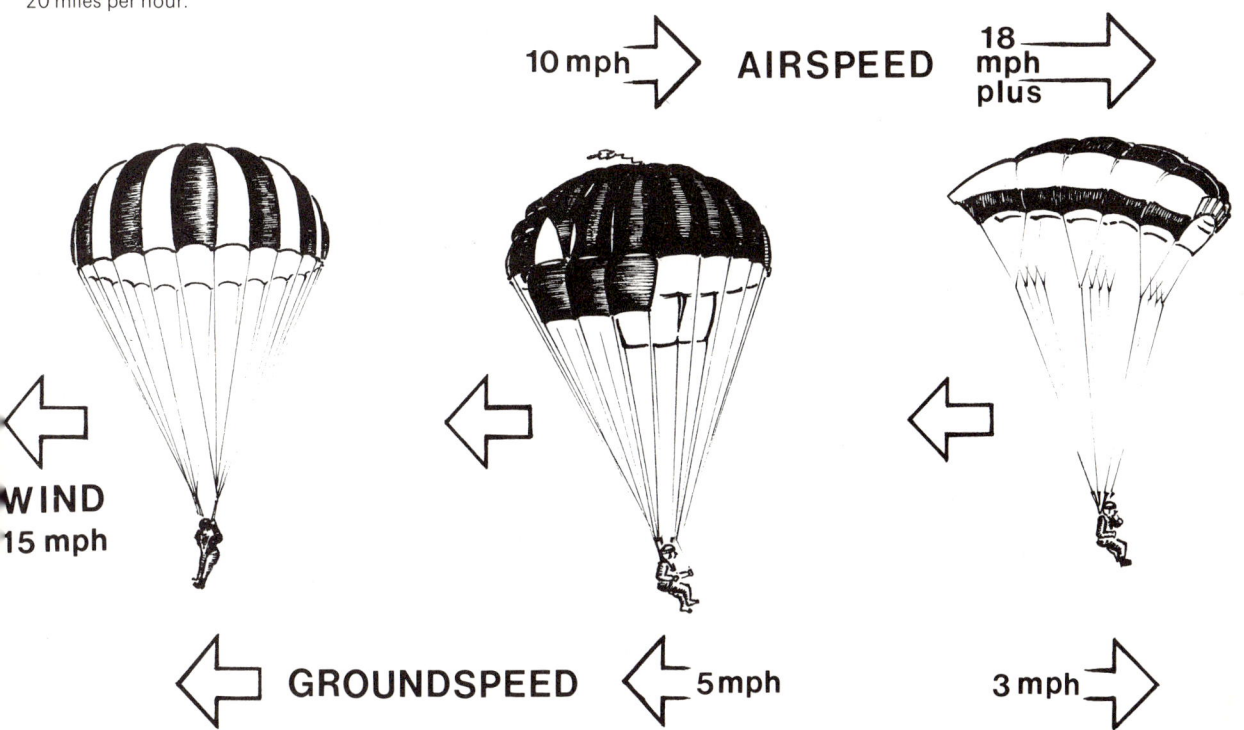

AIRSPEED 10 mph

AIRSPEED 18 mph plus

WIND 15 mph

GROUNDSPEED

5 mph

3 mph

arrangement of fabric tubes in a double surface canopy into which air is forced. This produces an aerofoil shape to make a simple inflated flying wing. The sink rate is much the same as the Para-Commander, but the glide ratio is more superior at about 1:4.5, about two-thirds that of a basic hang glider. It achieves this glide ratio by flying *through* the air – like any other sort of wing – at about 20 miles per hour, which means that, when flying against a wind of 20 miles per hour, the parachutist would be stationary over the ground and could step lightly to earth. This gives the Para-Foil great flexibility; but you never get something for nothing. The Para-Foil is no longer a simple parachute under which you can just sit there enjoying the ride back to earth, but an aircraft. You have to fly it. Para-Foils are controlled by pulling down the outer sections of the trailing edge either differentially or together. To turn to the right the trailing edge is pulled down on that side, using a toggle-ended line. To fly straight again the line is released. The glide ratio can also be controlled to adjust the approach path when coming in to land. This is done by pulling down on both toggles to droop both trailing edges at the same time. When coming in to a target landing the best results are obtained by

approaching using half-brake – both trailing edges being deflected downwards by a small amount. If you find that you are undershooting, you reduce the braking effect by letting the trailing edges float up again towards their normal position. If, on the other hand, you find you are overshooting the target, you apply more brake. But, and it is an essential but, because the Para-Foil is a flying wing, it will stall more definitely than a Para-Commander will. When you apply brake by pulling down the trailing edges, you are not only increasing the drag but also increasing the angle of attack, and, like all other aircraft, when the angle of attack is increased beyond a certain amount, the wing will stall. If you stall a Para-Foil on the approach, you will be dumped unceremoniously, and probably painfully, on the ground. The Para-Foil is, therefore, a 'chute for those that are expert, because, when you start any sort of parachuting, you will have enough to think about without having to worry about whether you are going to stall as well.

Landing a parachute
The first lesson in both parascending and parachuting is very much on the ground, because the need to land properly is common to both. It must be learnt before

flying, because once airborne you will not have time to work out how to do it. What you are endeavouring to achieve is to absorb an arrival speed, equivalent to jumping off a single-storey building without a 'chute, by landing with your body in the right position, followed by the landing roll; and your first rung on the ladder consists of practising it until you could do it in your sleep.

Body position
The correct body position avoids the landing load being taken out via one of your extremities, be it leg, elbow or even head. The feet and legs must be kept together as if glued, with the knees slightly bent. The elbows must be kept tucked in, and your chin must be pressed down on to your chest. Not only will this prevent you biting your tongue or jarring your teeth, but it will have the even more important effect of keeping your back rounded. Look in a mirror, and, when you think you look expert, practise jumping off a table or low wall, arriving with the flat of your feet on the ground, with the same compact body position maintained (Figure 6.3). Your arms should be held up, as though holding the risers to control your direction.

Landing
Although expert parachutists frequently arrive, and remain, on their feet, all your early landings should be completed with a landing roll. What this does is to absorb the shock progessively, starting with the soles, then the side of your glued-together feet, transferring the load immediately to the calf of the leg, then to the thigh on the same side, then to the back of your rounded shoulder and finally across to the opposite shoulder. The arms are still held up grasping the imaginary risers, which in a genuine landing you will be controlling. If you find that your landing roll has stopped before you arrived around onto the other shoulder, do it again, checking that your elbows are not sticking out and that you have not raised your chin off your chest. If you look up or put your head back, this has the effect of flattening your back, which then no longer wants to roll. When you start learning in your club, the instructor will have you practising the landing roll, not only to the left and right but as though you were facing into wind or were drifting over the ground downwind; and he is unlikely to be satisfied until you can do a good landing roll in any direction from a moving platform 4 feet high. It is worth getting out your oldest toughest clothes for this first lesson – and enjoying the luxury of a good hot bath afterwards!

Clothing
The clothing requirements are much the same as for the hang glider pilot. A well-fitting well-made helmet is necessary at the top end, and perhaps goggles as well, and good boots with support for the ankles at the other. These should never have lacing hooks, which could catch in parachute rigging lines (or hang glider bracing wires). Overalls or a jump suit are more suitable than jeans and anorak, being windproof and comfortable, with fewer loose ends to flap in the breeze. To start with, the club will probably be able to provide these items, so that you can save your money until you know exactly what you need to buy.

The two sports
Both parascending and parachuting are relatively inexpensive ways of flying, and both operate through clubs which provide training and the necessary equipment. Neither are activities of an essentially exploratory nature like gliding or aeroplane flying, where much of the charm is wandering off to new places; instead they provide their devotees with much more of a physical challenge, combined with the need for quick and clear thinking: they are sports for the young who want some excitement, but who are also prepared to work at gaining the necessary skill and sense of responsibility which keep them safe. Parascending and parachuting are also young sports, with a future full of new and interesting developments. But they have different objectives and, like gliding and hang gliding, in general attract different sorts of people.

Parascending
It was the Lemoigne parachute that made parascending possible. For years it had been realized that, if you could tow a parachute up to a suitable dropping height with a car, this could provide a cheaper method of training a parachutist than transporting him up in

Figure 6.2. The first thing to be learnt is how to land and roll so as to absorb the shock of a heavy landing without injury. It is essential that the feet are kept together and the knees slightly bent. The jumper should not look down at the ground to try to guess the moment at which he will land. He will almost certainly judge it wrong and will also be less relaxed.

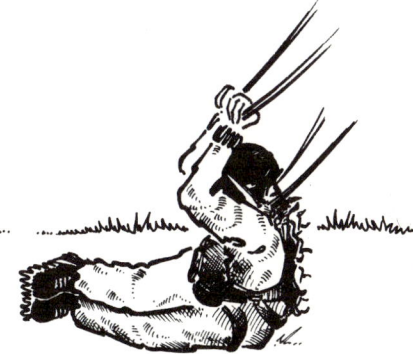

(a)

(b)

Figure 6.3. Parascending – the tow – (a) The Para-Commander 'chute is filled ready for take-off, and the helpers have just let go of the canopy as the tow starts; the batsman on the right having just given the signal to go. (b) Climbing on tow. Depending on the length the tow rope, heights of up to 2,000 feet can be attained without problems. (c) & (d) Parachutes of the Para-Commander type possess directional stability through their open gore arrangement, and can be turned and steered by the parachutist.

an aeroplane, even if several jumpers were taken up at the same time. It could also provide training in a more concentrated form, because the parachute would not have to be repacked between each sortie. Car towing was not possible with the classical symmetrical canopy 'chute because there was no means of controlling its behaviour, and on tow it was capable of swooping over sideways like a kite, taking the unfortunate hopeful with it.

With the arrival of the Lemoigne 'chute, towing became practicable, but there was no intention at the time of inventing a different branch of the existing sport of parachuting. But for some reason, probably the utilization of the aeroplane which was needed anyway for higher-altitude lifts, the tow method of getting beginner parachutists into the air did not catch on with the true jumper; instead the towing-up of parachutes attracted followers of its own, who in due course formed clubs and their own brand of flying for fun. Perhaps the biggest initial attraction of parascending is that it is probably the cheapest way for any group of people who want to fly to get into the air, plus the fact that there is no minimum age. The limit is one of weight. Most people under 14 years do not have sufficient weight to produce the necessary pendulum stability.

Almost all parascending is done in the seventy clubs in Britain which belong to the British Association of Parascending Clubs (BAPC). Many are Services clubs or those belonging to schools or groups, such as the Scouts. Most flying is carried out from disused airfields or quiet corners of operational ones, but parascending is also practised over water with boat towing. Each year there are interclub competitions and national championships; and as the newer Para-Foils in use can stay up in thermals there is more to this sport than may seem at first apparent. For the person who is either too young to fly

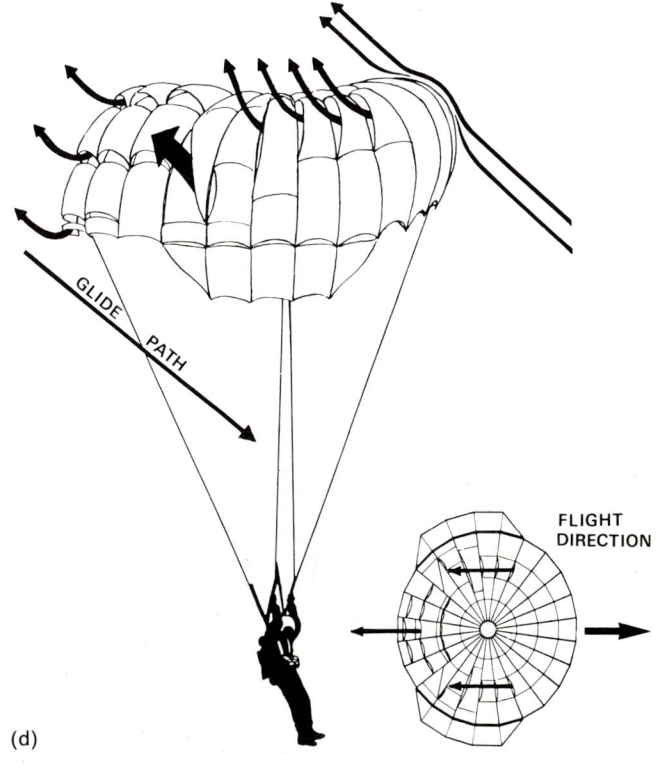

Figure 6.4. Flying a Para-Foil. (a) The jumper is pulling down on the toggles which droop the trailing edges either together or separately, to give him some control. A Para-Foil flies at about 20 miles per hour and will stall like an aircraft if the angle of attack is allowed to become too high. (b) A Strato-Star.

solo in other ways or who suffers from very limited funds, parascending offers a way of not only getting into the air but of progressing quickly. Given good weather and normal aptitude a youngster can make ascents to over 500 feet, releasing himself from the tow and controlling the parachute so as to make a good into-wind landing in the course of a weekend. It takes ten to fifteen ascents to reach this stage, so the newcomer should be prepared for an energetic couple of days. Because flying the Para-Foil is more difficult, Para-Commander experience is required before conversion to this 'chute, although the actual time for a bright and hard-working tyro from first hop to flying a foil can be around 7 or 8 days, or about seventy flights.

Ground equipment

Because the ground over which the towing takes place may be rough and because there may be considerable uploads on the vehicle, the tow car needs to be tough and to have four-wheel drive. A standard Land-Rover or equivalent does the job well, provided that the roof covering is removed. It is also sensible to check it over carefully for any sharp projections which could catch or tear the parachute when it is being carried back for the next flight. The tow rope is attached to the car via a tensiometer and a quick release. The tensiometer is important, so that the canopy will never be overloaded by the car being driven too fast in strong winds.

The tow line is braided nylon, although for early low-height tows ordinary sailing-dinghy sheet rope or a new rope called Parafil may be used. This is basically loose nylon fibres squeezed into a plastic-casing tube. It is flexible and strong and is good against ground abrasions, though care should be taken to avoid kinking it. The tow rope used is 300 feet long for early tows, increasing up to a standard 1,500 feet.

At the parachutist's end of the tow line, a webbing V yoke is attached, with the two arms of the V clipping on to the Capewell releases on the parachute harness just below the shoulders.

First flights

By now you will have become tired of practising landing rolls and of waiting for suitable weather. The problem is usually the wind. If it is too strong and gusty, you will find that the parachute has a will of its own and is hard to control, and you will be landing going backwards. Quite a lot of helpers are needed for parascending, and you will be expected to assist others to fly, just as they are now about to help you.

Apart from the instructor who drives the tow car looking backwards and is responsible for dealing with any problems you may have, a second 'observer' is needed to watch where the car is going, and a third to watch the tensiometer and to call out continuously the loading on the tow rope. At your end of the rope you stand facing into the wind with it attached to your harness via the V yoke; behind you the great colourful Para-Commander is laid out and held up by a helper at each side. One more helper is now needed, a batsman to signal to the tow car. When all is ready the signal, 'take up slack', is given, and the tow car moves slowly forwards until the rope is also taut. As the 'chute fills with air, the lines are held taut and you will feel the tug through your yoke and harness. Then the car drives off at a suitable speed. This will be quite slow, as there is already some wind filling the canopy, but, as the pull comes on you, you have to lean backwards and to 'mark time'. Usually only two or three steps are needed, and then you are airborne. Looking ahead you do not see any canopy, although you will probably hear it rustling; you are just floating up into the air. The height to which you will climb depends on the length of the tow rope and on the speed of the tow, but the instructor will probably take you to only about 50 feet for your first flight. To you, as the airfield and then the surrounding country spreads out all around, it will probably feel more like 200 feet. You look down the tow rope to the minute Land-Rover and then down at your own feet with nothing but space underneath them. By now the instructor will have slowed down and is gently lowering you to mother earth once more, but you probably will not notice this on your first flight until the ground suddenly seems to have got much closer. Then your feet touch so easily that you almost forget to do your landing roll, and the parachute collapses behind you with a quiet sigh. It is not, of course, always so simple. As you gain experience you will fly in stronger winds, and, after completing your landing roll, you may have to jump to your feet and to run around your canopy to twist it out of wind so that it will collapse.

After about eight to twelve flights you will do a ground exercise to teach you how to steer the canopy in free flight by adjusting the openings on the side to which you want to turn, in preparation for your first free descent from about 500 feet. For this you release yourself from the tow line, and watch the rope fall away into a minute snake towards the ground. You are now freely drifting on the wind, and will need to make small adjustments with the toggles to keep straight. Suddenly, the ground starts to rush up, and you are on it while still fiddling with the toggles to get straight. But your landing roll is now automatic, and you get to your feet again without difficulty and start folding up your 'chute before the helpers arrive.

Flying a Para-Foil
When you advance to the Para-Foil, you will probably be delighted with its performance and with the way in which it will progress into wind. But it does not like being flown slowly and will stall at speeds below about 18 miles per hour. This requires a different technique for landing. If you just allow the foil to fly until you touch the ground, as you have become used to doing with the Para-Commander, you will arrive fast and could easily hurt yourself. Instead, the foil has to be landed like a hang glider – or any other aircraft. Speed has to be reduced by flaring out. This is done by pulling down on both toggles, which has the combined effect of increasing both the braking drag and the angle of attack. If this is done too much or too high, the foil will stall, so good height judgement is needed, as well as a feel for how the foil is flying. Although you will be looking forwards and down for the landing, a quick glance upwards will tell you what the foil is up to. If it is overhead, it is fully flying, but, if it has receded behind you, it is either stalled or will be soon, and tension on the toggles should be immediately slackened, unless you are satisfactorily just about reaching the ground.

What next?
It may seem that quite soon the limit of opportunity in parascending will be reached, and there is little beyond getting very good at going up to about 1,200 feet on a 1,500 feet rope and coming down again. Certainly there are competitions, and water drops, but even these could have a limited appeal, after a few years. It all depends what you want. But recently it has been discovered that the Para-Foil can be persuaded to stay up in the thermals. Certainly, with a

Figure 6.5. First jumps are made with a static line attached to the aeroplane to pull open the parachute. In addition a manually operated reserve 'chute is always carried.

glide ratio of 1:4.5 it will come down fast between upcurrents, but because of its slow forward speed of 20 miles per hour it can utilize very small areas of lift. By using the brakes gently as ailerons, the foil will make turns of very small radius with the parachutist spiralling round, on a larger turning circle. Flights of 10 to 12 minutes have been made on foils in thermals, and, as techniques are developed, so flights of an hour or more should not be too difficult in the summer months.

Parachuting

Parachuting is a different sport from Parascending and is now probably wrongly named, because the attraction is not just coming down by parachute, but free fall. It is the delight of manoeuvring in the air in an entirely physical manner, like the birds, which makes the parachutist believe that his flying is the nearest to true human flight. He does not want to go to 700 or 1,000 feet but to 10,000 or 12,000 feet. He is not interested in making his parachute soar but in doing rolls or loops without a parachute at all at his terminal velocity of 120 miles per hour. At this speed the air is hard, and quite small movements of a leg or hand enable the skilled parachutist to control his body position precisely and even to alter its sink rate and airspeed. From 12,000 feet he will have a full minute of glorious flying before using his parachute at 2,000 feet to lower him sedately to earth.

In the early days of the sport most of the fun was endeavouring to land on a target. Apart from the limited appeal of this activity in the long term, it was hard to do with the parachutes of the time. But it was the efforts to achieve spot landing success that led to the development of steerable parachutes and delayed opening of the 'chute. This early free falling in turn led to the realization of the fact that the human body could be controlled in flight like any other aircraft.

Free fall parachuting is perhaps the most *potentially* lethal of all airsports because if opening is left until too late, the jumper will be killed. It is as simple as that; with other sorts of flying the aircraft can itself be manoeuvred or slowed, and, even in a calamitous arrival, it offers some protection to the occupants. But sport parachuting is in fact just as safe as other airsports, because the equipment used is good and the training is very thorough. As with all other airsports, it is the person who has advanced far past the training stage who is more likely to have accidents; when the standard human failings of complacency and carelessness begin to reappear.

Starting to jump

At parachute school you will have to learn not only about landing rolls but about how to depart correctly from the aeroplane which has transported you several thousand feet into the sky. It is a matter not only of diving cleanly into the limitless fresh air but also of ensuring that you do not open your parachute inadvertently inside the aeroplane or do not slip while positioning yourself on the wing in the surprisingly powerful slipstream. Having overcome those problems, you also have to know how to make your body assume a stable position in flight and also how to operate your reserve in the unlikely event of a malfunction of the main 'chute.

Several of you will go up together for your first jump, which reduces to some extent the inevitable feelings of over-excitement and apprehension, and you will be crowded onto the draughty floor of the doorless aeroplane. There will be an instructor with you who is responsible for hooking your static line securely to the aircraft, checking over both you and your parachute, and telling you when to go.

The first five or so jumps that you make will be with a static line. This looks after the worry everyone has about whether they would forget to pull the ripcord if they have never jumped before. When the static line reaches its full length of about 14 feet, it simply pulls out the bagged or packed 'chute, which then deploys fully in the slipstream. One minute you are hanging onto the wing strut in a shrieking gale, and seconds later you are floating calmly with the big rustling canopy reassuringly above you.

The stable position

To help the parachute deploy cleanly from its pack on your back, you should go into the stable, or full spread position, immediately on leaving the aircraft. As well as being safer it is more comfortable and avoids any possibility of your merely becoming a jumble of whirling arms and legs. As with the landing roll you

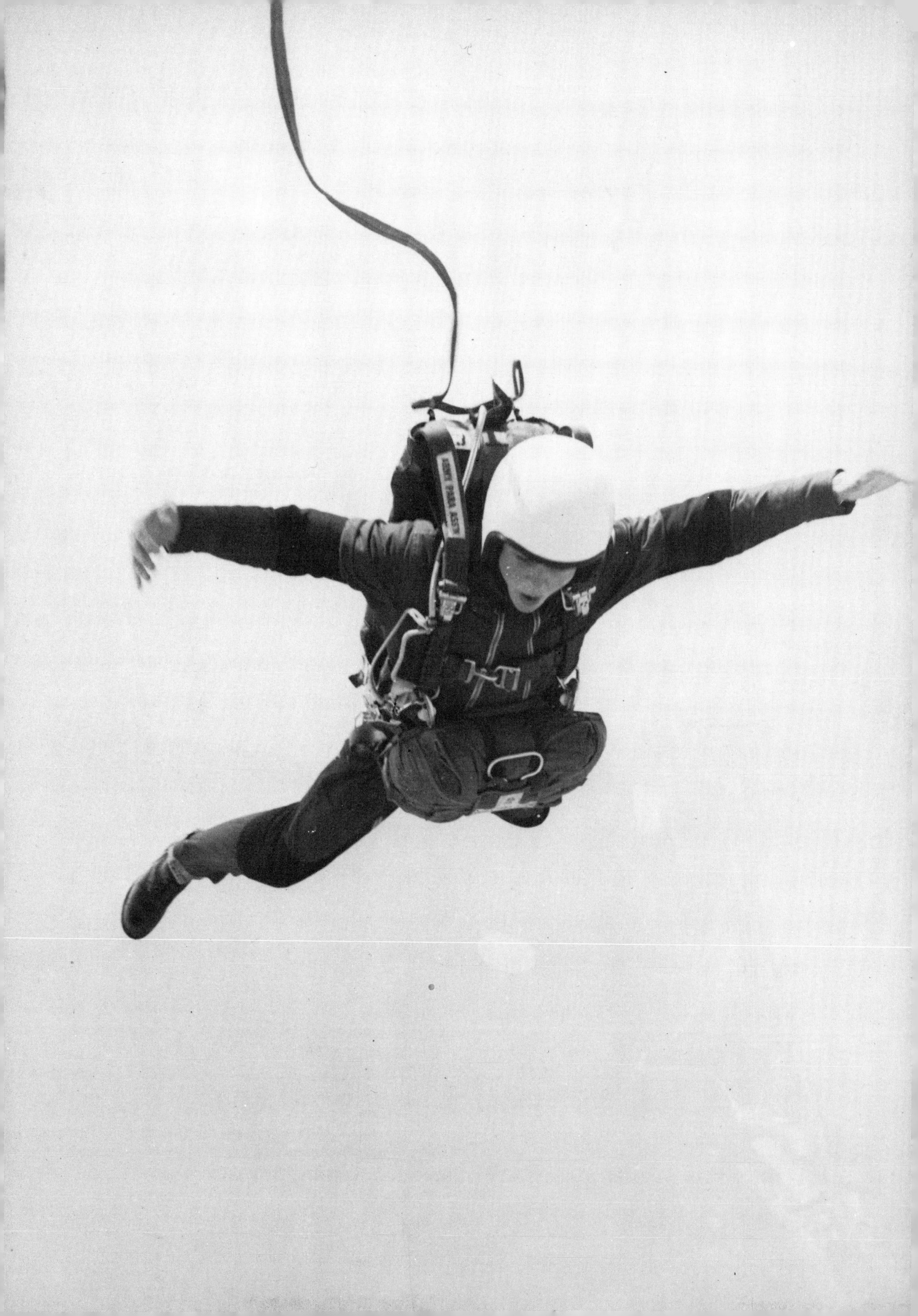

Figure 6.6. From the very first jump, even with static line opening, the jumper learns to adopt the stable spread position. If this arched-back attitude with the arms and legs pushed out is made, however the parachutist is falling, he will flip over into the spread position.

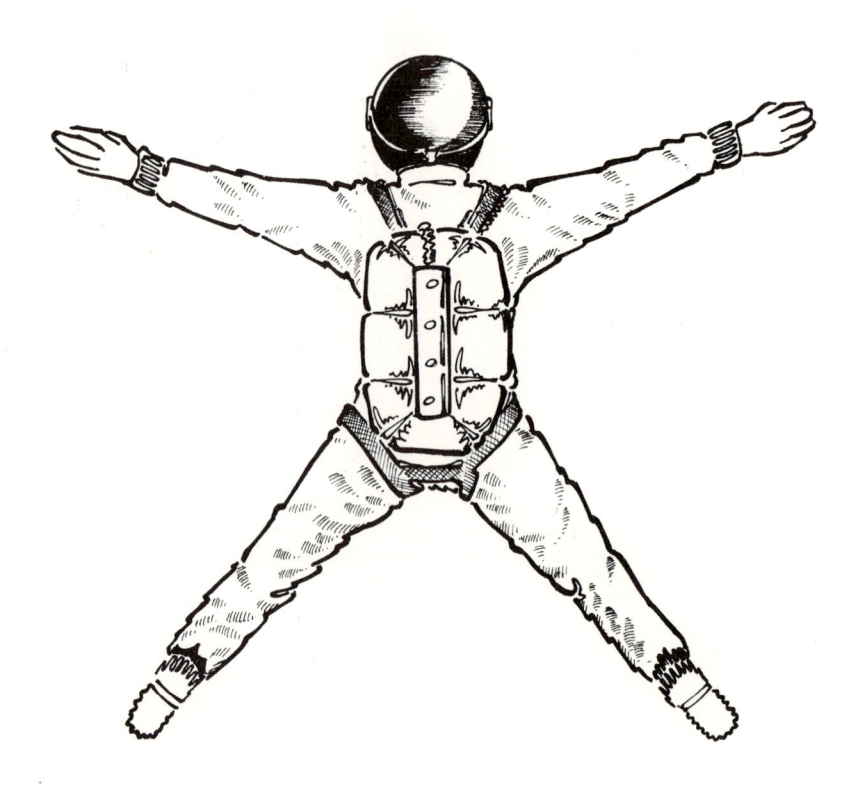

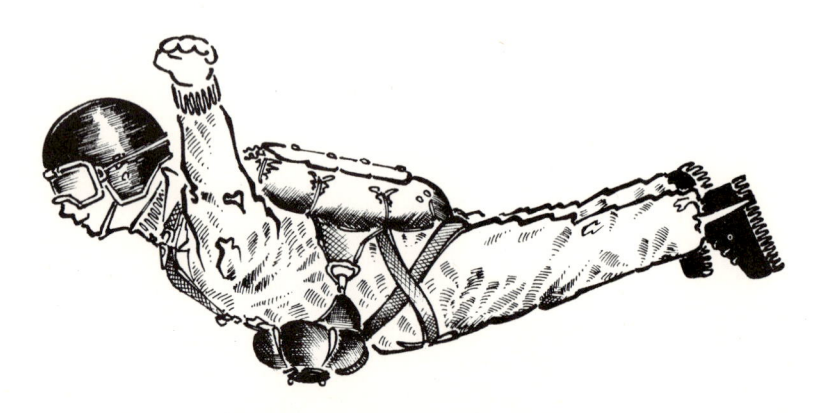

Figure 6.7. After the static line jumps, including several practices at pulling a dummy ripcord, the jumper can start free falling, responsible for opening his parachute at the intended time.

will have practised the stable position (Figure 6.6) in ground school and at home. The reason this spread position is called stable is that, regardless of how you are falling, if you force your arms, legs, and back into the correct attitude, you will immediately flip over into this position and will remain there.

The count

Almost all parachuting involves a critical accounting of time, because it is seconds, not minutes or hours, that are important. The object of the count is to enable you to calculate any intended delay time – 5 seconds, 15 seconds, etc. – before opening the 'chute, and to check that it is in fact opening in the time it should normally take. If it does not, then the reserve should be pulled.

The basis of assessing the passing seconds is to call out the words 'one thousand, two thousand' and so on until the required number is reached. This counting drill is so important that you will start doing it on your first jump, even though the static line is opening your parachute for you. On these early jumps you call up to four thousand, following this with the word 'Check' and a look over your shoulder to see if the parachute is opening properly. If by any chance it is not or does not within one further second, you pull the reserve 'chute on your chest. Exactly how you should do this will have been included in your pre-jump ground school, as will the reasons for possible malfunctions.

Free fall

After some static line jumps to the satisfaction of your instructor, you will then do a few more using a dummy ripcord, to show that you understand how and when the pull should be made. Then you will be allowed on your own to open the parachute yourself

Figure 6.8 To open the parachute the jumper should look down to put his hand correctly on the ripcord handle, moving his left arm forward so as to remain balanced. As soon as the ripcord is pulled he should return both arms to the stable spread position.

on 5 and then 10 second count delays.

Up to delays of 12 seconds your body will still be accelerating towards its terminal velocity of about 120 miles per hour (1,000 feet in about 6 seconds), and you will discover that the air has a surprisingly solid feel, so much so that seemingly insignificant, even inadvertent arm or leg movements will set you off in another direction, or in an extreme case will start you tumbling. Some of your body movements may be unintended, but a necessary one will have to be the withdrawal of your right arm from the stable spread position to pull the ripcord. With your left arm still outstretched sideways you would start to roll to the right, so you counter this by moving your left arm straight ahead; until you can return both arms simultaneously to the spread position (Figure 6.8).

As you build up the number of jumps and find more time to look around, you will begin to fly with an altimeter, usually mounted over your chest reserve. You still, and always, go on counting the seconds, but for longer delays, such as the 30 second delay, which is done from a jump height of 7,000 feet; this practice may become increasingly inaccurate. The altimeter reading should therefore override the count on the decision to open the 'chute when it reads 2,000 feet – or whatever other height had been previously decided on the ground.

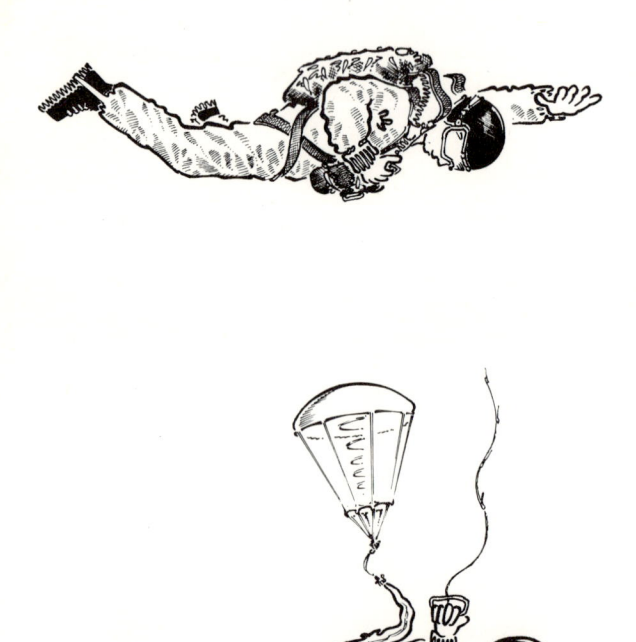

Becoming an aircraft: body control

Although it usually has to be held for only seconds, the stable spread position with the back arched and the head held back is tiring, so for longer steady falls the frog position is more comfortable. The differences will be seen in Figure 6.9. The lower position of the head enables the ground to be studied, although it should be appreciated that the descent rate is slightly increased.

From the stable and frog positions, turns, barrel rolls and forward and backward loops can be initiated, and with practice the art of body flying becomes a reality. It is even possible to glide forwards, as well as to fall through the air, by shaping the body into an aerofoil; this is known as the tracking position. The only problem with the delights of such flying is the demanding discipline of counting the time. Parachute opening can be left too late only once.

The first manoeuvre you will do is a turn, probably of 180 degrees. From the spread position gently rotate, or bank, your body from the waist in the intended direction. Quite slowly the horizon will move around. When you want to stop the turn revert to the stable spread position shortly before you reach the heading on which you wish to fly straight. After several turns you will probably want to increase the rate at which you go around. This is done by bending up the leg, from the knee, on the side to which you are turning, by tilting your hands at the wrists to make mini control surfaces and/or by pushing down the arm in the turn direction. If at any time you feel yourself becoming unstable, you should return immediately to the stable spread position and/or open the parachute.

Tracking is difficult to achieve if the maximum possibility of gliding at an angle of 35 degrees to the vertical is hoped for, but some skill in this manoeuvre is needed before going on to formation flying with friends and the challenge of relative work.

Relative work
The art, and certainly the skill, of relative work is a recent addition both to the fun of parachuting and to competitions. With landing accuracy becoming almost universal hits on the target with few misses, competitive parachuting could rapidly have become stale. Now the possibility of linking different formations, and making eight-man stars within 30 to 40 seconds of everyone leaving the aeroplane has introduced great new possibilities: the largest star ever was made in USA with thirty-one jumpers linked together. The aeroplane is left at a usual maximum height of 12,500 feet, as this is as high as it is sensible to jump without oxygen.

Relative work obviously requires considerable preplanning. The manoeuvres have to be decided, and

Figure 6.9. (a) & (b) Delayed free fall demands great accuracy of timing both by count and altimeter and/or stopwatch. While free falling the more experienced jumper will adopt the frog position which is less tiring, although it slightly increases the rate of descent.

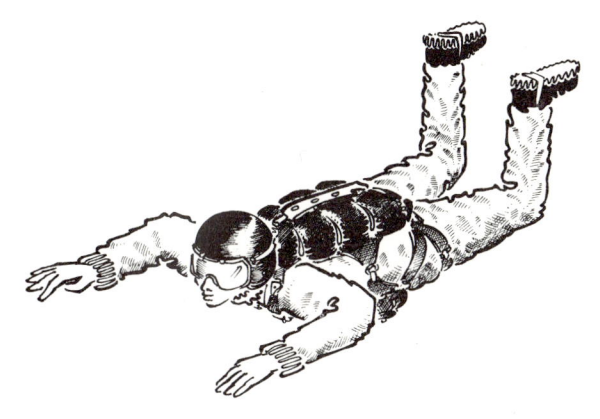

105

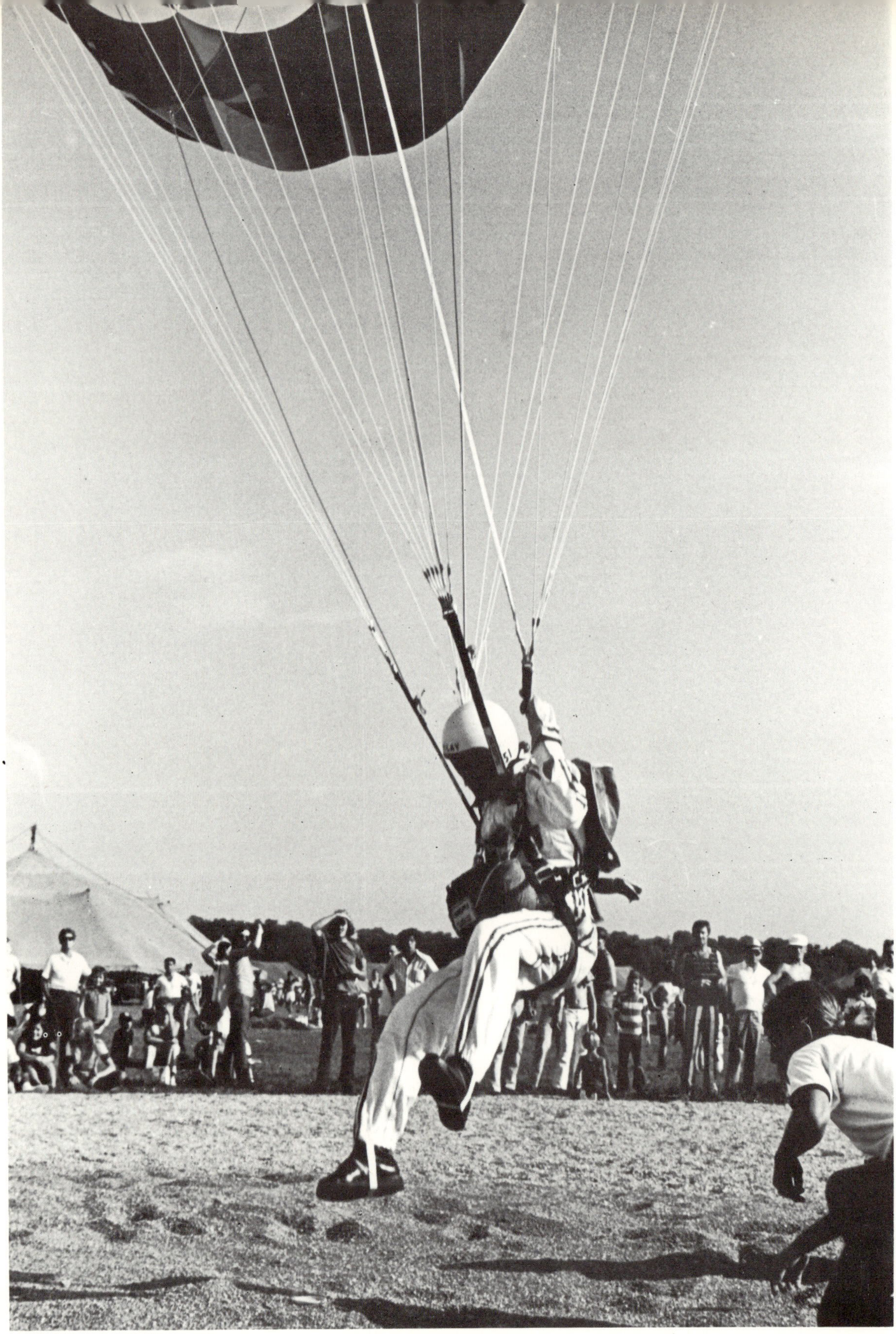

Figure 6.10. Using a Para-Commander type, landings can be made on a disc 10 centimetres in diameter.

the order in which the jumpers exit from the aeroplane determined. Someone has to be base man or pin man, on whom others formate, and the weights of jumpers have to be considered because a heavyweight will have a higher descent rate than the more slender built. For your first formation jump the instructor will make his way to you, and you should watch carefully the movements he makes to do this; because in a couple of jumps' time you will be expected to make the final link with the instructor yourself. To begin with your manoeuvres will almost certainly be too late or too large, so that you overshoot and ram the instructor or completely miss him. He, of course, will be in charge of the demanding clock, and when he breaks away it means that it is time to pull the ripcord. It is not difficult to imagine that, with a number of parachutists manoeuvring together, the risk of collision both before and after opening is considerable. To reduce this as far as possible everyone, on the break signal, turns 180 degrees to the right, and tracks away; then a quick look round to check that you are clear, and pull. If, in spite of all precautions, a canopy collision becomes imminent, the parachute should be turned or moved by pulling down on the toggles, just as they are used to manoeuvre for landing.

To many, body flying in formation with people you know and trust is fun, and any successful sortie gives a great feeling of achievement – because it is so demanding on the skill and co-ordination of both of you. In this sense parachuting has become true team activity with camaraderie enough to satisfy the most gregarious.

Is parachuting for you?
As with all varieties of flying the real reason for doing it is almost more important than anything else. A lot of people have a desire, almost a need, to fly, but either they do not know how to set about it or they cannot make up their mind what sort of flying it is that they want to do. What they actually try may also be determined by the size of their pockets and what is available near their home.

Some people are lucky in that they do know what flying they like, whether it be experimenting with new man-powered aircraft on the fringes of aeronautical knowledge or just visiting their friends at weekends in a flying motorcar. Their motives may be incomprehensible to others, but they are not suspect. It is in airsports like parachuting and hang gliding that the wrong motives for flying turn up more frequently. The parachutist can be easily visualized as a colourful person of courage and daring, and the newcomer may well want to jump so that he can see himself as that kind of person. This is the wrong reason for taking up any sort of flying, just as are doing it for a wager, wishing to commit suicide or spending a pool's win for the hell of it. No flying is safe unless it is done properly, and, although this may come as a revelation to some people, it is true. Most parachutists – and most other aviators – enjoy their flying because it is something they can really get their teeth into and can know the satisfaction that comes from developing skills. There is only one right reason for taking up parachuting or gliding or ballooning, because you really want to do it more than anything else.

Figure 6.11. The tracking position.

Figure 6.12 Relative work. The making of ten-man stars and other formations requires the jumper to manoeuvre like an aircraft. He can actually glide through the air, as against only falling, by adopting the tracking position Fig. 6.11.

ASSOCIATIONS

British Parachute Association
Address: Kimberley House, Vaughan Way, Leicester LE1 4SG
Telephone No.: Leicester 59778, 59635.

No. of members: 8,300
No. of clubs: 59
No. of display teams: 63
No. of jumps annually: 90,000
Minimum age for jumping: 16 years

The British Parachute Association (BPA) is the governing body of sport parachuting in the UK and is run by an eighteen-man council, supported by committees responsible for safety and training, competitions and forward planning.

Pilot licences and certificates
No parachutist licences are required. The BPA requires a medical certificate of fitness from a member's GP. A series of grades of competence are available.

Category I
He has been passed out on basic ground training (a minimum of 6 hours) and is ready for first static line descent.

Category II
(a) He has performed a *minimum of three absolutely stable observed static line descents* in the full spread position (counting throughout).
(b) Has completed a total of 13 hours of ground training in accordance with the BPA Minimum Ground Training Programme.

Category III
He has performed a *minimum of three successful and*

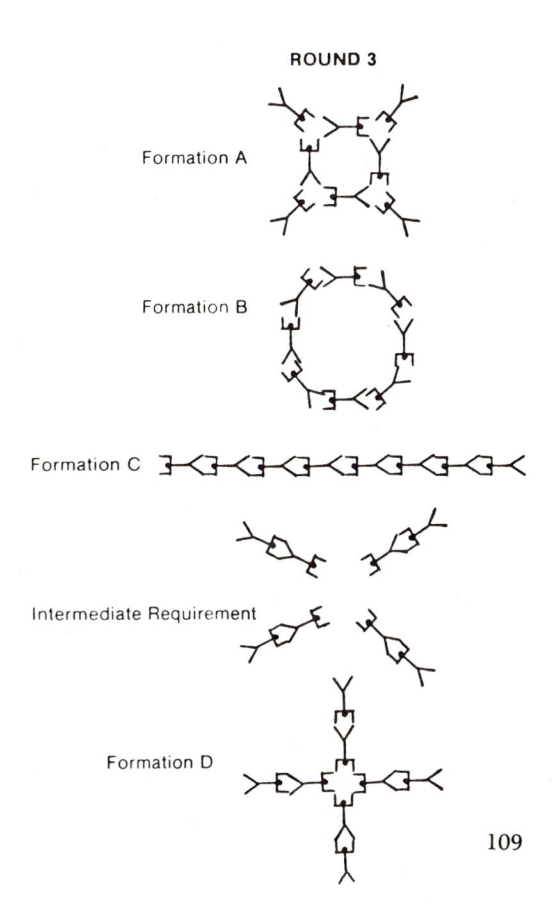

Figure 6.13. Some of the free fall competition positions.

Figure 6.14. To make formations successfully in the 40 seconds to 1 minute of time that is safely available, everyone must exit from the aeroplane as closely together as possible. This height is 12,500 feet, the greatest altitude that is practicable without oxygen.

consecutive, observed static line descents with dummy ripcord (counting throughout).
Category IV (5 seconds)
(a) Has performed a *minimum of five stable 5 seconds delayed openings* (counting throughout).
(b) Has remained stable throughout opening on each descent.
(c) Has looked at ripcord handle before and during the 'reach and pull'.
(d) Has achieved reasonable canopy handling.
Category V (10 seconds)
(a) Has performed a *minimum of five stable 10 seconds delayed openings* (counting throughout).
(b) Has learned to maintain heading during exist and in free fall.
Category VI (15 seconds)
(a) Has performed a *minimum of five stable 15 seconds delayed openings* in the following sequence.
 (1) Two flat stable (counting throughout).
 (2) After instruction in the use of instruments, three flat stable descents using instruments but continuing to count throughout.
(b) After successful completion of (a), he has demonstrated the ability to perform 360 degree turns in each direction, stopping on the aircraft heading.
Category VII (20 seconds)
(a) Has performed a *minimum of five stable 20 seconds delayed openings*.
(b) Has demonstrated his ability to recover from an unstable position leaving the aircraft.
(c) Has been introduced to spotting.
Category VIII (20 seconds)
(a) Has landed within 50 yards of centre of target on a *minimum of three 30 seconds delayed opening descents*.
(b) Has learned to track and to turn in a track.
(c) Has been cleared for self-spotting up to 7,000 feet.
On completion of Category VIII the student may be recommended for a FAI C certificate by his instructor and may be introduced to a Para-Commander or similar type high-performance canopy at which time cutaway drills (live) may be carried out in accordance with section 14, para 5 (d).
Category IX
(a) Has demonstrated to an instructor in free fall that he is fully in control of his movements, is aware of other parachutists around him and is capable of taking

avoiding action.
(b) Has demonstrated his ability to perform the following aerial manoeuvres: forward loops, backwards loops and barrel rolls.
(c) Has been introduced to relative parachuting.
Category X
(a) Has been cleared for unsupervised relative work having successfully demonstrated the following:
> (1) The ability to execute a link, followed by a backloop and a second link with a Category X parachutist approved by the CCI, on a single jump.
> (2) The ability to close third on a three-man group on two separate occasions.

(b) He has been cleared for self-spotted descents up to 12,000 feet.

Note: Up to and including Category VI, all students are to be observed and timed (from exit to full canopy development) by the instructor in the aircraft.

Training courses
Training is given in all BPA clubs either at weekends or for longer periods. Information is available from the BPA.

The British Association of Parascending Clubs
Address: 20–21 D'Arblay Street, London W1V 3FN
Telephone No.: 01–439 2465

The BAPC looks after the sport of parascending in the UK, including the training and qualifications of instructors, championships organization and distance record attempts.

No licences or proficiency certificates are required to fly. There are about fifty clubs, several of which run weekend training courses. Details are available from the BAPC.

7 Wind and Weather

Too often the weather becomes important only when you have to stay out in it; but whether you fly an aeroplane, a hot air balloon, a kite or a model you will do it better and have more fun if you know what the weather is going to do. Most people complain if the forecast is wrong, but not so many people are prepared to spend time finding out how the weather behaves so as to be able to make their own assessment. There is not a need to become a professional meteorologist and forecast for the whole country but to understand what is happening to the air in the locality over which you are operating, and for the next few hours. This is not difficult provided that you learn to recognize what you are seeing, and you are a good observer.

At all times the sky that you can see is telling you clearly what is happening to it, and yet some people are so unobservant that they will prepare to take shelter from a storm that could not possibly come their way or will fail to take a raincoat when the heavens are about to open, because the forecast said it would be dry.

All flying is weather sensitive to some extent. Man-powered aircraft are the most fussy, followed by balloons. Hang gliders can cope with a wide range of weather, apart from strong winds; and aeroplanes are rugged in this respect too, except that they can run into bad weather faster than anything else and maybe more rapidly than the pilot is prepared for. If the bad weather covers hills, then the situation may get out of hand very quickly.

Some people have difficulty in discovering what weather is coming and what is going because they are not very good at orientating themselves, so this is the first need if any sort of flying is contemplated. You have to get used to observing the sun, the wind and the cloud movements in relation to north; and to know where north is.

Getting lost in the air is even worse than flying slap into bad weather, so, until you have at least some idea of the direction you are facing, you should think twice about leaping into the sky. Some people seem to take a pride in professing to have no 'bump of locality', but this usually means that they never have taken the trouble to find the 'bump'. Others always appear to know where they are, and can locate themselves surprisingly well. It is not that they are clever but that way back, probably as a child, they became interested in tracking by the sun's direction or in telling the time by the length of shadows, and the unconscious process of noticing these things has continued ever since. The observant person will automatically note the wind direction each time he goes out or looks from the window even of a strange building and will appreciate if and when it changes. Without thinking he has related the wind to the position of the sun, even on a partly cloudy day. This feel for orientation is the first step towards understanding about the weather, because weather moves along with the wind, as well as just providing that warm summer breeze or unseasonal gale.

The weather that arrives will possess many of the characteristics of the region from which it has come. Northwest Europe not only is at a latitude where cold polar air mixes with warm air from more exotic parts of the world but is also a permanent half-way house between the moist Atlantic, with its moderate temperatures, and the hinterland of Europe with its hot continental summers and freezing winters. The south-westerlies that blow across Britain, have, for example, mostly come thousands of miles over Atlantic water, and from quite far to the south, so they can be expected to be generally mild and moist. Some winds are peculiar to a locality, such as the famous Mistral, that north wind that blows with immense strength down the Rhône Valley of France from the cold high Alps to the Mediterranean. In Britain there are no such notorious winds, but there is very often too much wind, and what the flier primarily wants to know is if or when the wind is going to get any stronger.

Sometimes a change in the wind direction is the first indication that a weather change is on the way. If it is, this will soon be reflected in the appearance of clouds – or the lack of them. The frequent changes in wind direction and strength occur because the air is spending its time blowing around great pressure systems – the well-known low-pressure depressions and high-pressure anticyclones. As these systems move across land and water, gently propelled by the rotation of the earth, and also of course growing within themselves or decaying, they bring the wind changes

112

Figure 7.1 Buys Ballot's Law. Christoph Buys Ballot (1817–90) was a Dutch meteorologist who discovered that, if you face the wind in the Northern hemisphere, the pressure will be lower away to your right hand. This makes it possible to visualize how the weather is behaving and if the forecast is running to time. Although Buys Ballot wrote his law stating that he stood with his back to the wind, this is of less value than facing it when you can see the weather that is coming.

along with them. With the confusing nomenclature that seems to to pervade so much of meteorology the air flows around a depression in an anticlockwise direction (in the northern hemisphere) and around an *anti*cyclone in a *clockwise* direction.

As the wind direction changes at any given point on the surface of the earth it is possible to tell in which direction the prevailing weather system is moving. This is useful information if it indicates that the cold front forecast as hellbent for your airfield now appears to be sliding away further to the north. There is a well-known law, Buys Ballot's law, which states that, if you are facing the wind (in the northern hemisphere again), the pressure will be lower away to your right hand. If, therefore, you are standing in the North Sea pointing to the southwest with the wind on your face, the centre of the depression will be away to the right (Figure 7.1). If it is a big depression, you will probably be in the influence of its moist and cloudy air, so, if you study the sky upwind (to the southwest) you will

113

probably see high cloud spreading up the sky, if it has not done so already. If, from the same place, on another day, you are facing into a north wind this will tell you that the depression is over Scandinavia and that there is an anticyclonic high over the eastern Atlantic. If the pressure is also slowly rising, you may soon be in the influence of its drier weather. A flattening or lessening of the cloud cover may help to confirm this.

Once you are used to orientating yourself and observing the passing weather, the time has come to relate your observations to the official forecasts and weather maps, so that you will be able to discover whether they are correct, whether the weather is running true to form, whether the expected rain is delayed, whether the front is coming in faster than expected or whether it is going to be a fine soaring day.

Thermals

Thermals are small-scale upcurrents produced as a result of heat from the sun warming the surface. They are the main support of the glider pilot, are treated warily by the balloonist and have the aeroplane pilot complaining of bumpy air. In parts of the world where the sun is high and strong, such as Texas and South Africa, thermals develop throughout the year, although they are stronger during their summer, when they rise to heights of around 15,000 feet. In north European countries they become usable in the spring, go up to heights generally in the region of 4,000 to 6,000 feet throughout sunny summer days, gently weaken in the autumn and die away for the winter.

Whenever the sun shines on the ground, it begins to heat the surface, which in turn warms the air above it. This does not happen in any sort of regular pattern because some varieties of surface heat up more readily than others. Dry tarmac or ploughed fields, for example, will become warmed more quickly than will dense woodland or damp marshes, and this can be quite well demonstrated with a model balloon, by sending it off over different sorts of ground, or when a cloud shadow is passing over as well as in sunshine, and by timing the length of the flights.

Air that is warmed becomes less dense than the surrounding cooler air and starts to rise. Now two things begin to happen. The rising air expands and in doing so cools, and on and near the surface air from all around flows in to replace the warmed rising air. As height is gained above the ground the air temperature lessens, and in clear air it does so at a rate of approximately 3°C per 1,000 feet. So the thermal is rising through air which is progressively cooling, but it is also losing its own warmth, and at a slightly faster rate. When the temperature of the thermal and that of the surrounding air have both cooled to the same value, it will be unable to rise further.

Because thermals are totally dependent for their existence on the sun, they cannot start until it makes its presence felt, usually around 09.30 to 10.00 in the morning, and they die away again in the early evening, as the sun loses its power. It is the discipline of this relatively short number of soaring hours in a day which has determined glider design to a large extent. Whatever flight the pilot wants to achieve he has to complete it while the sun is up; so the more efficient the glider and the faster it can fly, the longer the distance that it is possible for the pilot to go.

Sometimes the thermal will reach the same temperature as the surrounding air – or will rise into an inversion, or layer of warmer air – without cooling sufficiently to grow a cumulus on its head, particularly if the air is dry. But on most days cumulus clouds will appear and are good signposts to the lift. The reason that a thermal produces a cumulus cloud is that air, as it is progressively cooled, becomes increasingly less able to carry moisture in the invisible form of water vapour. When the air in the thermal reaches this stage, some of the moisture is condensed out into water droplets, producing a visible cloud. Because on any day the air over a considerable area is equally moist or dry, the clouds will develop at the top of each thermal at much the same height. This produces the uniform cloud base so typical of a good cumulus day.

If the air is fairly dry, particularly if it is also anticyclonic high-pressure air, the cumulus will remain small, flat and well separated all day, and it is a good sign of settled weather. The cloud base is also likely to be high, perhaps at around 6,000 feet. If, however, the air is moist, as it is more likely to be with

Figure 7.2. Thermals develop over ground that is heated by the sun and warming up the air over it. When warm enough the thermal will break away and rise and form cloud when it reaches condensation level — the level at which the air can no longer contain all the invisible water vapour that it is carrying. After the thermal has risen up into the soon fully grown cloud, there will be no more lift underneath, and the cloud will begin to decay away.

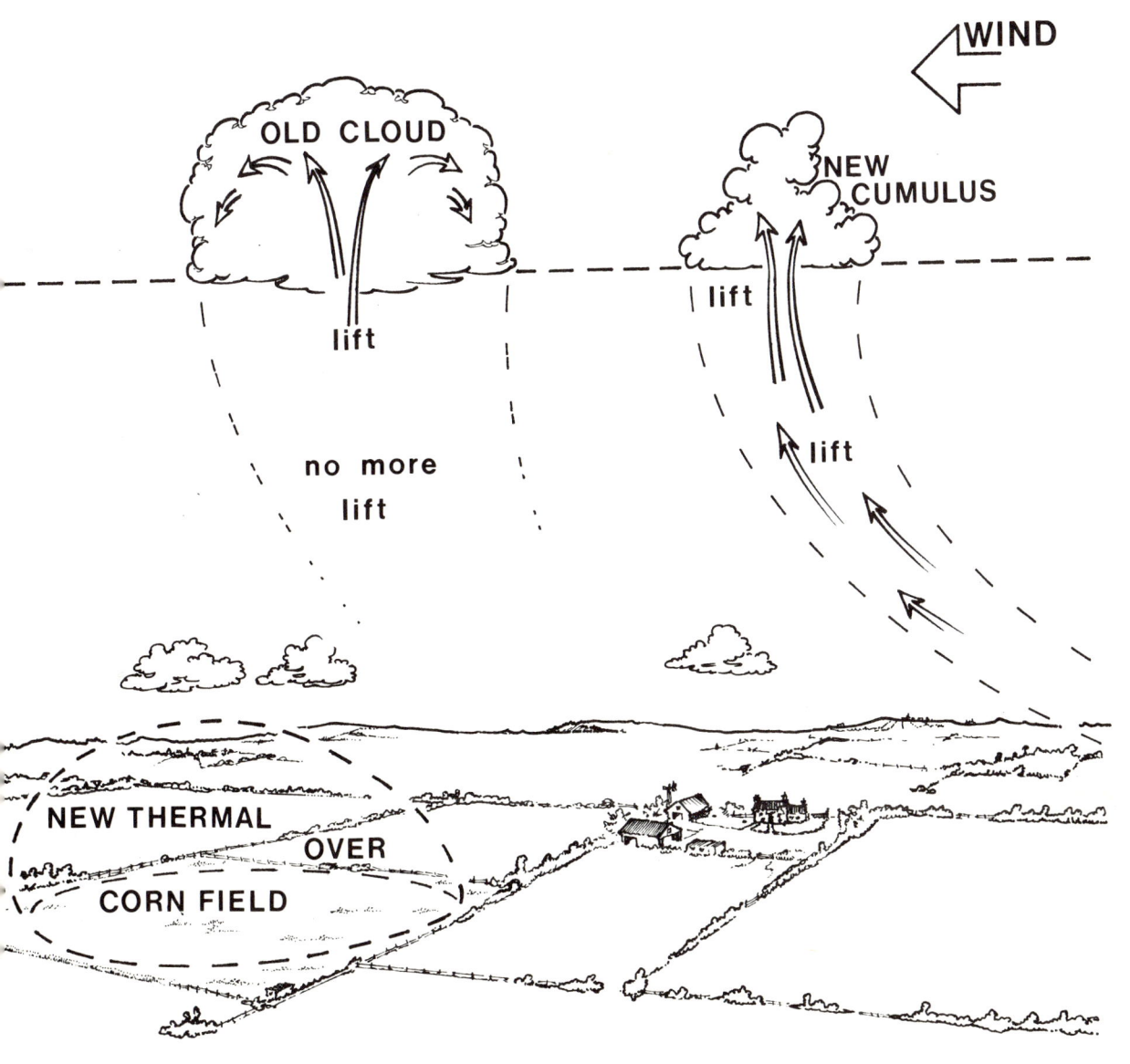

westerly winds from the Atlantic, the cloud base will be lower, perhaps only at 2,500 to 3,000 feet. The cumulus will look softer in appearance, be somewhat larger, and will have a tendency to run together or to overdevelop. When this happens, the amount of heat reaching the surface is considerably reduced, and thermals will rise only weakly or will cease altogether if the cloud has become thick. Without further supplies of warmed rising air to feed them the clouds will decay and evaporate, allowing the sun to break through. Now the whole process will begin again. The ordinary summer cumulus has a very short life, about 20 minutes. As the thermal reaches condensation level the cumulus begins to form and to grow, but within 8 to 10 minutes the tail end of the thermal has also reached cloud base and contributed its quota of moisture. Now, without any further supply the cumulus begins to collapse gently, flatten and evaporate, taking about 10 minutes to disappear. So the glider pilot has to work on the basis that at any given moment only half the cumulus in the sky are growing and therefore of any use to him. The other half may still look pretty, but they are a dead loss (Figure 7.3).

Even such small variations in the appearance of ordinary cumulus will provide considerable information on the weather generally. If during the middle part of the day cumulus disappears leaving a clear blue sky, the air moving across the country will be becoming drier and probably finer and more settled. If good cumulus in the morning develops into an ever-thickening grey mass which does not clear during the evening, the weather is unsettled, and the pressure will probably be found to be dropping. Should good weather be essential for the following day's activities, the forecast should be studied with care.

If the air is unstable, with the air temperature dropping steadily with height all the way up, the cumulus will grow tall and will do this rapidly. Sometimes on a clear morning with a well-washed blue sky, small cumulus will be seen to pop up quite early, around 09.00. This should be watched, for, if they turn into little towers and turrets, taller than they are broad, the chances are that the afternoon will be filled with squalls or thunderstorms, even if they stay away until then. Using thermals has become a well-established skill, since it was first appreciated some 50 years ago that warm air upcurrents were powerful enough to support a heavier-than-air machine, and a lot more has been learnt since about their structure. Most usable thermals have a diameter of about 1,000 feet or so and rise at rates between 3 and

Figure 7.3. Cumulus clouds grow near the top of thermals and indicate their presence. This cumulus is soft and fat with a relatively low cloud base, showing that the air is fairly moist. The slight lean visible in the distant clouds indicates that the wind is blowing from left to right.

Figure 7.4. If the air is very unstable, the heating strong and the air moist, the cumulus will grow into a cumulo-nimbus and will develop a self-stoking circulation of its own, drawing in air to feed itself. Thunderstorm cumulo-nimbus clouds grow to heights of over 30,000 feet, contain severe turbulence and icing conditions and throw out hail and cold heavy rain, as well as severe gusts.

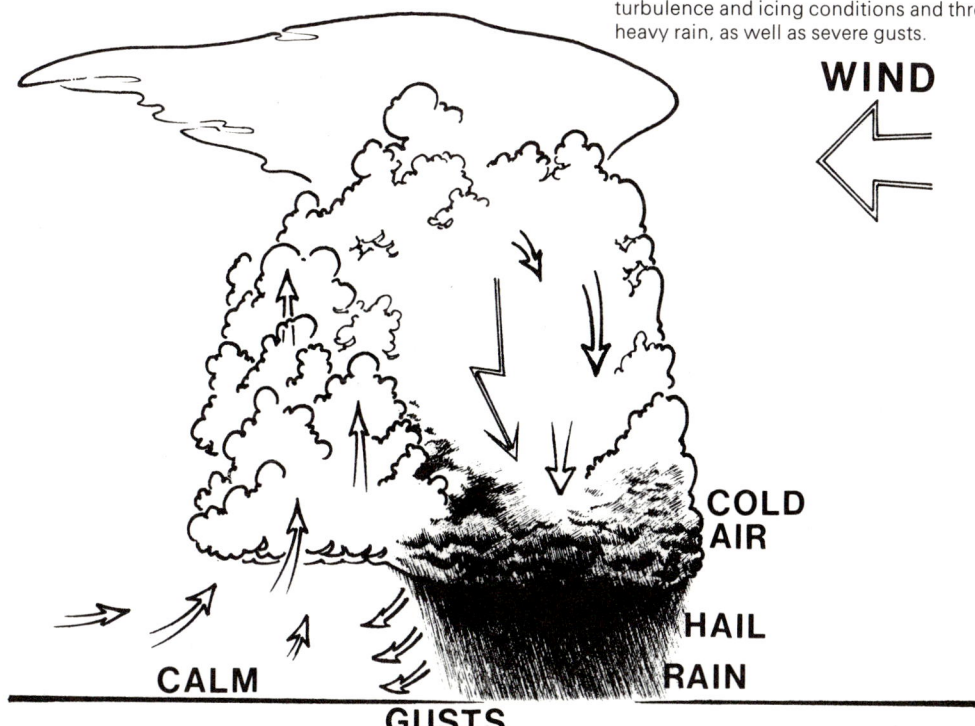

8 knots. Smaller or weaker than this and they would be quickly discarded by the glider pilot unless he could find nothing else. Stronger than 8 knots would be above average for Britain, only occurring on really good days. Once fully developed and rising freely the thermal often develops a doughnut-shaped structure with the air rising most strongly in the centre, and even downwards around the extreme perimeter. This accounts for the increased sink rate that is often met as you think you are about to enter a thermal. Because thermals are invisible it is often difficult to know which way to turn in order to stay in and circle fully in the lift. If you turn immediately, you will probably fly straight out of it again, so it is usual to wait a second or so; even then it is not always possible to know whether the centre is to your left or right. Sometimes help is given by the thermal itself trying to push the glider out by tipping it up on one wing. This means that the stronger lift is in the direction of the wing that was pushed up; so you push it down again and turn in that direction.

Because thermals become larger and stronger as they go higher, the glider pilot prefers to fly high in the best lift. This is not so easy for the hang glider pilot who mostly has to use them either near the ground before they have properly developed or over hills where they are distorted in shape. His only advantage is the very slow airspeed of the hang glider, so that it is easier for him to utilize small bits of lift than for the glider pilot. When a new thermal breaks away from its source, it drifts on the wind, rising initially only very slowly. If the wind is fresh and the terrain broken, the thermal will become turbulent and ragged; it is also more likely to be torn away from its source before it has sopped up all the warmth immediately available to it. Unfortunately, it is in just such fresh wind weather that the hang glider pilot is slope soaring on the hill and waiting for thermals to come. By the time the rough little thermal has reached the hill and drifted up the slope it will be difficult to use. The strongest part of the lift is most likely to be on the upwind side, because the drag effect of the surface of the slope will have slowed the thermal down on this side, where there may now be little except turbulence. In light winds with very good surface heating, thermals reaching the slope are much more likely to be large enough to resist the dragging effect of the hill face, and, by flying out from the hill into the wind, enough height may be gained to enable you first to S-turn into the wind and then to circle. In the late afternoon, when thermal activity generally is beginning to weaken, slopes facing the southwest

117

Figure 7.5. Sea breezes alter the weather to a considerable extent in summer in countries having extensive coastal regions. Cool air blows or is dragged in from the sea to replace that which has risen over the warm land. The effect of the sea breeze varies according to differences between the prevailing wind direction and the coastline.

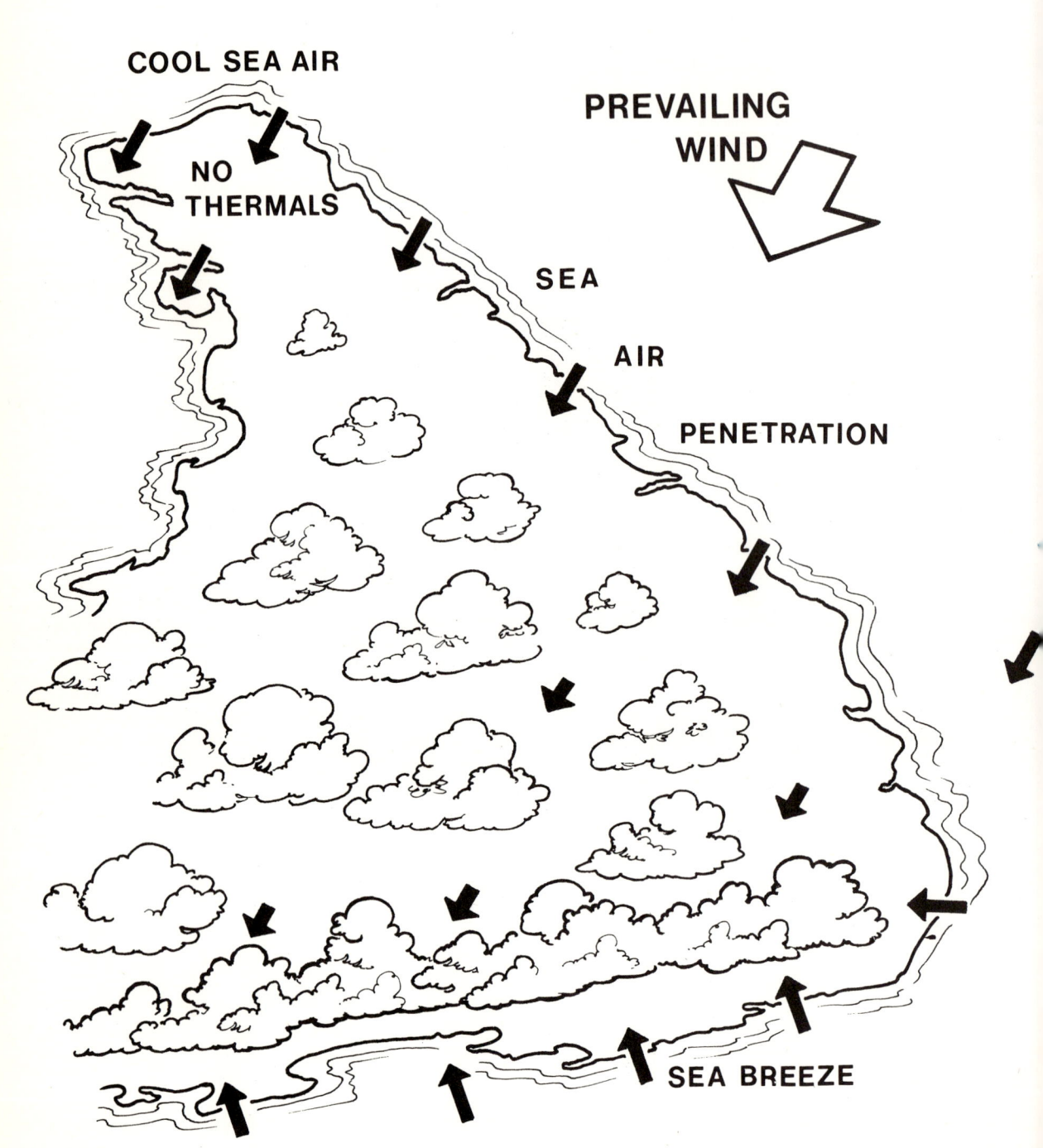

sometimes produce excellent, though gentle, thermal lift. The wind is lessening, and the accumulated warmth from the valley and slopes will find itself unstable relative to the now-cooling air over the hill top. No great heights will be attained either by a hang glider, a lightweight sailplane or a model, but flying in this sort of thermal lift is delightful.

Sea breezes

On an island, like Britain, or in any coastal area, many summer days will be affected by sea breezes. These are caused by thousands of thermals causing a general rising of the air over the land. Here, again, you cannot have something for nothing, so cooler air from over the sea moves in at low levels to replace that which is going up. If the thermal activity over the land is extensive and powerful, the sea air will be pulled steadily inland, perhaps for 20 to 30 miles, until it dies away later when the thermals die. The extent to which the sea breeze penetrates, and its character, will obviously be affected by the strength and direction of the prevailing wind. If, for example, the wind and sea breeze have a common direction, like a southerly wind blowing in over the south coast, there will probably be a fairly massive but simple penetration of cool sea air. But if the prevailing wind and sea breeze are to some extent opposed to each other, as with a northeast wind over the south coast, the two lots of air would interact with each other. Quite often this might take the form of a long line of solid-looking cumulus running parallel to the coastline and usually a few miles inland (Figure 7.5). This sea breeze front can be soared and sometimes will provide a fine easy glider ride for many miles. Equally, if the sea air penetrates inland beyond the gliding club, this will kill the local thermals. An understanding of how sea breezes develop is also of use to the aeroplane pilot, since by flying in the smooth sea air closer to the coast he will be able if he wishes to get away from all the bumps and turbulence caused by the thermals.

Wind on the hill

The air, like people, prefers not to be disturbed. But every hill, house and tree causes the air to burble around it, with mountains creating massive alterations to the normally smooth flow. Even the flattest of seas will slow down moving air close to the surface, producing a gradient effect. Where the moving air, or wind, is caused to divert because of some obstacle, such as a hill, in its way, it will either rise to go over the top or will flow around the sides. On the upwind side of the hill the air will be still relatively organized, but downwind, where it is endeavouring to re-establish a smooth progression, there will be turbulence made up of pockets of lower pressure air and back eddies.

For a very long time gliders have soared in the rising air produced by the wind blowing against a hill, reaching heights of two or three times that of the high ground above which they are flying. Now hang gliders are exploring the slopes and ridges abandoned by the glider when its performance and speed became more suited to the clouds than to the ground (Figure 7.6).

Not all hills are good for soaring. For a start it should be a long ridge rather than a hill so that the air finds it more trouble to curl around the ends rather than rise up over the top. The shape of the hill is also important. Ideally the terrain should rise steeply but curvaceously from flat unobstructed ground. The face of the hill should not contain marked discontinuities such as quarries or isolated large clumps of trees, although a completely wooded hill is no disadvantage – except for an unintentional landing! The crest of the hill should be rounded, and should remain reasonably level for some distance downwind. Much less suitable hills are hog-backed ridges, where the ground – and the hang gliders – falls away almost as steeply as they rose, and sharp-edged cliffs. Because the rising air finds it quite impossible to flow smoothly over such a sharp change in ground contour, it behaves as though the hill was rounded; at least most of the air does. The rest tries to fill the spaces that would otherwise be left, by moving the wrong way – downwards. The strength of downdraughts, eddies, turbulence and burbles should not be underestimated. Slope soaring altitudes are in feet or hundreds of feet rather than in thousands of feet, and it does not take many seconds to find yourself dumped ignominiously on the ground if you have allowed your aircraft – and that includes aeroplanes – to fly in the wrong bits of air.

In mountains, using lift from air being deflected

Figure 7.6. When the air meets a hill, it is forced to rise over it, and so provides a band of steady lift for enjoyable soaring.

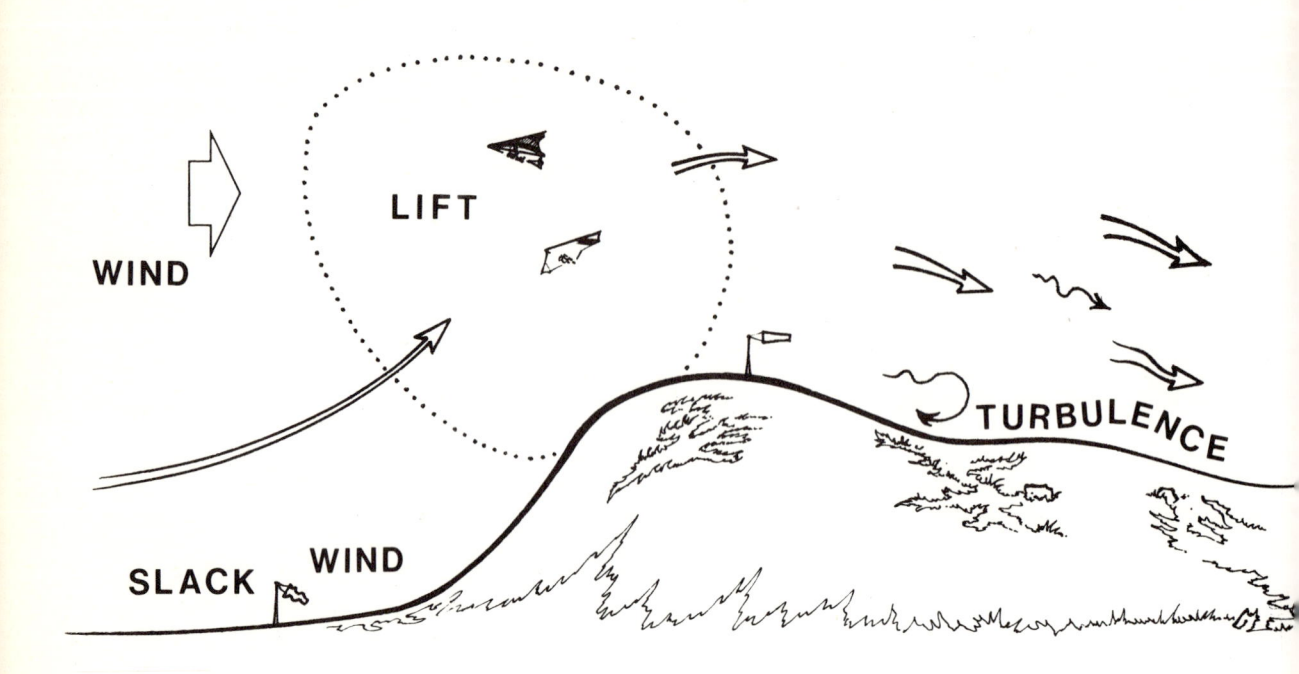

Figure 7.7. Waves over the Lake District in an easterly wind.

upwards over the terrain is often very complex, because the ground upwind of the ridge that you are soaring on will probably contain yet another mountain or hill instead of being flat. This upwind hill will have already modified the behaviour, and the strength and direction of the wind, so the ridge you believe should be facing the wind may not be doing so at all. Even if it is, and you are soaring high above it, this is where you should try to stay, because at a lower height the upwind hill may be creating a blanketing effect, causing all lift low down to disappear suddenly. Valleys are another problem when flying in mountains, because the wind blows either up them or down them and pays almost no attention at all to the direction of the prevailing wind at a higher level. The way the wind blows along a valley is determined to some extent by the shape of the terrain and its scale, but in general the wind will tend to blow up a valley during the day because warm air rises. In the evening and at night, the wind will blow or subside down the valley, as the air cools and increases in density.

Wind gradient

Whether there are hills around or not, the wind blows more slowly close to the ground than it does higher up, because of the drag of the surface and its obstructions. The easiest way to see this for yourself is to walk down the face of any hill facing into the wind; near the foot the air will be relatively calm.

The problem of wind gradient is that it is most marked at the very height that you will be wanting to fly slowly, as when coming in to land. Now, although normally the *airspeed* of an aircraft – any aircraft, including a Para-Foil – is not altered by changes in wind strength, it is so affected if the change in wind speed happens suddenly. It amounts to the aircraft suffering a temporary loss in energy, and this is reflected in some small loss in airspeed. Obviously, if the presence of a wind gradient is anticipated and if the aircraft is brought in to land with a sufficient margin of speed, there will be no difficulty. It is only if the effect of wind gradient is not recognized or if it is underestimated and the aircraft is brought in near the minimum acceptable approach speed that the arrival will be heavier or more sudden than expected.

Waves

As well as the relatively small-scale disturbances around hills and other surface features, the air is capable of developing large-scale undulation or waves, much as can happen in water. Waves in the atmosphere may be caused by winds at a given level blowing strongly over air that is moving more slowly but are more commonly produced by the presence of mountains. The wave, or series of waves develops downwind of the mountain, in much the same way as waves can be seen downstream of a boulder in a fast-flowing river. In the air, waves are often vast in dimension, reaching to 50,000 feet or more and continuing to exist for many miles downwind. On the upgoing side of the waves the lift is often, and characteristically, strong and smooth, and for the pilot equipped with oxygen it provides a magnificent ride. On the downgoing side of the wave the downdraught may also be smooth, but it can also be powerful enough to down a large jet, let alone a small aeroplane or glider. Because a wave system is created by a stationary mountain, it also remains stationary over the ground, with the wind blowing through it. At high levels this wind is invariably much stronger than at lower levels and can easily be blowing at the same speed as that at which the aircraft is flying, or even at a higher speed. To remain in the upgoing part of the wave the aircraft has to match its airspeed to the opposing speed of the wind over the ground *at that height*. This means that, if you allow the aircraft to slip back into the downgoing part of the wave, you simply may not be able to fly fast enough to return upwind into the lift. The only hope, in this case, is to turn downwind and to reach the upgoing part of the next wave in the series – provided the terrain is suitable and you do not run out of land.

Back to the weather

Flying without understanding the weather and how the air behaves is like driving a car without understanding the road system and signs: it is extremely dangerous. In the air you are not only in the weather but part of it. If you use it and its energy correctly, you will get more flying. It will also be cheaper flying, because you will be able to keep your glider airborne longer for each launch charge; even a small aeroplane will use less petrol if engine power can be supplemented by thermals. Money and time will also be saved by avoiding wasted journeys – because you know the wind is going to strengthen and will become too strong for ballooning or parachuting or even flying models – which is an excellent way of learning about the weather (Figure 7.8, a and b). Until you start to fly, the weather that moves so constantly across the sky may seem inconvenient, or good for sunbathing, or just miserable, and not really anything much to do with you. But it is your playground, whether you are using it to bounce off cloud tops in your home-built single-seater, to drift by balloon in the dawn of a fine summer morning or to search for the innermost energy of invisible thermals.

Figure 7.8. (a) Air flows over and to the lee of mountains much as water in a river flows over and past boulders, forming a system or series of waves. These can provide lift up to over 45,000 feet but equally can produce regions of downcurrent powerful enough to bring down a large jet. (b) Wave systems are often characterized by smooth-edged lenticular clouds which remain almost stationary in the sky.

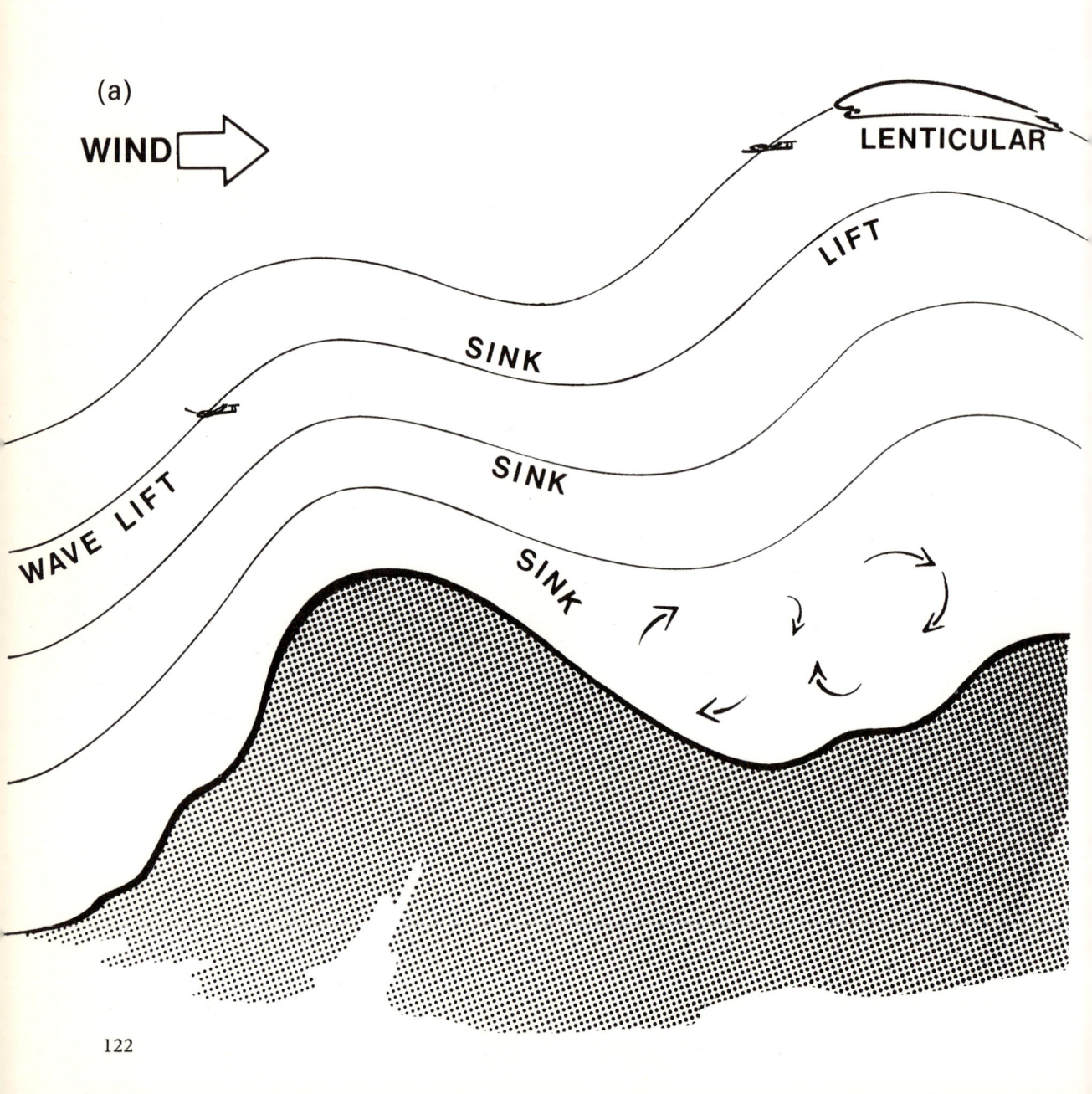

(a) WIND ⇨

LENTICULAR

LIFT

SINK

SINK

WAVE LIFT

SINK

(b)

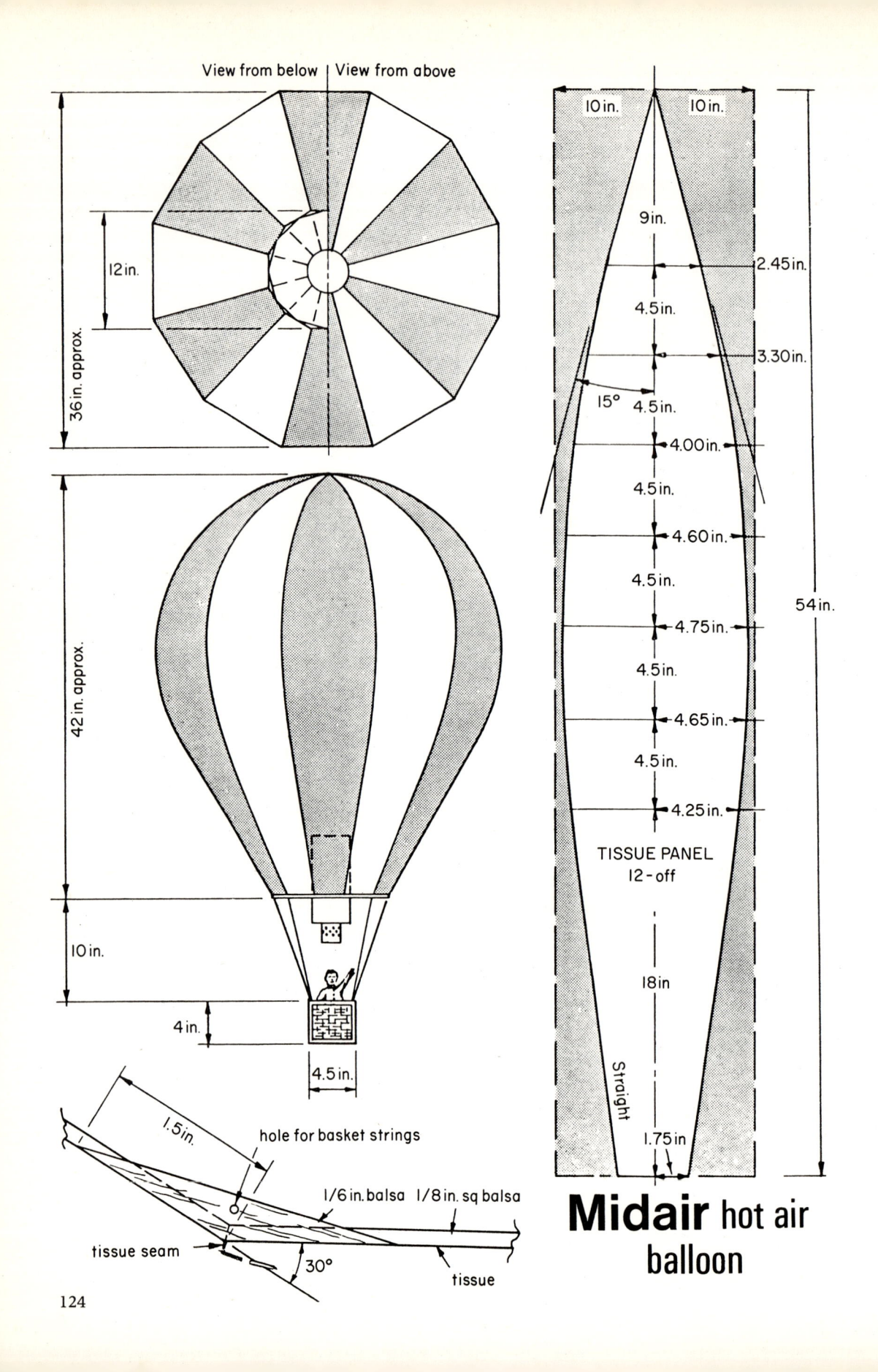

Midair hot air balloon

Figure 7.9. Behaviour of air on a small scale can often be observed by playing with models.

Hot air balloon. Rapid climbs can be expected if they encounter any thermal lift, but several spaced out over a few hundred yards on a warm day can often show when a new thermal takes off.

Making and flying the Midair balloon from a design by S. T. Midson

Normal commercial tissue paper, available in sheets of 30 inches × 20 inches, is used to make the envelope and the numerous colours available can be used to advantage. The twelve panels are made from six sheets of tissue each formed by joining two standard sheets along the 20 inch length, to give a $59\frac{3}{4}$ inch length by 20 inches wide. Tissue paste or PVA glue should be used for the envelope — the plastic spouts from the small size PVA glue containers are handy when gluing seams.

Fold one sheet in half, lengthways, and mark out one panel to use as a pattern. A free-hand smooth curve is adequate between the marked points, but at no time must the panel go outside the 30 degrees inclusive angle at the point or a pumpkin-shaped balloon will result. Fold the remaining sheets and pin the pattern to them, making sure that they are flat and all pins are in the *waste* material. Cut out carefully to ensure all panels are the same shape.

Lay the first panel flat on a table, then run a *thin* line of glue down the right-hand curved edge. Place the next panel on top of it and press the edge onto the glue. Fold this panel in half along its centreline, so that the left-hand edge lies above the glued seam, then run the next line of glue along the new right-hand side curved edge and repeat until all twelve panels have been glued into a concertina-like shape. The left-hand edges of the top and bottom panels should then be glued to complete the envelope.

If you are heavy-handed with the glue, sufficient will soak through the tissue to fix adjacent seams together; in order to prevent this, newspaper should be inserted to keep the layers apart.

Cut the last 1 inch of the point off, and, when the glued seams are dry, open the balloon up and glue on a disc of tissue 3 inches in diameter to make a neat cap. A hair dryer can be used to inflate the envelope at this stage to give a taste of things to come! For neatness the envelope can be turned inside out, but the outside seams make very useful grips when handling, and it is recommended to leave them as made.

Make the opening framework from $\frac{1}{8}$ inch square balsa, cut to length to match the panel, and glue to the edge of the tissue. Cut and add the angled joiners when dry — for this job a fast drying cement is best.

For the purist the basket could be made from scale-size cane, but the author's is made from a simple balsa framework covered with thin paper.

The 'balloonist' is up to you, but he must be light — thin card is the most suitable material. This size of envelope produces about $4\frac{1}{2}$ ounces of lift.

Launching the balloon requires two persons. Firstly, choose a still day and plenty of open space, then starting at the upwind edge of the area, pull the envelope open using the seams as grips, and hold in the flight attitude. Hold over a heat source, such as a small camping gas stove, and the balloon will fill completely until you find yourself holding something weightless; when lighter than air, release it to the mercy of the winds.

The balloon will rise at about 5 feet per second and will sink at about 4 feet per second in *still air*.

Flights on a short, fixed, tether in the open are not practical. If, however, the operator carries the end of the tether along with the wind and balloon, it will remain in its safe correct flight attitude — a further method of controlling height and flight length is to attach a string tether which the balloon lifts until the weight of string in the air balances the balloon lift, the length remaining on the ground being pulled along by the balloon. Lift produced varies with a number of factors and the length and weight of the string must be found by trial and error — a piece of wood on the end, fastened so that it cannot catch as it is pulled along, can also be used.

It should be noted that, although the drawing shows the position for a burner, it is not advisable to use one in a balloon on public land.

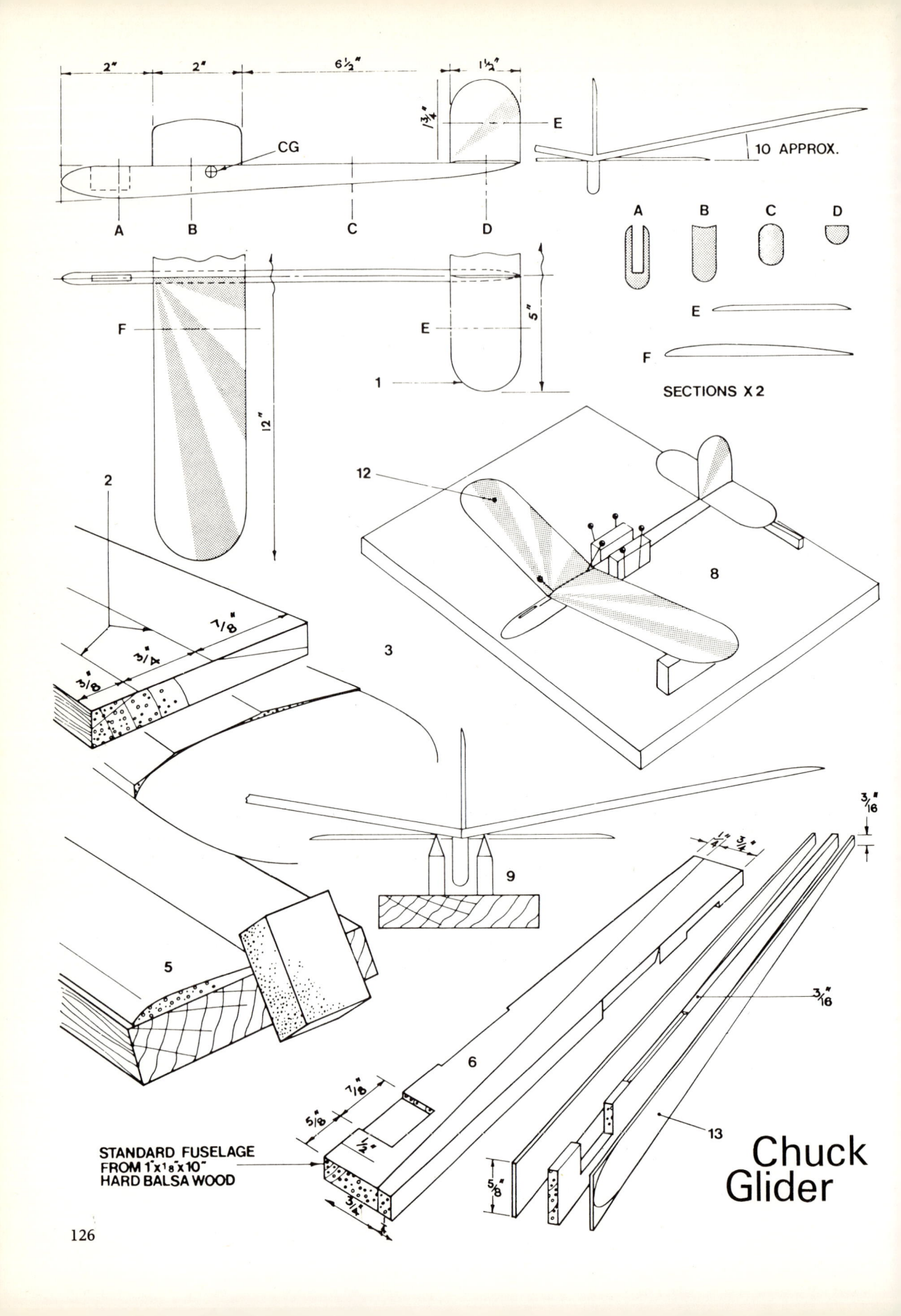

Chuck Glider

Figure 7.10. *Chuck Glider.* A very simple glider, too small and too light for any except gentle winds, but flown from a hilltop it may be persuaded to soar – or show where there are only downcurrents or turbulence.

Figure 7.11. *Peter Powell Kite.* The two-line stunter kite is very controllable and so can be positioned and flown to discover how the air is behaving over a hill or cliff – and it can cope well in fresh winds. But do not fly it in thunderstorms or near overhead cables.

Making and flying a simple chuck glider

Draw out to full size on balsa, or use a card template.

Sand the wing to give an aerofoil section, mainly on the top surface.

Make a simple assembly jig as shown, and use it to sand the root end of the wings to obtain the correct dihedral angle. Make the wing attachment bevel on the fuselage the same way.

Cement the fuselage strips together, and carefully sand the wing attachment position to fit, ensuring that it will give a positive angle of incidence.

Cement the wing and fuselage together.

Taper the edges of the tail surfaces and cement in position.

Waterproof the tail and fuselage with a thin coat of clear dope, and dope lightweight tissue over the wings. Hang up to dry.

To fly it, adjust the nose weight with Plasticine until the flattest glide angle is obtained when the glider is gently launched at a slight downward angle in calm conditions.

If the wing does not appear to provide lift, slit the rear of the fuselage and insert a 1 millimetre balsa wedge under the tailplane trailing edge.

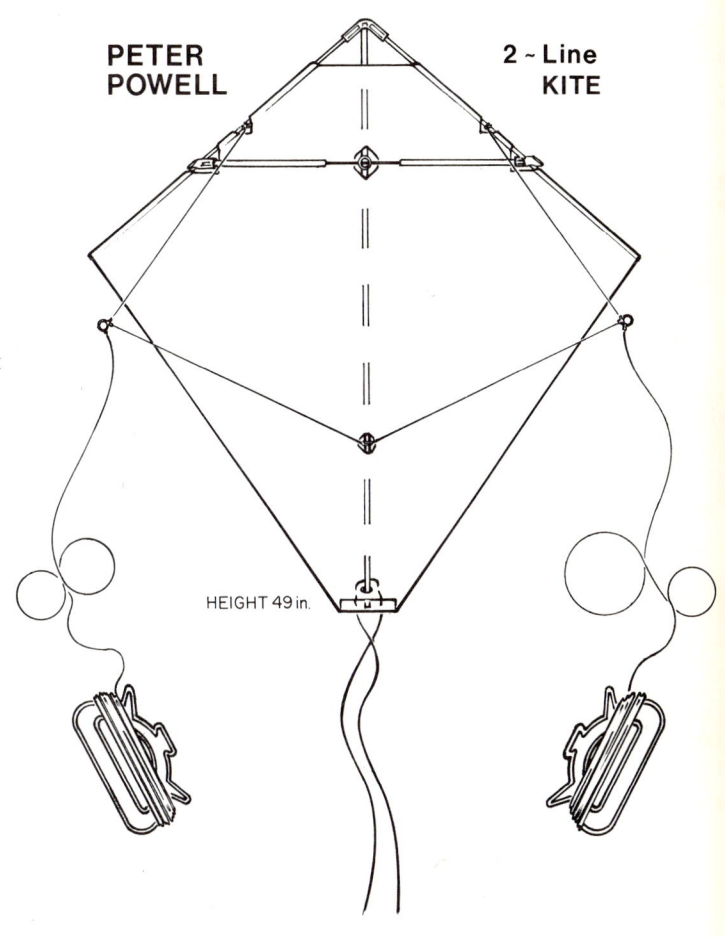

Appendix 1   Rules of the Air

(a) Meeting head on. Both aircraft break or turn to the right.

(b) Converging. The aircraft which has the other on its right gives way. This is often best done by turning to go behind the aircraft which has right of way as this glider, 177, is doing.

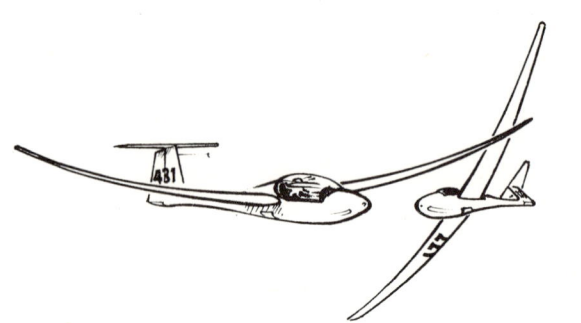

(c) Overtaking. The overtaking aircraft is responsible for keeping clear.

(d) Landing. The lower aircraft has the right of way. Unless the higher aircraft can follow in at a safe distance, it should climb away and go round again.

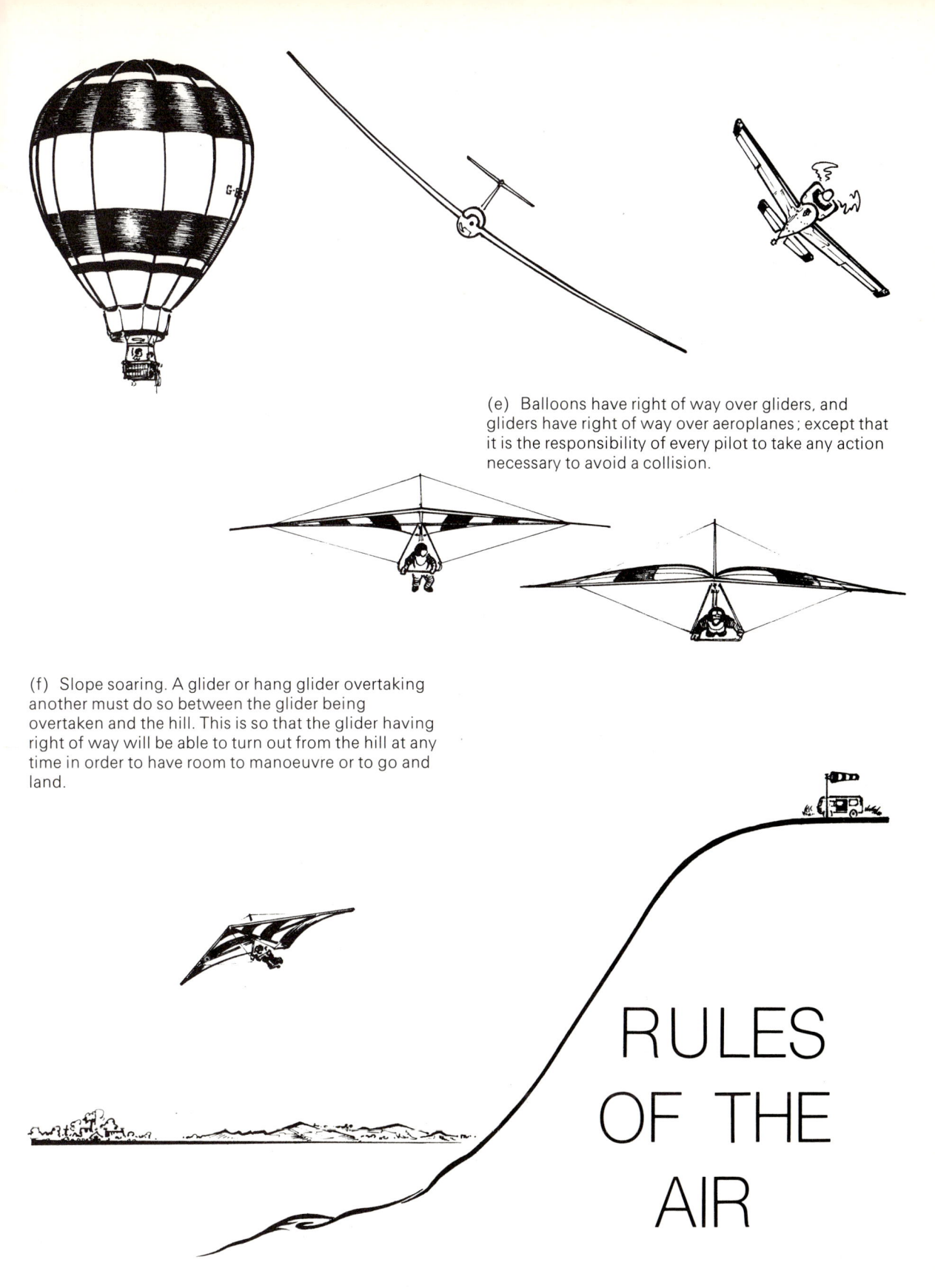

(e) Balloons have right of way over gliders, and gliders have right of way over aeroplanes; except that it is the responsibility of every pilot to take any action necessary to avoid a collision.

(f) Slope soaring. A glider or hang glider overtaking another must do so between the glider being overtaken and the hill. This is so that the glider having right of way will be able to turn out from the hill at any time in order to have room to manoeuvre or to go and land.

RULES OF THE AIR

Appendix 2   Example of Medical Standard (BGA)

Part A

TO BE SIGNED BEFORE STARTING TO FLY AS PUPIL OR SOLO PILOT

I hereby declare that I have never suffered from any of the following which I understand may create, or may lead to, a dangerous situation in flight.

Epilepsy, fits, severe head injury, recurrent fainting, giddiness or blackouts, unusually high blood pressure, a previous coronary, I am not taking insulin regularly for the control of diabetes.

I further declare that, in the event of my contracting, or suspecting, any of the above conditions in the future, I will cease to fly until I have obtained medical opinion.

Signed .... Date............

Name in Block Letters...................................
....

If you cannot sign the above declaration, you must, *before flying*, obtain the signature of your *regular* GP or that of an approved CAA PPL medical examiner.

I am the regular GP of the applicant/I am a CAA medical examiner (delete as appropriate)

I understand that the applicant wishes to fly in sporting gliders, but has been unable to sign the above declaration. In my opinion it is safe for him/her so to fly.

Signed..
Date............

Name and address...
(Block Letters..
....

Applicant's name (Block letters).......................
....

Part B

The following conditions may cause you difficulty while flying. If you suffer or have suffered from any of these you are advised to take medical opinion.

Chronic bronchitis, severe asthma, chronic sinus disease, chronic ear disease, eye trouble, (for example, inability to read a car number plate at 25 yards, corrective glasses may be used), regular severe migraine, diabetes in any form, rheumatic fever, kidney stones, psychiatric disorders, severe motion or travel sickness, any condition requiring the regular use of drugs (include any medication whatsoever).

You are further advised that (a) if you normally wear glasses you should always carry a readily accessible spare pair and (b) minor illnesses, drugs and the donation of blood will probably make you temporarily unfit to fly.

Appendix 3 Addresses

The addresses below are additional to those for national associations for each sport, which will be found at the end of the relevant chapter.

Fédération Aéronautique Internationale
   The FAI is the international controlling body for airsports
   6 rue Galilée 75782 Paris,
   France

Royal Aero Club of the United Kingdom
   A member of the FAI and the controlling body for airsports in Britain
   Kimberley House, Vaughan Way, Leicester

Civil Aviation Authority
   The CAA is the government body controlling aviation in the United Kingdom
   Shell Mex House, Strand, London WC2

Air Registration Board
   The ARB is the authority looking after the airworthiness of aircraft in the UK.
   Brabazon House, Redhill, Surrey

The Helicopter Club of Great Britain
   The National association looking after rotating wing sport flying.
   The Secretary, Rocky Lane Farm, Henley-on-Thames, Oxon. RG9 4RE

The Society of Model Aircraft Engineers
   The national association for aeromodelling in the UK.
   The Secretary, Kimberley House, Vaughan Way, Leicester

The General Aviation Safety Committee
   The body promoting safety in flying in the UK.
   Church House, 33 Church Street, Henley-on-Thames, Oxon. RG9 1SE

Royal Aero Club

"SAFETY THROUGH KNOWLEDGE"

The Air Education and Recreation Organization
AERO is the body which promotes aviation in schools and youth groups.
Cawarden House, 118 Upper Chobham Road, Camberley, Surrey

The Air League
The body promoting aviation in general. Produces *Air Pictorial* magazine.
4 Hamilton Place, London W1V OBQ

Index

A
Aerobatics, 49, 51, 100, 104
Aeronautical chart, 60
Aerotowing, 39
Airbrakes, 29, 35, 37, 46
Air racing, 52
Airships, 89
Airspeed, 15, 98, 120
Airspeed Indicator, 19, 37
Altimeter, 19, 26, 37, 84, 104
Andrée, Saloman, 89
Angle of attack, 14, 40
Anticyclones, 112, 114
Audio variometer, 19, 27

B
Balloon basket, 79, 81
Balloon capacity, classes, 79
Barograph, 39
Battens, 11
Billow, 10
Blaue Maus, 26
Breenwave, 23
British Association of Parascending Clubs, 97
British Balloon and Airship Club, 91
British Gliding Association, 46
British Hang Gliding Association, 16, 20
British Parachute Association, 109
Bungey launching, 40
Burner, 83, 84, 85
Buys Ballot's Law, 113

C
Capewell releases, 98
Car towing, 39
Cassutt IIIM, 52, 53
C-FL Canard, 23
Championships, 88, 97
Check list, 17, 44
Chuck glider model, 126
Cloud base, 114
Cockpit check, 43
Code of Good Practice, 25, 47, 91
Cold, 19
Compass, 61
Controls, 40

Cross country flying, 26, 28, 40
Cumulo-nimbus, 117
Cumulus clouds, 19, 26, 114

D
Dagling, 30
Deflexers, 10
Delayed drops, 103
Delta Silver, 17, 25
Depressions, 112, 113
Drag, 14, 28, 40, 72, 74
Drift, 15

E
Epoxy, 28
Evans VP-1, 54

F
Falke SF.25B, 42
Fatigue, 19
Fédération Aéronautique Internationale, 17, 72, 131
Fibre-glass, 28
Final glide, 28, 36
First solo, 43
Flaps, 29
Formation jumps, stars, 107, 109
Formula 1, 52, 55
Free fall, 103
Frog position, 104
Full spread position, 100

G
Gas balloons, 89
Gipsy Moth, 48
Glass fibre, 28
Glide ratio/angle, 26, 28, 35, 92, 100, 104
Gliding clubs, 26
Goodhart Manflyer, 73
Gossamer Condor, 74
Ground effect, 72
Groundspeed, 15, 98
Grunau Baby, 27

H
Harness, 14
Helium, 89

133

Helmet, 10, 83, 95
Hill soaring, 13, 18, 40, 119
Homebuilt aircraft, 49
Hot air balloons, 77
Hydrogen, 89

I
Icarus V, 24
Instructing, 48
Instruments, 36

J
Jalbert, Domina, 92
Jupiter, 71

K
Kirby Kite, 31
Kittiwake, 62
Kremer, Henry, 67, 72
Kremer prizes, 71, 76

L
Landing, Landing flare, 10, 43, 85, 92, 99
Landing roll, 93, 95
Launching, 40
Lemoigne, Pierre, 92, 97
Lenticular clouds, 122
Leonardo da Vinci medal, 92
Lilienthal, 9, 26, 77
Lippisch, Alexander, 66
Lowe, Robert, 54

M
MacCready, Paul, 74
Magnetic deviation, 61
Magnetic variation, 61
Manflyer, 73
Map reading, 60
Medical Standards, 130
Midair Model balloon, 124
Mistral wind, 112
Montgolfier, Etienne, 77
Moonraker, 21
Motor glider, 40
Mountain soaring, 120
Mufli, 67

N
Nicolaides, John, 92
Nomex, 80
Nylon fabric, 80, 89, 90

P
Parachutes, 36
Parachutes, steerable, 92, 100
Para-Commander, 92, 96, 97
Parafil, 98
Para-Foil, 92, 98, 99
Peter Powell Kite, 127
Pik-20, 33
Pilcher, 9
Pitch, 14
Pitts S-IS, 49
Popular Flying Association, 52
Potter, John, 71
Private Pilot's Licence, 48
Proficiency Badges, 16, 20, 25, 46, 48, 109
Propane gas, 77, 81
Puffin, 71

Q
Quicksilver, 22

R
Radio, 15
Ram air parachute, 92
Reflex, 10
Relative work, 105
Reserve parachute, 100, 104
Rhön mountains, 26
Rip cord, 100, 103
Rip panel, 83
Rogallo, Francis, 9
Roll control, 15
Rollason Beta, 53
Royal Aeronautical Society, 69, 76
Rozier, Pilâtre de, 77
Rules of the Air, 128

S
Sand ballast, 89
Schwinguin, 66
Scorpion, 22

Sea breezes, 118
Simulator, 10
Slope soaring, 13, 18, 40, 119
Spin, spinning, 43
Squalls, 116
Stability, 10
Stall, 14, 16, 43, 93, 99
Static electricity, 89
Static line, 100, 103
Stork, 72
Sumpac, 67
Syndicate ownership, 35, 54, 88

T
Tail parachute, 29
Terminal velocity, 100
Test flying, 40, 57
Tether training, 13
Thermals, thermal soaring, 18, 26, 36, 40, 84, 99, 114, 117
Thunderstorms, 116
Tip draggers, 9
Toucan, 71
Tow, Tow car, 26, 39, 96, 97, 98, 99

Tracking, 104
Trail rope, 87, 88, 90
Tug pilot, 48
Turns, 15, 40, 72, 104

V
Valley winds, 119, 120
Vampyr, 26
Variometer, 19, 27, 37, 84
Vintage gliders, 40
Volkswagen engine, 40, 57, 90
VP-1, 54

W
Warm front, 64
Waves, 120
Weight shift control, 9
Wills Wing Cross Country, 21
Winch, launching, 26, 39
Wind gradient, 120

Z
Zlin 526-AFS, 50

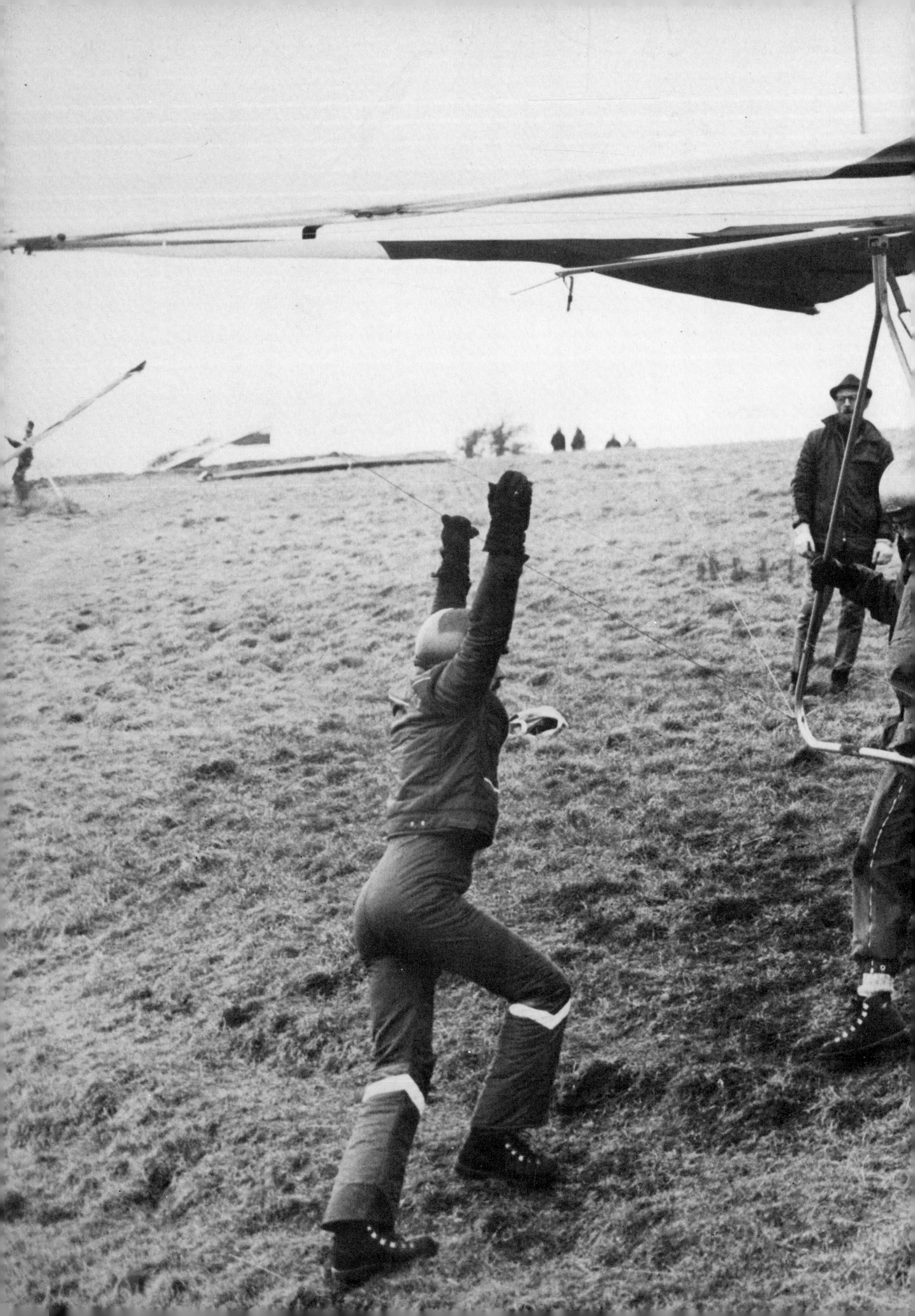